GOVERNMENT AGAINST ITSELF

GOVERNMENT AGAINST ITSELF

PUBLIC UNION POWER AND ITS CONSEQUENCES

DANIEL DiSALVO

OXFORD
UNIVERSITY PRESS

OXFORD

UNIVERSITY PRESS

Oxford University Press is a department of the University of
Oxford. It furthers the University's objective of excellence in research,
scholarship, and education by publishing worldwide.

Oxford   New York

Auckland   Cape Town   Dar es Salaam   Hong Kong   Karachi
Kuala Lumpur   Madrid   Melbourne   Mexico City   Nairobi
New Delhi   Shanghai   Taipei   Toronto

With offices in

Argentina   Austria   Brazil   Chile   Czech Republic   France   Greece
Guatemala   Hungary   Italy   Japan   Poland   Portugal   Singapore
South Korea   Switzerland   Thailand   Turkey   Ukraine   Vietnam

Published in the United States of America by
Oxford University Press
198 Madison Avenue, New York, NY 10016

© Oxford University Press 2015

Library of Congress Cataloging-in-Publication Data
DiSalvo, Daniel.
Government against itself : public union power and its consequences / Daniel DiSalvo.
pages cm
Summary: "Daniel DiSalvo contends that the power of public sector unions is too often inimical to the
public interest"— Provided by publisher.
ISBN 978–0–19–999074–0 (hardback)
1. Government employee unions—United States. I. Title.
HD8005.2.U5D575 2015
331.88'1135173—dc23
2014020729

1 3 5 7 9 8 6 4 2
Printed in the United States of America
on acid-free paper

To Daryl

CONTENTS

ACKNOWLEDGMENTS

I could not have written this book without a lot of help from many quarters. I'm blessed to have been challenged, inspired, and supported by many friends and colleagues. And I confess to exploiting their kindness and generosity.

I'm indebted to Fred Siegel, one of the great chroniclers of America's cities. Fred is among a vanishing breed of New York intellectuals, the sharpness of whose pen is matched only by the depth of his concern for his fellow urbanites. He was the first to encourage me to explore the fascinating world of public sector unionism. My City College of New York colleague, Rajan Menon, read the entire manuscript and provided enormously helpful feedback. His willingness to wrestle with a subject far from his own interests and guide me around numerous pitfalls went far beyond the call of duty, collegiality, and even friendship. Terry Moe of Stanford University provided me extensive comments on the manuscript and took the time to engage me in a long-running email correspondence. Terry's outstanding work on teachers' unions in particular and public sector unions in general has shaped my thinking on these subjects. Martha Derthick of the University of Virginia helped me frame many chapters, offered sage advice about the book's organization, and pointed me to many helpful sources. My book is a vain attempt to live up to the brilliance of Martha's analyses of the politics of public policy.

The Manhattan Institute of Policy Research has generously supported my research on public sector unions. I have learned a tremendous amount from the institute's senior fellows and staff. These include but are by no means limited to Larry Mone, Howard Husock, Michael Allegretti, Brian Anderson, E. J. McMahon, Nicole Gelinas, Steve Malanga, Steven Eide, and

Scott Winship. Bernadette Serton, the Manhattan Institute's book director, gave me valuable advice about how to frame the book and smoothed the prose of a few chapters into respectable shape. The Manhattan Institute has helped me find outlets for my work, which allowed me to see how it would fare in the marketplace of ideas. Other people have also helped me test my ideas in the public square, especially David DeRosiers of RealClearPolitics, Josh Greenman of the *New York Daily News*, and Yuval Levin of *National Affairs*.

A number of other scholars and writers have been generous enough to read and comment on parts of the manuscript, including James Ceaser, Andrew Biggs, Steve Savas, Nick Salvatore, Charles Lane, Ray La Raja, Chris Edwards, George Mitchell, Reihan Salam, John Krinsky, Eric Lupfer, and the two peer reviewers enlisted by Oxford University Press. Their probing questions and stern editorial suggestions have made the book much stronger in many places.

Many members of the American Bar Association's Labor and Employment Section, especially George Crisci, were generous enough to explain to me the finer points of labor law and contract negotiations. I also benefited from research assistance from Clara Garcia Beltran and Fai Tsoi.

Finally, I'd like to thank my editor at Oxford, David McBride. I owe him a debt of gratitude for encouraging me to write this book, for sending my manuscript to two thoughtful reviewers, and for his expert editorial hand, which guided the manuscript to publication.

GOVERNMENT AGAINST ITSELF

THE BATTLE OVER COLLECTIVE
BARGAINING IN GOVERNMENT

Meticulous attention should be paid to the special relations and obligations of
public servants to the public itself and to the Government .... The process of
collective bargaining, as usually understood, cannot be transplanted into the
public service.

— *President Franklin D. Roosevelt*

[It is] impossible to bargain collectively with the government.

— *AFL-CIO President George Meany*

When one thinks of millionaires, one usually thinks of corporate executives, real estate moguls, high-profile lawyers, tech wizards, professional
athletes, and investment bankers. One does not think of police officers, firefighters, or school teachers. Yet public employees are one of the
fastest-growing groups of millionaires in the country. And this isn't just
because a million bucks isn't what it used to be. Today, upon retirement in
their mid-50s, cops, firefighters, and teachers will be paid handsome pensions and receive healthcare coverage until they die. If one calculates the
value of their net worth to include their retirement packages, many have

already become millionaires.[1] Indeed, those who spend their entire careers in public service are often among the highest earners in their states upon retirement. Eight states pay on average over $1 million in pension benefits to a retired worker, and 23 states pay about $750,000 or more over the course of a worker's retirement.[2]

Take the case of Glenn Goss. At the age of 21, Goss joined the police force in Delray Beach, Florida. In 2005, he retired at age 42, after 20 years on the job. He had achieved the rank of commander, and his final salary was $90,000 a year. Upon retirement, he began receiving a $65,000 annual pension, which is guaranteed for life and indexed for inflation. His retirement package also includes a healthcare plan worth approximately $10,000 a year. If one considers that male life expectancy in the United States is approaching 80 years, Goss will be receiving his pension and health benefits for another 38 years.

Still in his 40s and in good health, Goss decided to return to work even after he was officially retired. Rather than launch a new career, however, he went back to police work in Highland Beach, a neighboring community from where he used to work. The job he took was nearly identical in terms of salary and benefits to the one he left. (This practice is commonly referred to as "double-dipping.") Put it all together and an estimation of his current net worth is $2 million.[3]

As another example, look at the arrangement that Michael Hirth has secured. A 55-year-old fireman in Hallendale Beach, Florida, he participates in a Deferred Retirement Option Program. It allows him to "retire" but continue working. Under this program, Hirth receives his pension and salary simultaneously. He can also direct pension dollars into a fund that guarantees an 8 percent annual return. Year after year, if the fund doesn't perform to that benchmark, the state of Florida (and ultimately its taxpayers) is on the hook for the difference.

Finally, consider the case of Joe Smith, a gym teacher and longtime football coach at Addison Trail High School in DuPage County, Illinois. He earned more than $184,000 in the 2008–09 school year. Under contractual provisions, his 35 years of teaching experience and master's degree boosted his salary. Now retired, he enjoys full pension and healthcare benefits.[4]

Stories of such lavish compensation may make some readers indignant. (A personal favorite is the lifeguard in Newport Beach, California, who retired at 51 years old with a $108,000-a-year pension.[5]) For many people struggling in the private sector—to say nothing of the unemployed—these arrangements appear outrageously inequitable, especially since these same workers are footing the bill for public employees through their tax dollars. During the Great Recession, government employees became the envy of many workers toiling in the regular economy, where the average salary hovers around $51,000 a year and benefits are much less generous, if workers have them at all.[6] Indeed, the job security, pension and health benefits, and work schedules that most public employees enjoy are things that most private sector workers can only dream about. And these differences from the private economy are not altogether new. One journalist remarked 30 years ago that "Altogether, [public employment is] one sweet deal: generous pay and benefits, lifetime job security, meaningless performance evaluations, and, last, but not least, protection from all the swings of fortune that affect workers in private industry."[7] Yet, facile indignation about such inequities is not the most important thing about these examples.

By all accounts, Glenn Goss is a decent cop, Michael Hirth a competent fireman, and Joe Smith a dedicated teacher. And they are far from our best-rewarded public servants. Pointing out their levels of compensation is not intended to attack these people personally or public employees generally. Government workers are hugely important. They put out fires, ensure our safety, and teach our children. We want good, well-qualified people doing these jobs. The difficulties stem from the fact that there are *millions* of similarly compensated public employees across the country. Government employment accounts for more than 20.3 million jobs—17 percent of total US employment—with the vast majority of these jobs in state and local governments.[8] The focus of this book is therefore more on the latter than the former because that is largely where the action is. (In addition, the scope of collective bargaining in the federal government is much more limited than it is in most state and local governments where it is practiced.)

The aggregate cost of public employee compensation (including pay, pension, and healthcare) has contributed mightily to creating a fiscal burden that threatens to weaken state and local government across the country.[9] The best current estimates of the unfunded pension liability for state and local government is around $3.2 trillion—or approximately 21 percent of total US gross domestic product. And that doesn't include healthcare liabilities, which are harder to estimate but probably add another $1 trillion, which by itself is equal to about one-third of state and local government revenue.[10] Furthermore, the rate at which government workers are retiring is faster than the rate at which people are retiring in the private sector. By 2030, the number of retired public workers will equal the number of people employed by state and local government. Therefore, state and local governments are allocating larger shares of their budgets to retirement benefits (pensions and healthcare) to their past and current employees.[11] And even as state and local government jobs have declined by some 671,000 positions since 2009, spending by state and local governments has increased by $200 billion.[12] As expenditures on benefits increase, they "crowd out" government spending on parks, education, public safety, and other services on which the poor and middle class rely. In short, government costs more but does less.

What contributed to creating this situation? There are, of course, many explanations. But the most important is that Goss, Hirth, and Smith all belong to unions. More specifically, they belong to public employee unions. These unions have been particularly adept, due to the advantages they enjoy over other interest groups, in securing better pay, benefits, and job protection for their members.[13] And many of these items are connected, since salary increases translate into higher pension liabilities. Pursuing their interests in politics and at the bargaining table has often translated into Samuel L. Gompers's famous labor dictum: "More."[14] Clearly, that's great for our public servants. However, it's not so good for everyone else. The problem with unions in the public sector is that in order to serve the interests of their members, they hamstring government's ability to address social problems, reduce inequality, and enhance social cohesion.

As James Madison remarked long ago: "The great desideratum in Government is such a modification of sovereignty as will render it sufficiently neutral between the different interests and factions ... and at the same time sufficiently controuled itself, from setting up an interest adverse to that of the whole Society."[15] Unfortunately, public sector unions constitute just such an adverse interest: too often the pursuit of their interests compromises the public's interest in low-cost but highly productive government that sensibly allocates scarce resources. It is for these reasons that Franklin Roosevelt and George Meany, both great champions of organized labor, opposed collective bargaining with unionized government workers.[16] Both were concerned about its negative implications for democratic practice, the health of public finances, and the quality of government services.

The stakes involved in permitting collective bargaining and unionization in public sector labor relations—things that sound technocratic and boring—are nothing less than whether democratic politics and fiscal responsibility can ever, for very long, be combined.[17] Organizing government employees—most of whom have nearly life tenure—into interest groups to then negotiate and lobby government provides a motive for government to grow beyond what is required to keep up with increases in population and to cost more than is necessary to attract and maintain a competent public workforce. Fiscal integrity is hard to maintain under such conditions, as a given level of tax revenue ends up purchasing fewer public services. Furthermore, government tends to grow in ways that do not always rebound to the benefit of citizens who rely on government services. Doing anything to counteract such trends becomes even harder in largely one-party states and cities where public sector unions are deeply intertwined with the dominant political party. In sum, the extent and proper structure of American democracy is at stake.

That said, just because this book examines some of the adverse consequences of public sector unionism does not imply that there are no other threats to democratic health in the United States. Far from it. The machinations of ideological individuals, business corporations, and citizen associations with considerable political resources also present grave challenges to the public interest. An uninformed and uninterested public and a press corps obsessed with the horse-race aspects of political campaigns rather than the substance of public policy present still other hazards. And people can take their pick of a long list of other problems. There's party polarization, income inequality, dysfunctional political institutions, lingering racism, and ethically challenged politicians. Readers should rightly be concerned about them. And good books have been written on all of these topics.

However, one can be critical of all of these things and still believe that public sector unions are part of the full landscape of problems afflicting American politics. Accepting that public sector unions do not necessarily chime with fiscal integrity, social solidarity, and healthy democratic practice does not require one to reject other sources of American democracy's difficulties. For instance, believing public sector unions are problematic by no means precludes the belief that corporate America exercises too much power or that wealthy individuals have captured too much of the nation's wealth over the last 30 years. These claims are simply not mutually exclusive. Therefore, admitting the obvious, that there are other problems with American democracy, should not distract us from the study of government unions.

THE POLITICS OF PUBLIC SECTOR UNIONISM

After the 2010 Tea Party elections, American politics was consumed by disputes over public sector labor relations. Major political battles occurred in New Jersey, Wisconsin, Ohio, New York, Illinois, and California among other places.[18] To balance their budgets, governors across the country demanded that public employees accept salary freezes, furlough days, and less generous pension and healthcare benefits. Republican Chris Christie of New Jersey and Democrats Jerry Brown of California and Andrew Cuomo of New York wrestled with government workers' unions over wage and benefit concessions that would close budget deficits without raising taxes. Other governors, such as Republicans Scott Walker in Wisconsin and John Kasich in Ohio, sought to go further and enact structural reforms eliminating collective bargaining with most state workers' unions, halting government collection of union dues, and giving agency managers greater workplace discretion to hire, fire, discipline, and reassign workers.[19] These proposals sparked massive protests by unions and their allies.

These fights often split along partisan lines. Republicans attack and Democrats defend the unions. For instance, Senate Minority Leader Mitch McConnell (R-KY) has remarked that public sector unions create "an inherent and undeniable tension between those who believe in limited self-government and those who stand to benefit from its growth." They are also, he argues, "the reason so many state and local municipalities are flat broke" and are "behind the unsustainable expansion of public pensions."[20] On the other side, President Barack Obama accused Wisconsin Governor Walker of launching an "assault" on public employees with his collective bargaining reform proposals and that it is "important to recognize that public employees make enormous contributions to our states and our citizens."[21] Such divisions are hardly surprising given the parties' ideological positions. One cross-national study has found that American parties mirror parties in other democracies, where left-wing parties are consistently more generous toward public employees than right-wing ones.[22]

Therefore, the unions and their allies in the Democratic Party have countered efforts to alter the status quo with massive resistance. Protests in Madison, Wisconsin, lasted for weeks—swelling in size on some days to 70,000 people and dominating national and international news coverage. Democratic state legislators fled to neighboring Illinois to prevent a vote on Walker's proposal but succeeded only in postponing legislative defeat. The unions then spearheaded recall elections of a number of Republican state senators and Governor Walker himself before the scheduled conclusion of his term in 2014. Yet Walker won the recall election by more than he won his initial election. Many of the state senators were returned to office as well. The battle was all the more curious insofar as Walker had to spend huge sums of political capital to achieve what in the end was a modest reform compared to states such as Indiana and Michigan who passed right-to-work laws that are much tougher on both public and private sector labor organizations.

In Ohio, the Republican-dominated legislature and Republican governor passed a similar law—one that in fact went further than Wisconsin's in restricting collective bargaining insofar as it did not include a carve out for police and firefighters. The unions and their allies responded quickly by putting the new law on the ballot in a referendum, vastly outspending and outmobilizing the measure's supporters, and defeating it handily.

Yet, not all conflicts between elected officials and unionized government workers have pitted Republicans against Democrats. The Democratic Party is in fact divided over this issue and faces a real political conundrum.[23] Liberal Democrats want to use public sector employment as a model that the private sector should emulate. If this approach costs more, they argue that taxes should be increased on Wall Street financiers, corporate businesses, and wealthy individuals to underwrite it. Meanwhile, centrist Democrats want more effective services in order to reduce pressure for tax increases. Sometimes they seek to use the promise of improved services as a bargaining chip for tax increases. (Centrists worry that overly taxing Wall Street and the rich will cause finance firms and wealthy individuals to restructure their compensation packages to avoid higher income taxes and thereby weaken the already unstable tax bases of states like New York and California that rely extensively on taxing the wealthy to fund their governments.[24])

In some manifestations, the axis of the Democrats' division plays out depending on which branch of government Democrats find themselves in. Democrats who occupy executive positions—mayors and governors—have been forced by recent budget pressures to turn their backs on their erstwhile union allies. At the same time, Democratic representatives in city councils and state legislatures have stuck by the unions. In Chicago, the 26,000-strong teachers' union called a strike to protest a longer school day requested by Democratic Mayor Rahm Emanuel, President Obama's former chief of staff.[25] Conflict between the mayor and the Windy City's teachers has continued, as Emanuel ordered the closing of 54 schools and layoffs of 2,100 teachers to address the city's looming public pension crunch. It is ironic that some public sector workers now risk losing their jobs due to the high cost of benefits their unions consistently demand.

The Democrats' divide over public sector unions is also apparent in education. President Obama and his Secretary of Education Arne Duncan's Race to the Top Program has pushed states to adopt policies opposed by teachers' unions, including promoting charter schools, common core standards, and more rigorous teacher evaluations.[26] Race to the Top has sparked major conflict between teachers' unions and Democratic governors and mayors around the country. Education policy also pits two core constituencies of the Democratic Party against one another. On one side are the teachers' unions; on the other are racial minorities. African Americans and Latinos, while supporters of elements of the teachers' unions' agenda such as higher spending, taxes, and increased teacher pay, disproportionately favor school choice, vouchers, online learning, and tax credits to fund private school tuition—all things the teachers' unions are dead set against.[27] Former Los Angeles mayor Antonio Villaraigosa, a former teachers' union organizer, remarked in a high-profile speech that "the most powerful defenders of the status quo are the teachers unions. They intimidated people, especially Democrats, from doing anything about reform."[28] There is likely to be future friction between teachers' unions and minorities—if not the groups that claim to represent the latter such as the National Association for the Advancement of Colored People (NAACP)—given the wide gaps in their preferences on many educational policy issues.[29]

Reflecting on the tensions within his party, Chuck Reed, Democratic mayor of San Jose, the home of Silicon Valley, has even gone so far as to say that "there's a difference between being liberal and progressive and being a union Democrat."[30] Reed is among a number of California Democrats who have locked horns with public sector unions. They include San Francisco public defender Jeff Adachi, former assembly speaker Willie Brown, former state senate speaker Gloria Romero, former Los Angeles mayor Antonio Villaraigosa, and, according to someone off the record, Governor Jerry Brown.[31] Back on the East Coast, unions protested New York Governor Cuomo's efforts to create a new, and less generous, pension system for new hires and has defended the expansion of charter schools. And Connecticut Governor Dannell Malloy has struggled with his state's unions in an effort to balance the state's budget. All told, the big change is that public employee unions operated mostly behind the scenes for the last few decades. Today's policy battles have put them squarely in the national spotlight.

Conservatives and Liberals

For some conservatives, government is always too big and public employees are overcompensated loafers. On the other side, liberals lionize public sector unions but don't always face up to the financial consequences of unions' wage and benefit contracts. Yet such attitudes, which are caricatures of themselves, don't take us very far. I have no stake in trashing Republicans or helping Democrats, or vice versa. My aim is to understand the rise and role of public sector unions in American politics and follow the evidence where it leads. Looking beyond partisan disputes, this book offers a case for skepticism about the benefits of public employee unionization and a way to think about the future of unionism in government.

A premise of this book is that the analysis of public sector unions must be shorn of mythology and separated from the legendary struggles of private sector labor in the mid-twentieth century. Rather, public employee unions must be analyzed with the same detachment as when studying other interest groups in American political life, each of which has its own set of incentives, goals, and constraints. Many studies of organized labor, especially those examining the private sector, have a tendency to romanticize union struggles pitting David (the workers) against Goliath (large companies). However, teachers, cops, and corrections officers lack the victimhood status of industrial workers battling capitalist barons. This may partly explain why scholars have devoted so little attention to the study of public sector unions. Today, there is a more vigorous discussion in the public square than there is in academe about the advantages and disadvantages of unionized government.[32] This discussion was sparked by the 2008–11 recession, the fiscal problems of American governments, and Republicans' efforts to exploit the issue for political gain.

Therefore, I believe that an unvarnished account will interest people across the political spectrum—liberals as well as conservatives, public employees as well as those in the private sector. Indeed, public employee unions' effects on state and local government present an ensemble of issues that impact all of us. To craft such an account, I translate academic scholarship into prose accessible to the layperson, compile media stories and think tank studies, rely on government documents, and bring to bear my own research on the subject. Yet, getting beyond partisan snipping requires first engaging the arguments of both sides.

Since the 1930s, Republicans and conservatives have not been keen on either unions (public or private) or expansive government. Therefore, unions composed of government workers that seek to increase taxes and expand government are particularly anathema to them. Attacking unions strokes many conservative erogenous zones. Conservatives are likely to find my skeptical and at times critical treatment of public sector unions congenial. Yet, my hope is that it will refine and enlarge their views on what is a complex subject without simple solutions.

The last generation of conservatives defined themselves against government. Their central goal was to reduce government's size. Yet, simply swinging the budget axe and punishing public servants are misguided responses to current problems. While cuts must sometimes be made, we need a sensible approach that doesn't gut services that many citizens depend on. Nor will bashing public workers improve the economy, revive cities, or solve the slow-moving pension crisis. Such blunt approaches will limit conservatives' ability to participate in the important conversation about how to improve government productivity in the future, which is arguably the number one domestic issue. In simply focusing on the size of government, some conservatives missed a chance to examine and engage the real problems citizens confront, which require government action.

Too often conservatives are unwilling or unable to admit that some government programs are necessary and sometimes do a great deal of good. Furthermore, some conservatives are too quick to believe that public sector unions are at the root of both dysfunctional bureaucracy and the growth of government. The truth is that these are complex issues and there is no single explanation or easy solution. While public employee unions do impact these outcomes, their role is more nuanced and limited, as I explain in later chapters. Being satisfied with simple explanations will only serve to exclude conservatives from the crucial debate about how to make government more productive in the face of tight budgets. Instead, conservatives need to engage in the nettlesome details of public policy.

To that end, conservatives should also be attentive to the many possible unintended consequences of making big changes in public sector labor relations. For instance, moving too quickly to reduce public employee compensation could reduce the quality of the government workforce on which citizens depend. This can have a negative impact on the production of human capital—especially in the school system—which would ultimately rebound to weakening the private sector. Business needs well-educated workers. Public schools will provide most of them. Conservatives also want government to regulate business efficiently and effectively. Yet, if government cannot hire and retain good people, the wait times for licensing, permitting, and regulatory approval will grow longer. Starting and running a business or charitable enterprise will become more difficult. Conservatives also value public order. But if police training programs are cut, corruption and incompetence can ensue, undermining law and order. And these examples are just for starters.

On the other side, the ideas, values, and instincts of most Democrats and liberals have long tied them to unionism. They struggle to see a difference between public and private sector unions. They scorn the notion that America would be better off if public employee unions were less powerful or didn't exist at all. To the contrary, as *Washington Post* columnist Harold Meyerson put it, such unions "are the linchpin of progressive change in America."[33] In this view, public employee unions provide political balance in society and are the bulwark against broader injustice in the world.[34] The unions help preserve a slice of the middle class that would otherwise be plunged—through conservatives' efforts to privatize government work—into the vicious race to the bottom.[35] Furthermore, the safe, orderly, predictable, and egalitarian workplace they've created is the model for the private sector.

Most Democratic politicians still see giving up on government unionism as political suicide. The unions are core financial contributors to their party and its candidates. They staff the get-out-the-vote drives that get minority voters to the polls. Without them, many Democrats hold, the GOP and big business would dominate American politics.[36] Few liberal Democrats are willing to concede that collective bargaining in government has any downsides at all. Centrists admit there are problems but are likely to want to change the subject. The Democrats face a real contradiction within their coalition, insofar as the unions are powerful and they rely on them during election time. Many Democrats will remain reluctant to criticize the unions because they have strong incentives not to. Therefore, making the case that they too should be skeptical of government unionism is a high peak to climb.

For instance, defenders of public employee unions, such as former Clinton-era secretary of labor Robert Reich, have charged that humble public workers are being targeted as "scapegoats" for the nation's recent economic misfortune.[37] They argue that most public employees live modest lives and aren't paid much better than workers in the private sector. The act of criticizing public servants thus distracts attention from rising income inequality and corporate executives who are the real culprits behind today's economic woes. Yet, being highly critical of corporate misbehavior should not stop one from recognizing the downsides of unionized government. And as long as public sector unions persist, they will offer ample opportunities for conservatives to distract attention from liberal projects.

In some ways, I hope that more liberals than conservatives read this book. In fact, I'd argue that liberalism's political future depends on considering this issue. As historian Walter Russell Mead has pointed out, "Public sector union support, however attractive in the short term, is a poisoned chalice in today's world."[38] Insofar as liberals want government to do more to create more equal opportunities, protect citizens from market failures, and lift up the poor, having to defend the costs and inefficiencies imposed by public sector unions is a major drag. The Achilles heel of American liberalism is that it occasionally turns a blind eye to the dysfunctional aspects of public monopolies. (On the other hand, big-business Republicans tend to overlook the problems with private sector monopolies.) When American government performs poorly, so does American liberalism. And with government likely to face tight budgets at all levels for the foreseeable future, a central debate in American politics will be about how to make government more productive. Democrats cannot carry government unions' water and participate effectively in that debate at the same time. In short, how to deal with the public sector unions in their midst presents Democrats with a real challenge, as they must rely on the unions' power but need to confront that power to make important policy changes.

My hope is that this book will prompt readers to reconsider their views on unionized government. I hope it will lead them to question whether the benefits that accrue to public workers through unionization and collective bargaining outweigh the costs to taxpayers and those who rely on government services. (In today's polarized political environment, it is even hard to get people to admit that there are trade-offs among policies they support.)

To prompt such reconsideration, I show that there are indeed serious trade-offs involved in a commitment to activist government that provides an array of goods and services to its citizens—especially the middle class and the poor—and a commitment to unionism and collective bargaining in the public sector. The problem is that the two commitments often work at cross-purposes, making it nearly impossible to consistently champion government workers and advance the public interest.[39] Finally, as government unionism generates stories of influence peddling and excessive salaries for public workers, it becomes a cause for citizen skepticism about government in general, which undermines the trust in government that grand liberal projects of state activism require.[40]

Democrats believe that government can do a great deal of good in society. They believe in the value of technocratic expertise in staffing the bureaucracy. However, if government is tied down by previously negotiated work rules, if the unions make it politically difficult to eliminate ineffective programs to make room for new policy experiments, and if the costs of employees benefits devour the budget, then no matter who is elected, there will be a big gap between what government wants to do and what it can do. Transferring rights and resources to government workers and their unions only makes it more difficult to provide those things to the broader public.

As long as the Democratic Party depends extensively on public employee unions, it will be a less effective advocate for the vast majority of working-class Americans who don't have government jobs. The Democratic Party might be better served—and the public better served as well—if it gave up defending the status quo and developed a long-term strategy to raise living standards across the board.[41] It cannot advocate effectively for working-class Americans when the labor movement is dominated by public employees, many of whom are white-collar professionals with college degrees.[42] Without having to defend lifetime employment and generous pensions for public workers, Democrats could talk more persuasively about the things government can and should do—especially for the downtrodden. Excessive entanglement with government unions transforms the Democratic Party into a conservative party resistant to changes in the way government operates. Reinventing government, once a prominent Democratic slogan, is drained of all serious content.[43]

Public attitudes regarding unions in general and public sector unions in particular are in flux.[44] Before 1960, public attitudes toward unions were favorable.[45] Yet, in 2009, for the first time in the modern era, less than half of Americans told pollsters that they approved of labor unions.[46] In a 2012 *Education Next* poll, only 22 percent of Americans thought that teachers' unions had a positive effect on schools, while 40 percent thought they had neither a positive nor a negative effect. When asked a binary question (positive or negative impact), 51 percent of Americans said the unions had a negative impact and 49 percent said they had a positive impact. That stands in stark contrast to teachers themselves, 71 percent of whom said unions had a positive impact.[47] Even in labor-friendly California, citizens have soured on public sector unions, as 44 percent said they caused more harm and 39 percent more good, which was part of a net 16-point swing in attitudes about labor unions from positive to negative over the past two years.[48] However, according to a *USA Today*/Gallup poll, 61 percent of Americans opposed ending collective bargaining for public employees in 2011. A *New York Times*/CBS News poll that same year produced nearly identical public support of collective bargaining—with only a slight majority of Republicans favoring limiting the practice.[49] Yet, a Clarus Group poll found that 64 percent of Americans thought that unions should not represent public employees—and 42 percent of Democrats felt the same way.[50] (The extent, then, to which citizens understand all that is involved in collective bargaining—rather than it just being a nice-sounding phrase suggesting that we should all work together—remains untapped by pollsters.)

In addition, the states where citizens complain the loudest that their taxes are too high correlate almost perfectly with the states where public employee unions are strongest.[51] All told, Americans appear poised to decide whether they believe public sector unions have positive impacts on policies they care about.

THE SCHOLARLY LITERATURE

Given its importance to American politics, the phenomenon of public sector unionism has been understudied. Yet, scholars have not completely neglected it. Economists have developed the most extensive literature on the causes and effects of it. They have examined unions' effect on employee compensation, government spending, administrative efficiency, "threat effects" on nonunionized departments, and more.[52] However, many such studies are over 20 years old and originated in the period when public employee unionism was just taking off.[53]

One might look to historians for an extensive treatment of the subject. Alas, they have devoted little attention to public employee unions. One finds nary a mention of public sector unions in American history textbooks.[54] Labor historian Joseph McCartin has remarked that those in his profession are "poorly equipped to explain the rise or persistence of organizations like AFSCME or the NEA … [because] there is almost no literature on such unions in our field."[55] While there are enough books on the United Automobile Workers (UAW) and biographies of Walter Reuther to fill a shelf, there are no academic treatments of the American Federation of State, County, and Municipal Employees (AFSCME) or biographies of its fierce leader Jerry Wurf. To be fair, Richard Kahlenberg has written a fine biography of Albert Shanker, the tough liberal leader of the American Federation of Teachers.[56]

And political scientists have not done any better. Most of their studies date back to the 1960s and 1970s, when urban politics was still at the forefront of the discipline and conflict over collective bargaining rights peaked.[57] David Greenstone made only passing reference to government workers' unions in his classic analysis of organized labor in American politics.[58] Recent studies of labor politics by Margaret Levi, Taylor Dark, and Herbert Asher note the growth of public sector unionism.[59] However, they do not analyze the causes or consequences of that growth and focus almost exclusively on private sector unions. Other recent studies don't make a distinction between private and public sector unions at all.[60] The treatment of labor unions in the interest group literature also makes no distinction between public and private.

There are a couple of important exceptions to this neglect, however. Terry Moe is currently the leading scholar of the effects of teacher unions on education policy in the United States.[61] His outstanding book, *Special Interest: Teachers Unions and America's Public Schools*, is by far the most in-depth treatment of public sector unions. His work is especially important because teachers are the largest number of public employees, constituting 6.9 of the 17 million state and local government employees in 2010. Moe makes a powerful case that the unions have used their political power in a variety of ways in a host of institutional settings to stymie education reform for 30 years, all the while pursuing and winning better pay, benefits, and work rules for teachers. Another exception is Sarah Anzia, whose work examines teacher, police, and firefighter unions in off-cycle elections and shows how they often get their way.[62] Together, Moe and Anzia have also explored the effects of government unionization on the costs of state and local government and how public sector unions shape the politics of public pensions.[63]

Finally, sociologists have also largely ignored public sector unions. However, there are a few notable exceptions. Paul Johnston's early book offered a pioneering reconceptualization of unionism in government.[64] More recently, Joshua Page has written a fine book on California prison guards. Page shows how the guards have won huge salary and benefit increases, encouraged tough-minded penal policies, and encouraged the extensive growth of prison construction in the Golden State.[65] Jake Rosenfeld has also made some revealing comparisons of public and private sector unions and shows how the former do not provide many of the broad-based benefits to working-class Americans that the latter once did.[66]

Why have scholars neglected to carefully study the causes and consequences of public employee unionism? Perhaps college-educated teachers and the "bad proletariat" of cops and corrections officers lacked the emotional appeal of industrial workers battling capitalist barons. It might also be that dealing with public sector unions' unique features would require revising the traditional story of organized labor in the United States—a traditional story to which many historians have become rather attached.

Furthermore, treating government workers' unions separately greatly complicates the dominant view of organized labor, which holds that all union members should be subsumed under the term "workers." This is the standard approach among those who treat labor as an interest group.

Unionism in the Public versus Private Sectors

There are unions in the public and private sectors. However, unions representing government workers are different from those found in the private sphere.[67] Too often in public discourse and academic analyses they are conflated, which badly distorts reality. One of the premises of this book is that there are stark differences between unions of teachers, cops, and firefighters and those of steelworkers, carpenters, and coal miners. These differences mean that public sector unions deserve separate treatment and study. Furthermore, these differences mean that the attitudes one holds—whether positive or negative—toward unions in the private sector *cannot* be transplanted to those in the public sector. The economic, legal, and moral case for the two species of unions is very different.[68]

One big difference is the nature of preexisting job protections in the public sector, namely, civil service laws, which were enacted before collective bargaining statutes and unionization. Civil service laws partially regulate promotion and compensation decisions and provide far more extensive protections for employees from arbitrary firing, transfers, or disciplinary actions by managers. Workers in the private sector usually lack such protections. This obviates to a significant extent the need for further protections and work rules adopted through collective bargaining. Civil service statutes were adopted to address another problem in public sector labor relations: the rise of spoils systems, where people were hired, fired, assigned tasks, and paid based on political connections.

Another difference is that governments are able to borrow more cheaply than business firms—think of tax-free municipal bonds—and can access new revenue through taxation. This softens the impact of swings in the economy. Private sector workers and their unions, however, remain fully exposed to the business cycle. During the great recession of 2008–11, a greater percentage of private sector workers lost their jobs than workers in the public sector. In addition, many public sector "layoffs" during the recession were, in fact, people encouraged to retire early with guaranteed pension benefits. Over the long haul, the likelihood of being laid off is far higher in the private than in the public sector. Even without unionization and collective bargaining, then, jobs in the public sector are likely to be better protected and more stable than those in the private sector.

Yet, the most fundamental difference between public and private sector collective bargaining—a process that determines the legally binding contractual agreements for the terms and conditions of employment—is that public sector unions can exert greater influence on their employers (i.e., the government) through the political process.[69] The unions can thus exercise influence on both sides of the bargaining table. This alters the structure of collective negotiations by relaxing the incentives of managers to drive a hard bargain. Unlike private sector unions, who have a natural adversary in the owners of the companies with whom they negotiate, the antagonist of public sector unions is far weaker. When private sector unions negotiate with owners, the owners have powerful incentives to keep profits for themselves. There is no such opportunity for agency managers when they negotiate with public sector unions. In many cases, management will even benefit from elements of the contract negotiations. Furthermore, managers acting in negotiations are often the agents of politicians elected with union support.

Even in the case of large corporations, where ownership and management are separated, there are still powerful institutional incentives for managers to drive a hard bargain with workers. These include the transferability of ownership through stocks, boards of directors with stock holdings, shareholder meetings, and takeover threats from other firms. In the public sector, few such mechanisms exist to pressure government negotiators. Voters are usually far less well informed than corporate board members or stockholders. There are few possibilities for exit and buyouts are nonexistent.

The extent to which citizens can indicate their preferences for state and local government by "voting with their feet" and moving to places that offer a more preferable mix of public policies is limited and therefore offers a weak check on the unions.[70] This is because the public is often ill-informed about public policy in general and public sector labor relations in particular and there are serious personal, social, and economic costs to moving. Therefore, the number of people voting with their feet on the basis of opposition to public employee compensation and the high taxes needed to underwrite it is likely to be very small.

With few external pressures, most government agency managers have little stake in contract negotiations. Therefore, they have never been as hostile to union organizing nor as tough of negotiators as managers and owners in the private sector. There is little history of "union busting" by government managers. They do not hire scabs, interfere with union elections, enlist strikebreakers, or otherwise seek to disrupt union practices. No one has ever heard of the Pinkerton's Detective Service cracking the heads of office clerks. And because government doesn't go out of business, once government workers are unionized, they usually stay unionized.

Furthermore, markets provide a natural check on private sector unions. At Boeing, for instance, the machinists' union in Seattle ran into significant limits on the pay and benefit package it could demand. Paying too much for labor could over the long term make Boeing uncompetitive vis-à-vis its rivals, such as AirBus. If the machinists rejected Boeing's final offer, the airplane manufacturer threatened to move construction of its planes to South Carolina, a state with lower labor costs and weak unions.[71] On the other hand, because government is the monopoly provider of many services, such as education and security, there is no such market counterpressure. In many cases, government is the monopoly or near-monopoly provider of the good or service and it is unable to change its location.

Public sector unions also try to select those who will sit across the bargaining table from them by engaging in electioneering. "We elect our bosses, so we've got to elect politicians who support us and hold those politicians accountable," the AFSCME flatly states.[72] The unions' participation in the campaigns and elections of the politicians with whom they will eventually negotiate gives them a degree of influence that unions in the private sector can hardly imagine. These unions provide large sums of money to candidates, mostly Democrats but sometimes Republicans, at all levels of government and make massive independent expenditures on campaign advertisements. To top it off, they provide the foot soldiers for voter registration and get-out-the-vote drives. Finally, between elections, they engage in extensive lobbying efforts to win legislators' support.

Consequently, public sector unions are fundamentally political entities.[73] Almost all decisions relevant to their members—such as pay, work rules, benefits, and hiring and firing—are ultimately political decisions.

When public employees unionize, they are driven to try to manage the people (legislators) who are supposed to be managing them (for the sake of ordinary voters). Not surprisingly, then, they have become political powerhouses in states and cities across the country. However, their exercise of power has strained governments' finances and taxpayers' wallets. In the wake of the Great Recession, state and local governments across the country have been forced to increase taxes, raise nuisance fees, run budget deficits, or some combination of all three. Some, such as Vallejo, Stockton, and San Bernardino, California, and Detroit, Michigan, have declared bankruptcy. Detroit has the dubious honor of being the largest municipal bankruptcy in US history. Others teeter on the edge.[74]

Furthermore, given public employees' generally higher levels of education and experience, they can still be powerful forces even without collective bargaining rights. This is why in many places where they lack such rights—or before they gained them—public employees often formed associations to pressure government to attend to their interests. As one legal scholar points out, "Public employees ... can and normally do participate in determining the terms and conditions of employment. Many can vote ... and present arguments in the public forum. Because their terms and conditions are decided through the political process, they have a right as citizens to participate in those decisions which affect their employment."[75] Thus, even without collective bargaining, public employee unions still have their First Amendment right to organize and participate in the democratic choices of their employer, the people.[76]

Unlike private sector unions and other interest groups, public sector unions get "two bites at the apple." It is this problem that distorts democracy and ill-serves the public good. Unlike other groups in American political life, public sector unions get to collectively bargain with their employers (the first bite) and then they get to influence those on the other side of the bargaining table through electioneering and lobbying (the second bite). Private sector unions only really get the first bite as they try to improve the material conditions of their members. The vast majority of what private sector unions win directly for their members is won at the bargaining table. Of course, as everyone knows, private sector unions participate extensively in politics. However, they participate to secure a far broader agenda than things directly affecting the terms and conditions of employment for their members on the shop floor. Think of the American

Federation of Labor–Congress of Industrial Organizations (AFL-CIO)'s efforts to raise the minimum wage (a wage no union worker would accept), influence US trade policy, and shape the immigration debate. Other interest groups—such as the National Rifle Association or the Sierra Club—get to lobby but they don't get to collectively bargain.

Public sector unions are different. They can win things at the bargaining table through political activity. That means endorsing candidates; donating money to their campaigns; lending them experienced staff; manning phone banks; turning out their members to vote; and running issue ads on radio, television, and the Internet. It is not altogether surprising that political scientist Terry Moe found that teacher union political activity was almost single-handedly responsible for the feeble results of the education reform movement over the last 25 years.[77] Michael Hartney and Patrick Flavin also found that as teacher union political activity increased, the likelihood that states would enact reform-oriented education policies—such as school choice and performance pay for teachers—declined significantly.[78] Public sector unions can serve their own interests well but often at the cost of the public's interest in a government that costs less and does more. Therefore, the two bites at the apple, coupled with informational advantages government unions enjoy, distort democracy because they give the unions a leg up on everyone else.

Therefore, the favorable impression created by the words "collective bargaining" is largely a misleading one in the public sector. Those words convey a notion that the public interest is realized insofar as government (elected) officials fully press for the interests of the public (children in schools, citizens in need of various government services) and the unions press for the interests of workers (better salaries, benefits, and working conditions) and through collegial negotiations end up with a just mean between the two sides.

However, the deck is stacked against this outcome. The incentive structure on both sides is not equal. Public officials have only limited incentives to push wholeheartedly for the interests of those who depend on government services. It is also the case that elected officials—operating in areas of uncertain outcomes with short-time horizons and harried staff—don't always know what would be in the best interest of citizens and the government. Furthermore, they are often tied to the unions through campaign contributions, as well as being lobbied by them. On the other hand, the unions and their members know far more precisely what they want and are vigilant in its pursuit. The result, then, of collective bargaining negotiations in the public sector is a powerful tendency to privilege the union position from the outset.

A final advantage public sector unions enjoy over their private sector counterparts is that the productivity of government work is very hard to measure.[79] When unions in the private sector negotiate with firms, the productivity measures of workers are clearer and the basic facts about the firm's financial health are not really in dispute. Agreement on such things helps restrain negotiations. In the public sector, the unions have an advantage because they can always claim that the productivity measures are bogus and that more tax revenue is available. Because many public employees are white-collar (or at least pink-collar) employees, performance metrics are very complex. So are the government's finances. In political disputes, unions representing such workers can fudge the numbers—even though government budgets are public information and there is usually no money hidden in private accounts—to improve their position in a way the private sector unions can't.

All told, at the level of first principles, it is not immediately obvious what exactly the broader benefit to the American people is to allowing its government workers to unionize and collectively bargain. That they benefit government workers themselves by transferring resources to them is clear—that's what unionization is designed to do and it would be surprising if it didn't do it, at least in some measure. Yet, the fact that there is no readily apparent and easily grasped answer to the question of the broader public benefit of government unions might be a reason union leaders avoid the issue or dismiss it as absurd.[80]

As is discussed at length in chapter 10, one must be attentive to the differences in the arguments that hold that the unions benefit government workers themselves and those that are said to benefit the broader citizenry in some way—as proponents of unions often conflate them. These two sorts of claims are distinct and sometimes in tension. At bottom, there is a contradictory conception of the nature of government work that informs public sector unionism. In one view, government work is a dog-eat-dog world where workers need protection from managers. In another view, people—many of them highly trained professionals and experts—work for government to serve the public good, that is, to enhance the security, prosperity, and well-being of their fellow citizens, and there is little risk of exploitation.

The Case for Public Sector Unions

Before proceeding, it is important to present, albeit in brief, the arguments usually marshaled *in favor* of public sector unions so that readers have a perspective from which they can weigh the arguments and evidence offered in this book. There are seven major arguments invoked to support public employee unionism. They are as follows:

1. Public employee unions help achieve "labor peace" and make their employers more efficient organizations. This means that permitting unionization and collective bargaining will reduce strikes, lockouts, "job actions" (such as "sick-outs" or working to code), and the sabotage of employer equipment. In short, collective bargaining with unions is the most effective way to organize public labor markets.

2. Unionization provides a vehicle for "industrial democracy," meaning the active participation of workers in the governance of their workplace.[81] As Walter Lippman once put it, "Without unions industrial democracy is unthinkable. Without democracy in industry, that is where it counts most, there is no such thing as democracy in America."[82] In this view, collective bargaining is an instrument of democratic self-government, as New York Senator Robert Wagner argued in the 1930s.

3. Unions provide public employees with representation in the political arena, enhancing workers' "voice" in the broader democratic process. Some extend this claim to argue that unionized government has now become necessary to achieve political balance in American democracy by holding up the flagging private sector labor movement and underwriting the Democratic Party. Without government unions, Republicans and big business would run roughshod over the nation.

4. Unionization reduces the power inequalities between employer and worker. This is accomplished through the negotiation of detailed work rules that constrict managerial discretion and shield workers from the potential abuse of that discretion.

5. Unionization improves government workers' lives by increasing their salaries and benefits.

6. Collective bargaining is a fundamental social and economic "right" of all workers, similar to rights to education and clean air and clean water.

7. Government union power provides a bulwark against the tendency of politicians to underinvest in public goods. Insofar as government unions perform this function, they help prevent a "race to the bottom," whereby states in America's federal system compete to cut labor costs and services to make themselves more attractive to business investment.

Each of these arguments has its merits and a powerful appeal because they invoke participation, representation, rights, and democracy—some of the deepest values of modern American society. At the end of the day, readers will have to judge for themselves whether the claims on behalf of government unionization stand up to scrutiny and are sufficiently powerful to outweigh the costs imposed on the public.

A Personal Note

Beyond this subject's obvious importance to the functioning of American government and the red-hot politics surrounding it, I became interested in it partly for personal reasons. I'm from a union family and my workplace is unionized. My paternal grandfather, an immigrant from Sicily, was a member of the steelworkers' union in Pittsburg. My father was a member of a carpenters' local. As a professor at the City College of New York in the City University of New York system (one of the Empire State's two public university systems), I am required to pay representation fees to a union as a condition of employment. (Such is the stipulation of an "agency shop.") One could see this story as the classic version of the Italian immigrant family narrative: from work in industry to the skilled trades to white-collar professional. Indeed, the differences between my experience and those of my father and grandfather are striking. Like professors elsewhere, I spend my time teaching classes, conducting research, and performing administrative service to the college—hardly back-breaking work. At the union hall I went to as a boy with my father, the focus was on bread-and-butter issues of capturing more of companies' profits in wages and benefits for carpenters, painters, and plumbers. Most of the members' highest educational attainment was a high school degree—my grandfather had no formal schooling after age 10.

My union, the Professional Staff Congress (PSC-CUNY), pays close attention to the state budget, not profit margins. Led by people with PhDs who are materially comfortable compared to workers in the old industrial unions, its union meetings are known to veer into debates about such things as American foreign policy in the Middle East. In addition, I see the consequences of unionization every day in the way the university operates. Because it is never wise to bite the hand that feeds you, I'll say only that the City University of New York has more rigidities in the management of its workforce than most institutions of higher education. Faculty and staff therefore devise ad hoc "workarounds" that bypass the formal procedures, which often serve to decrease transparency and increase dysfunction. Personal relationships become the coin of the realm, which is paradoxically exactly what all the formalization of rules and procedures was designed to eliminate.

Other people at the City College of New York (CCNY)—and at other public workplaces—see it too. Allow me one example. After seeing me on a television program discussing these issues, a female painter from the Facilities Department dropped by my office during her coffee break. She wanted to tell me about her experiences in CCNY employ. At first I thought she was going to attack what I'd said the night before— this is, after all, New York City, a union town that's famous for its sharp elbows in political discussions. Yet, to the contrary, she was elated that someone on television had articulated what she had been feeling. (She was even more astounded that I was on the CCNY faculty). In her late 40s with a strong Queens accent, dressed in a white t-shirt and white painters' pants, she was clearly a strong woman who had worked hard in a profession dominated by men. She told me that she'd been working at CCNY for about a year—mostly, she said, because of the attractive pension and health benefits. But she hated it. She couldn't believe how much time it took to do anything. She couldn't believe what people were paid for what little work, in her telling, that they did. Many were there, in her account, just to get the pension. She couldn't stand the detailed rules. She felt insulted because they didn't allow her to prove how fast and how talented a painter she was. The combination of unionization and government employment was undermining her pride in her craft. And she worried that the poor upkeep of many buildings was a disservice to the lower-income, immigrant, and first-generation college students who were enrolled at CCNY.

At the same time, the issue of public sector unionization is a controversial topic that generates a lot of heat. I know firsthand how passionately people feel about the issue. One of my colleagues emailed me to say that my analyses were "devoid of any human feeling" and "demagogic"—hardly the usual polite scholarly critique. Attacks from public employee union leaders and their allies have been even stronger. Barbara Bowen, the president of PSC-CUNY, the union to which I pay representation fees, called some of my arguments "upside-down" and "diametrically opposite the vast majority of [my] colleagues."[83] At a public debate on these issues with former New York State senator Richard Brodsky, an official from AFSCME District Council 37, which represents some of the lowest-paid public workers in New York City, launched a full-scale assault on me and my arguments. A leader of the teachers' union in Worcester, Massachusetts, also reacted vehemently to a speech I gave, disputing the notion that there could be any discrepancy between what was good for kids and what was good for teachers. New York City's civil service newspaper, *The Chief-Leader*, ran an editorial trying to discredit me by calling me a "Neocon" and "ideological."[84] In short, to write about this subject, especially taking what is a minority position in the Big Apple, one has to develop thick skin.

Ultimately, I wrote this book to explain to family members, colleagues, friends, and engaged citizens that the values that underpin their support for unions in the private sector cannot easily be transposed to the public sector. In fact, those values often work at cross-purposes for an active government that shields citizens from the ravages of the market and supports society's least fortunate.

THE GOVERNMENT UNION
DIFFERENCE

Public sector labor relations are complex matters. They involve not just salaries, wages, and benefits of employees but also management's prerogatives and the things that public agencies are tasked to perform. Government is a unique employer not easily comparable to organizations in the business world. In government it is harder to measure efficiency and productivity for agencies and workers because they often lack clearly defined goals and missions—to say nothing of the objective measurement of success used in the private sector, namely, profit. When employee unionization is added into the mix, more complications arise. How unions are defined and measured and how to define and measure their effects on workers' wages and benefits, government productivity, and political activity present formidable challenges for social scientists. The studies are multiple and sometimes contradictory. Getting a clear picture is hard.

To help organize such disparate material into a coherent tableau, I present four themes in this chapter to provide a framework for thinking about the role of public sector unions in American democracy. These themes are then braided into the chapters that follow. Taken together and buttressed by the existing evidence, they reveal significant tensions between the public interest and the interests of public sector unions.

DEMOCRACY

The first theme is *democracy*. The oldest critique of public sector unionism is that it compromises the sovereignty of democratic government and distorts the democratic process.[1] When most people think about how democracy is supposed to work, they imagine citizens voting in competitive elections for candidates offering distinct policy platforms; the winners then take office and set about implementing their agenda through the bureaucracy. To be sure, this is a stylized picture that overlooks many other distortions. Yet, unionizing government workers vastly complicate it. In collective bargaining negotiations with the government, the people's elected representatives partially cede control of the bureaucracy to unelected labor leaders. Many policy choices are then the outcome of negotiations between officeholders and unions, rather than the expression of the people's will channeled through their representatives.

Huge information asymmetries help explain many outcomes. The "rationally" ignorant public pays little attention to public sector labor relations, while the unions are preoccupied with it. Law professor Richard Epstein has described collective bargaining in government as "an unfair match" between voters on one side and public officials and unions on the other because politicians can "escape voter wrath by granting public employees highly favorable, but less visible," pay and benefit packages.[2] Furthermore, over the long term, negotiated work rules can even push public policy down paths that neither elected officials nor voters truly desire.[3] There is also evidence that unionized portions of government end up overstaffed, while other sectors are starved.[4] Democratic accountability does little to restrain government union demands.

Furthermore, insofar as public employee unions are unique interest groups, they can distort democratic elections and legislative processes. Government unions make campaign contributions and organize get-out-the-vote drives to elect politicians who then act as "management" in negotiations over pay, benefits, and work rules. The result is a cycle that is hard to break. Politicians agree to generous contracts for public workers; those workers then pay their union dues—a portion of which are funneled back into those same politicians' campaign war chests. Such an arrangement sets government on a glide path toward growth.

Public sector unions also enjoy a number of advantages over traditional interest groups when it comes to political influence. First, they have easier access to policymakers through the collective bargaining process, while other interest groups must fight for such entrée. Second, government unions can more easily mobilize their members for electoral participation than other interest groups can. Third, most interest groups must devote a great deal of time and effort to fundraising. Public sector unions, on the other hand, enjoy a steady, reliable revenue stream, as union dues are deducted directly from members' paychecks—often by government, which drastically reduces the unions' administrative costs. These "agency fees," which are often the monetary equivalent to union dues, must be paid by all members in a bargaining unit regardless of whether they join the union or not.[5] Therefore, they act as strong incentives—if not outright coercion—for workers to join the union. These advantages usually allow them to defeat any reform coalition seeking to roll back any of their gains in collective bargaining rights, job security, or compensation. Few other interest groups possess such an arsenal of resources. Bringing them all to bear can reduce the quality of the democratic process.

All of this means that when it comes to public sector labor relations, unions representing government workers, elected officials, and agency managers can combine to create a uniquely powerful "iron triangle." Iron triangles are part of an important tradition of analyses of American politics.[6] Interest groups representing farmers, gas and oil companies, banks, auto manufacturers, real estate firms, and so on all seek to exercise influence with elected officials and the bureaucracies that regulate their industry. Debate and discussion inside iron triangles is often technical and confined to experienced insiders. And, as critics often point out, the interests and policy preferences of insiders often differ substantially from those of the general public.[7] To the extent that powerful interest groups succeed in insulating policy decisions from citizen pressures, they are able to do so because they have the means and motive to tirelessly pursue their goals, while the attention of the general public is too episodic and underinformed to have much of an impact. While iron triangles that diminish democracy are to some extent inevitable given the structure of American political institutions, public sector unions can make them even stronger and more exclusive.

Finally, to the extent that public employee unions have saddled state and local government with long-term liabilities in the form of pension and healthcare commitments, they restrict the range of democratic choice. Today, states and localities are budgeting more but deciding less, as large slices of the public fisc are already spoken for. In California, for example, the share of general fund revenues used to pay pensions and public employee healthcare has doubled in the last decade, crowding out other spending priorities the public and politicians might entertain. The problem is especially grave because the number of retiring government employees is growing faster than the number of retirees in general. So while budgets grow in size, what government can do with those funds is more limited. This is a recipe for voter skepticism and distrust.

EQUITY

The second theme is *equity*. As public employee unions became political players in states and cities throughout the country, they widened the gap between the worlds of private and public sector work. In the former, cut-throat competition and increasing inequality are the order of the day. In the latter, middle-class security and greater egalitarianism persist. Take the hypothetical cases of Pam and Maria (based on averages in the public and private sectors). Both are administrative assistants who are pretty good at their jobs. Both have roughly the same levels of education and experience. But Pam earns about $4,000 more a year than Maria—and also has greater job security (a form of compensation), more paid vacation days, a pension plan, and healthcare. Maria's job is more tenuous and she lacks a pension plan and health insurance. What explains the difference? Pam belongs to a union and works in a government agency, while Maria works for a small business. It is hardly fair that two workers should receive such disparate treatment simply because one works for government and the other works in the private sector.

These imbalances are most evident when it comes to employee benefits. While the average public sector retirement pension is only about $30,000 a year, most people in the private sector have no pension savings at all. Since

2002, for every $1-an-hour pay increase, public employees have gotten $1.17 in new benefits, while private sector workers received just 58 cents in added benefits. And the smaller pension figure doesn't accurately capture what is going on. In California, for example, state workers often retire at 55 years of age with pensions that exceed what they were paid during most of their working years. In New York City, firefighters and police officers may retire after 20 years of service at half pay—which means that, at a time when life expectancy is nearly 80 years, New York City is paying benefits to 10,000 retired cops who are younger than 50 years old.[8] Indeed, the city now pays out more for retired than active police officers each year. In addition, under the "defined benefit" pension plans that prevail in the public sector, recipients do not have to shoulder any of the financial risk, which is borne by taxpayers.[9]

Consequently, as one union leader put it to me, "pension envy" is real. A pollster who ran focus groups in New Jersey about people's views on the financial crisis reported that he found more anger at public sector compensation than at Wall Street. According to him, "I had one guy in a focus group go on a rant about the pension his father, who was a retired cop, got from the town, that the pension was way too generous."[10] Clearly, if citizens are singling out their family members for criticism, the generosity of pensions, especially for those in the protective services, is a problem. And it is not just that such inequities allow Republicans to pit working people against each other.

As the recession subsides, private sector workers cannot continue to be asked to pay taxes to sustain benefit levels they have little hope of ever receiving. Talk about "bringing the private sector up to the public standard" is farfetched. The forces required for such a transformation simply don't exist in contemporary society. If anything, signals suggest, the two worlds of work are more likely to diverge further.[11] Therefore, the imbalances between the public and private sectors will have to be addressed on the public sector side. This doesn't imply a race-to-the-bottom but rather a series of reforms to enhance equity. In some cases, this might even mean paying higher salaries but reducing pension and healthcare benefits for public employees.[12] It might mean paying higher starting salaries and slowing the rise in the pay scale, which tends to be very generous to workers who spend their entire careers in public employ.

On a broader scale, such inequities also appear in places with and without unions. The *Washington Post* compared two very similar wealthy suburban Washington, DC counties and found that the one where public employees were strong had larger budget deficits, higher taxes, and greater political sclerosis.[13] In Maryland, where collective bargaining with public employees is legal, the Montgomery County government faced a $1 billion deficit, which was nearly 25 percent of the spending plan in 2010, which it addressed by raising taxes. Over in Virginia, where public sector collective bargaining is prohibited, there was a far smaller budget deficit, which was resolved with prudent cutting. The difference was an explosive growth in government spending on public employees over the previous decade. For instance, Montgomery teachers' salaries nearly doubled, rising at almost triple the rate of inflation, between 2000 and 2010. Teachers in Montgomery now make about 20 percent more than those in Fairfax, and the former spends about 20 percent more on schools than the latter with no noticeable improvement in student outcomes. Apparently, politicians endorsed by the teachers' union in Montgomery were so appreciative of its support that they donated money to the union rather than the other way around. The Montgomery versus Fairfax comparison reveals the inequities in government that public sector unions help impose on citizens.

Finally, unlike private sector unions, those representing government workers generally serve to make people with college educations and a degree of affluence a bit better off. While the benefits that public sector unions win for their members in terms of wages, healthcare, and pension benefits, although substantial, tend to be smaller than those won by unions in the private sector, government unions don't do much for workers with high school diplomas and limited skills because they don't represent very many of them. According to political scientists Jan Leighley and Jonathan Nagler, as the percentage of public sector union members increased between 1971 and 2004, the fraction of union members in the top third of the nation's income distribution increased by 24 percent, while the proportion of unionists in the bottom third of the distribution declined by 45 percent.[14] This is because better-educated and more affluent workers are more likely to belong to public rather than private sector unions.[15] A labor movement dominated by public sector unions does not reduce political inequality by boosting the voter turnout rate among their less educated and working-class members. Consequently, sociologist Jake Rosenfeld argues that "as unions concentrate in the public sector, their historical role representing those with comparative low education and income levels is reduced."[16]

EFFICIENCY

The third theme is *efficiency*. The issues here are how public sector unions shape how effectively government performs core functions and at what cost. One long-term problem is that government has become very expensive for taxpayers and these expenditures have been directed at things that do not increase economic growth. One group of economists reports that "since 1950, state and local spending has grown ... fast enough to double the size of state and local government every 8 or 9 years."[17] Such growth would be justifiable if it were improving infrastructure, which can increase economic efficiency and spur growth in employment. But that hasn't happened. Spending on things like bridges, roads, prisons, hospitals, and mass transit has remained constant as a percentage of gross domestic product since 1950. This suggests that *almost all* of the growth in state and local spending has gone to employee compensation. In addition, Northeastern University economist Barry Bluestone has shown that, between 2000 and 2008, the price of state and local public services has increased by 41 percent nationally, compared with 27 percent for private services.[18]

Many states have increasingly resorted to debt financing to cover generous public services. And there is a correlation between debt and public sector union strength. Economists Richard Freeman and Eunice Han found that "states with public sector bargaining laws have higher debt-to-state gross domestic product (GDP) ratios and slightly higher deficits than states without such laws."[19] High debt means higher interest payments and lower bond ratings, which is not good for anyone except bankers, as governments are unable to use those tax dollars for other purposes—or return them to citizens through tax cuts. Consequently, the costs of that debt are constricting states' ability to do other things. For example, a report from the New York State comptroller points out that:

> *The cost of borrowing increasingly crowds out other State expenditures.* In 2011-12, New York paid $6.8 billion in State-Funded debt service, which amounted to approximately 5.1 percent of All Governmental Funds receipts. Growth in State-Funded debt service, at an average annual rate

of 9.4 percent over the last 10 years, has far outpaced average annual growth in State spending on both education (5.3 percent) and Medicaid (5.1 percent) for the same period.[20]

And states with stronger public sector unions tend to have higher debt loads and consequently higher interest payments to serve that debt.[21]

Unlike unions in the private sector, government unions have incentives to push for more public employment, which increases their ranks, fills their coffers with new dues, and makes them more powerful. Therefore, they consistently push for higher taxes and more government activity. Over the long term, this can stifle economic growth and pit public and private sector unions against each other. In New York State, some private sector unions joined a coalition backing Governor Andrew Cuomo that aimed to improve the state's business climate and push back against the state's powerful public employee unions. The president of the Building and Construction Trades Council of Greater New York, Gary LaBarbera, said, "We're advocating for a fiscally sane economy in New York" and that "at times there will be competing interests between public- and private-sector unions .... But without a fiscally sound environment, we will not be able to attract new businesses to the city; we'll continue to lose business."[22] For the New York City Council campaigns in 2013, a similar coalition of private sector unions and business leaders formed to counteract the influence of the public sector union–dominated Working Families Party.[23] And in New Jersey, even after Governor Christie battled the Garden State's teachers' union, he racked up re-election endorsements from the state's private sector unions, especially those in the building trades, which are often the more conservative among private sector unions and have a history of occasionally aligning with Republicans.[24] The difference is that private sector unions depend on economic growth and public sector unions depend on government growth. The two are sometimes at odds. Furthermore, sometimes private sector unions also seek government contracts, say, for road construction, and want tax revenue directed to projects they care about rather than into the pockets of their public sector union counterparts.

Within government itself, public sector unions have shaped the conditions of their members' employment in ways that give them shelter from the economic storm that rages in the private sector. In the private sector, intense competition, constant evaluation, long hours, and pay-for-performance standards are the norm. By comparison, the public sector is an oasis of regularity, predictability, and security. Because public employee unions are most powerful at the state and local level, where most people actually interact with government, they give shape to that experience.

Take the clearest example of inefficiency: the inability of school administrators to fire incompetent teachers. Indeed, protecting such ineffective workers has the effect of weakening the overall public workforce. Stanford University economist Eric Hanushek found that if even middling instructors could somehow replace the bottom 5 to 8 percent of American teachers, the United States would be catapulted to nearly the top of international math and science rankings.[25] Such a change would be a herculean feat given the strength of the job protections unionized teachers enjoy. Therefore, in this area as in others, citizens will have to muddle through with government that performs less than optimally.

Public sector unions have also vigorously opposed pay-for-performance and other efforts to instill greater accountability. Competition, flexibility, and transparency receive lip service, but in collective bargaining negotiations, when the chips are down, the unions scuttle the actual policies that would make these abstract values a reality. The teachers' unions provide a clear example. As political scientist Terry Moe has shown, the teachers' unions have used collectively bargained work rules to design the organization of America's schools to serve teachers' interests rather than those of students.[26]

The unions have pushed for and won rules that allow senior teachers to take the jobs of junior teachers (regardless of merit); that require junior teachers to be laid off before senior teachers (so-called last-in, first-out); that limit the number of faculty meetings per year; that require principals to give advance notice before visiting classrooms to evaluate teachers; that specify (down to the minute) the time outside of class that teachers have to prepare; and that give teachers a liberal number of "personal" days with pay (so students must be taught by substitutes). The rules teachers' unions negotiate literally define how America's schools are run. The result, Moe writes, is a huge "disconnect between what the public schools are supposed to do and how they are organized to do it."[27]

The long-term consequence is that two worlds of work—one private, one public—have developed. The protected aspects of the public world have reduced efficiency in the delivery of public sector services. Ultimately, the poor and the middle class who send their children to public school, rely on cities to collect their trash, commute to work using public transportation, and depend on various forms of state support get the short end of the stick. They are paying more in taxes and receiving less in services. If government were more efficient and effective, it could provide more services and support to those who really need them. And all sensible people should oppose policies where the overall costs outweigh the benefits. The problem is that public sector unionism and collective bargaining are too often at odds with commonsense policy and effective government.

PURPOSE

The fourth theme is government *purpose*. By increasing the costs of government, public sector unions skew its priorities. For instance, 60 percent of Washington State's budget goes to pay the salaries and benefits of the state's employees.[28] This part of the budget is thus off limits to policymakers, since it is governed by union contracts. Governments are thus budgeting more dollars but deciding less, as huge portions of budgets are fixed costs.[29] Furthermore, union demands for greater employee compensation redirects monies that could be used for other purposes. For example, in Massachusetts, hundreds of millions of dollars in school funding have never reached a classroom because they have been used to pay for the healthcare of education workers. This sort of situation helps explain why the major increases in spending on education over the last 30 years have had so little effect on student performance.

Such "crowding out" or redirection of government spending is most evident in the skyrocketing costs of public employees' pensions. By one estimate, the unfunded pension liability of the states is currently $3 trillion. Another estimate found that the states have unfunded liabilities of about $980 billion—nearly double what they officially claim.[30] For example, in 2009, New Jersey's unfunded liability was $130 billion, which was more than four times the state's 2008 fiscal year budget. California, which faced a $25.4 billion budget gap in 2011, paid $100,000-plus pensions to more than 12,000 state and municipal retirees in 2012.[31] Meanwhile, the cost to local government of employing a worker has soared. For instance, in San Jose, the average cost of a full-time worker is $142,000 a year, up

85 percent in 10 years. A sanitation worker in New York City now costs $144,000 annually, up from $79,000 a decade ago. The result is that government cannot spend tax revenues on other purposes.

The reordering of government priorities is painful. Around the country, governors and mayors have been forced to propose cuts to education, policing, fire protection, healthcare programs, and other social services. The city council of Philadelphia currently faces the agonizing choice of whether to lay off 2,350 teachers in a school system with 131,000 students or to address the city's $5 billion unfunded pension liability with $120 million in new revenues from an extension of an 8 percent sales tax.[32] These sorts of tough choices are facing elected officials in many parts of the country. Sacrificing a huge swath of states' and cities' education, health, and poor relief expenditures to pay for the benefits of a vastly smaller slice of people that happened to have worked for government is hardly a wise allocation of scarce resources.

Looking Ahead

The conflict between the interests of government unions and the public interest is profound. The long-standing hope that the two could be reconciled rested on questionable economic projections and an outmoded demographic model. The increased cost to taxpayers of public employment is only one of public sector unionism's principal effects. Government workers' unions have also had a significant impact on the character of the labor movement, the business climate, and government's productivity and efficiency. Ultimately, they have shaped the way that American democracy works. The fundamental question, to put it grandiloquently, is whether unionized government works for the people or the people now work to pay for unionized government. This is a question of serious concern to liberals and conservatives, Republicans and Democrats, and private and public sector workers.

To set the United States on a path to compete globally, adjust to rapid technological change, and assist those most in need of government support in the twenty-first century, American government has to make government more flexible and responsive. Moving in that direction will be contentious, since the unions have a huge stake in preserving the status quo. Other countries are facing similar challenges in dealing with government unions.[33] It's not just California's prison guards that pose a problem to fiscal sanity and effective services, but also unionized British police officers, French railworkers, and Mexican teachers. Yet reconfiguring government labor relations will contribute to the long-term project of creating a government that can balance American society's aspirations and economic dynamism and social compassion.[34]

THE UNSEEN RIGHTS REVOLUTION

Organized labor in the United States has been transformed. It is no longer concentrated in the private sector with blue-collar workers in manufacturing and the building trades filling the ranks. For the first time, in 2009, more public sector employees (7.9 million) than private sector employees (7.4 million) belonged to unions—even though there are five times as many workers in the private as in the public sector[1] (Figure 3.1). The American Federation of State, County, and Municipal Employees (AFSCME) has approximately 1.5 million members and the National Education Association (NEA) 2.5 million, dwarfing the United Automobile Workers (UAW) and the US Steel Workers. The iconic image of a union member, the beefy white ethnic in a hard hat and steel-toed boots, is an anachronism. A majority of unionized workers are now employed by the government and are more likely to be teachers, police officers, and firefighters than carpenters, autoworkers, and coal miners.[2] This has changed the face of organized labor.[3]

At their peak in the United States, more than a third of nonagricultural workers belonged to unions. Yet at the same time, government workers counted for only a tiny percentage of unionized workers.[4] When the conservative American Federation of Labor (AFL) merged with the radical

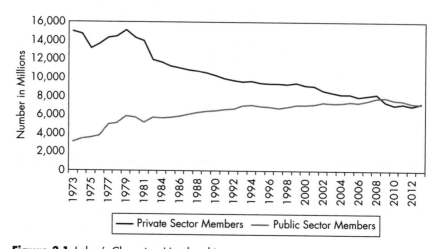

Figure 3.1 Labor's Changing Membership.

Source: CPS, Unionstats.org, Barry T. Hirsch and David A. Mcpherson.

Congress of Industrial Organizations (CIO) in 1955, few public employees were union members. In government labor relations, civil service rules specified the conditions of hiring, promotion, and work. Legal barriers in many states forbade government workers from joining unions, and where they could join unions, union rights were highly restricted. All states banned strikes by public workers. And government employees were from populations—such as white-collar professionals and women—that had little attachment to unions. The dominant understanding regardless of political viewpoint—from labor leaders to conservative Republicans—was that collective bargaining would interfere with the sovereignty of government by delegating a piece of policymaking authority to union representatives in collective bargaining negotiations. In sum, before the 1960s, public employee unions were severely restricted and constituted a minor portion of the total unionized workforce. Most policymakers were hostile to them. In such a weak position, the leader of the United Federation of Teachers (UFT), Albert Shanker, referred to public unions' activity as "collective begging."[5]

Beginning in 1958 and running through 1984, public employees' unions gained the right to organize and bargain collectively, with the majority of states enacting measures favorable to collective bargaining for public employees. In 1959, only three states had collective bargaining laws for state and local employees. By 1980, 33 states did.[6] The percentage of public sector workers covered by collective bargaining laws shot up from 1 percent in 1960 to 66 percent in 1990.[7] Today, only three states, Virginia, North Carolina, and South Carolina, completely proscribe collective bargaining in the public sector. Utah allows workers the "right to present proposals," which is more like a "meet and confer" law than collective bargaining. The rest permit it for at least some public servants (usually teachers and those in the protective services, such as police officers, firefighters, and corrections officers), and most states have extensive legal provisions permitting "agency shops" and "dues check-off" (meaning the government's collection of union dues).[8] Yet, there is considerable occupational variation in which workers enjoy collective bargaining rights. For instance, firefighters enjoy the widest collective bargaining rights and nearly 77 percent of them are unionized.[9] State statutes were supplemented by local ordinances. The growth of public employee unions and their membership followed hard on the heels of the legal changes. Less than 10 percent of full-time public employees were unionized in 1960. By 1980, it was 36 percent.[10] That percentage has remained strikingly stable over the last three decades, as government workers' unions have consolidated their position[11] (Figure 3.2).

Public sector unions are now potent political forces in big cities, state capitals, and Washington, DC.[12] They participate in the development of public policy through collective bargaining, which empowers them to share in government's decision making about how and at what price government employees will perform public services, and they shape public policy through their extensive lobbying and electioneering

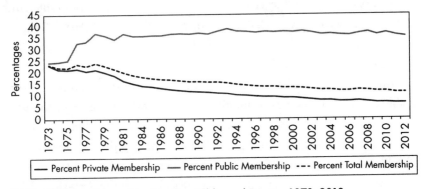

Figure 3.2 Total Union Membership: Public and Private, 1973–2013.

Source: CPS, Unionstats.org, Barry T. Hirsch and David A. Mcpherson.

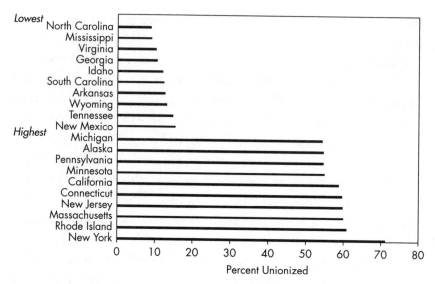

Figure 3.3 Public Sector Unionization Rates by State, 2012.

Source: CPS, Unionstats.org, Barry T. Hirsch and David A. Mcpherson.

efforts. In recent campaigns and elections, the power and energy of the labor movement emanated from public sector unions. They are among the largest donors of money to candidates, mostly Democrats but sometimes Republicans, at the state and national levels and make important independent expenditures on campaign advertisements.[13] Consequently, in 2011, Republican governors in Wisconsin, Ohio, Indiana, and elsewhere sought to enact reforms to reduce the power of public sector unions (Figure 3.3).[14]

What we have, then, is a major political development—what political scientists Stephen Skowronek and Karen Orren call "a durable shift in governing authority"—that cries out for explanation.[15] How did public sector unions become the heart and soul of the labor movement and among the more powerful interest groups in American politics? I address this question in three parts. First, I explain the political conditions that enabled the legal changes in many American states from 1958 to 1984. I then analyze the patterns of state legislative coalitions that formed to pass major collective bargaining legislation. Finally, I discuss how the rise of public sector unionism should make us reconsider the traditional story about the decline—numerically and politically—of the American labor movement.[16]

THE GROWTH OF PUBLIC SECTOR UNIONS

From Massachusetts Governor Calvin Coolidge's breaking of the Boston Police Strike in 1919 through the 1950s, most politicians, labor leaders, economists, and judges did not believe that collective bargaining was proper in the governmental arena. Courts across the nation generally held that collective bargaining by government workers should be blocked on the grounds of sovereign immunity and unconstitutional delegation of powers.[17] Even many of the icons of the labor Left, such as New York Mayor Fiorello LaGuardia and President Franklin D. Roosevelt, were opposed to public employee unions.[18] In 1935, Roosevelt signed the National Labor Relations Act, which provided substantial federal government support for private sector unions but excluded public ones. Its aim, in the words of its sponsor, New York Senator Robert Wagner, was "encouraging the practice and procedure of collective bargaining."[19] Yet Roosevelt drew a line when it came to government workers. "Meticulous attention," the president insisted, "should be paid to the special relations and obligations of public servants to the public itself and to the Government .... The process of collective bargaining, as usually understood, cannot be transplanted into the public service."[20]

LaGuardia and Roosevelt feared that democracy would be compromised by the peculiar nature of public sector unionism. Overall, opponents' view of public employee unionism and collective bargaining rested on the *essentiality* of government service. As a matter of duty, public services, they argued, must not be imperiled by strikes. It also seemed natural to maintain that the people (i.e., the government) cannot strike against *the people*.[21] To the extent that government employees were organized, they belonged to various sorts of associations, most of which also included managers.

There is a debate over the extent to which it was the legal changes of the 1960s and 1970s that led to the growth of government unionism. Most analysts find that the new laws, considered as external factors, were the most important cause.[22] However, even if legislative changes did increase the number of unions and the size of their membership, the prior question of how the laws themselves came into being remains unaddressed. As two scholars put it, "If the public policy did cause the increase in unionization among state and local government employees, then the task is to explain the emergence of the public policy."[23] In sum, how the collective bargaining laws actually passed has received far less attention from economists.[24]

Four conditions provided the impetus for the legal changes bringing collective bargaining into government, the conversion of employee associations into unions, and the explosion in the number of government employees belonging to them. The first was the weakening of the party machines at the state and especially the city level.[25] The principal means for breaking the machines was the enactment of civil service laws to deprive them of control over patronage—the exchange of government jobs for political services—which was their lifeblood. In many of America's large cities, party machines dominated the selection of people for government jobs. Chicago Alderman Vito Mazullo explained how the system operated in his southwest-side ward:

> I got an assistant state's attorney, and I got an assistant attorney general. I got an electrical inspector at twelve thousand dollars a year, and I got street inspectors and surveyors, and a county highway inspector. I got an administrative assistant to the zoning board and some people in the secretary of state's office. I got ninety-five precinct captains and they all got assistants and they all got jobs. The lawyers I got in jobs don't have to work precincts, but they have to come by my ward office and give free legal advice to the people of the ward.[26]

In turn, those selected for patronage jobs were expected to be loyal to the party and provide votes, funds, and campaign work. Machine politicians opposed the enactment of collective bargaining legislation because they feared it would undermine their operations. As economist Gregory Saltzman points out:

> Union contracts requiring just cause for discharge would make it harder for officials of one political party to fire workers who had been hired by the opposing party. Similarly, seniority bidding rules would make it harder for officials to use the threat of transfers, job assignments to dirty duty, and assignments to work on holidays to pressure current employees to contribute labor or money to the party in power. Finally, union contracts could also prohibit the assignment of specific patronage duties that had previously been routinely expected.[27]

Insofar as the aim of public employees' associations was to professional-
ize the government workforce and end such practices, patronage systems
for the first half of the twentieth century separated the Democratic Party
and the aspiring public sector unions.

The movement to eliminate patronage began in the late nineteenth
century and reached its apogee in the 1950s. While reformers largely succeeded by the 1930s in much of the West, in the industrial states of the
Northeast and the lower Great Lakes region, where private sector unionism
was flourishing, the patronage system hung on. Machines ruled the roost
in New York, Pittsburg, Jersey City, Philadelphia, Baltimore, St. Louis,
Cleveland, Chicago, Albany, and many smaller cities. By the end of the
1950s, however, a new generation of reformers had put the old machines
on the defensive in most of their strongholds.[28] The reformers sought to
"sever the link between the ward politicians and the dispensation of [gov-
ernment] services."[29]

Under the rule of the party machines, turnover in government employment was often high, connected as it was to election results. The instability
of public employment meant that a sense of professionalism could never
take hold.[30] The pressure on the machines thus came from civic groups, the
press, and public employees' associations, which demanded greater professionalization of the workforce. They hoped a more professional workforce would draw in talent, increase efficiency, and reduce corruption. In
the early years, the leadership of the AFSCME "saw itself as part of a great
movement to reform government," one of whose principal aims was "the
extension of the merit system to all nonpolicy determining positions in all
government jurisdictions."[31] One effect of the rise of civil service reform
was that public employees gained nearly lifetime job security. Civil service reform was a precondition for unionization because it gave workers
a long-term interest in their jobs and facilitated their capacity to express
collective concerns. The professionalization of the workforce also under-
mined the old city machines. Political scientists Edward C. Banfield and
James Q. Wilson reported that by 1961, 52 percent of cities with populations over 500,000 had nearly all employees under civil service protections. Only 41 percent of cities with populations between 10,000 and
100,000 had no civil service protections at all.[32]

The passage of state and local civil service reform measures provided
a greater degree of job security and prestige to government workers than

they had previously enjoyed.[33] Civil service rules, based as they were on the idea of merit in hiring and promotions, also regularized government work. Winning a job was now based on competitive exams and qualifications rather than personal connections. Advancement and raises occurred on regular schedules that were publicly available. Civil service rules became the floor for public workers in terms of job protections and regularized work rules. In New York State, for example, in 1941, government employees won the right to a hearing if faced with disciplinary charges; in 1955, all competitive class employees were eligible for tenure; also in the 1950s, public pensions guaranteed by the state constitution were made available to all full-time employees. Once accustomed to such protections, union efforts to secure more of them appeared only natural.

As patronage systems were displaced by civil services rules, the Democratic Party (and sometimes the Republican Party) needed new sources of voters, campaign dollars, and foot soldiers. Fortunately for it, the barrier between Democrats who had previously relied on the patronage system and public sector unions was also dismantled. The growth of unions in government offered new resources. And the Democrats had things to offer public workers: new collective bargaining rights, stricter enforcement of civil service rules, and social services aimed at working-class citizens. In sum, the demise of patronage gave politicians the incentive to link arms with the public sector unions and make them bigger and more powerful to increase their own electoral fortunes.

The second condition was the reconfiguration of state legislative districts. The Supreme Court's decisions in *Baker v. Carr* (1962) and *Reynolds v. Sims* (1964) dramatically shifted power in many states from rural to urban voters over the course of a decade. Prior to the Supreme Court's intervention, many state legislatures repeatedly failed to redraw their congressional and state legislative districts despite the population shifts detailed in the US Census. In 1960, districts in Alabama reflected population distributions from the 1900 census. Only New Hampshire and Wisconsin approached the "one man, one vote" standard the court set. (In this light, it is not surprising that Wisconsin was the first state to enact a statewide collective bargaining law). At the other end of the spectrum, the smallest counties in California had over 400 times as much representation in the state senate as Los Angeles. In sum, the court's decisions created a massive redistribution of political representation in the states.

The shift in representation, not surprisingly, had significant consequences. One study found that it redistributed approximately $7 billion annually in funds from rural to urban counties.[34] Because more liberal Democrats hailed from urban areas and were more sympathetic to unionism than their rural counterparts, the shift aided the fortunes of public employees. This was partly because private sector unions and associations of government employees (that had not yet converted themselves into unions) were far more prevalent in the cities. Students of teachers' unions have found that teachers organized into associations (NEA) or unions (AFT) and began negotiating with school boards in the large cities before the passage of mandatory collective bargaining statutes. The urban teachers' unions then lobbied heavily for the passage of duty-to-bargain laws. Once the laws passed, unionization quickly spread to the suburbs, as well as smaller cities and towns.[35] Urban legislators' newfound power allowed them to respond more directly to the demands of public employee unions. Political scientist James C. Garand found that from 1945 to 1984, one of the strongest predictors of increased size of state government was the voting power of public employees.[36] And from 1950 to 1980, Democratic control of state government outside the South (where party competition was just beginning) was correlated with greater welfare spending.[37]

The third condition underpinning the changes to come was economic and demographic change. The postwar period witnessed a major spike in government jobs. Between 1960 and 1976, state and local government employment went from 11.2 to 15.3 percent of the nonagricultural workforce.[38] In other words, between 1960 and 1970, employment in state and local government rose from roughly 6 million to 10 million.[39] There were simply more jobs in the public sector than heretofore. In addition, the Depression generation was extremely fertile, which resulted in the now famous "baby boom." To educate, protect, house, and provide public spaces for so many new citizens, government had to grow.

The increase in the number of jobs, combined with increasing demands on employees, elicited calls for change in how employees were treated. This was most evident in education. The number of students entering the schools in the 1950s and 1960s shot up. In the United States, approximately 77.3 million babies were born between 1946 and 1964.[40] Consequently, the demand for people to work in the schools—as teachers, principals, and administrators—increased dramatically. It is not surprising that some of the first public employees to unionize and some of the most militant, displaying almost an eagerness to engage in illegal strikes, were teachers. In the late 1960s and 1970s, strike activity by teachers increased dramatically. From 1958 to 1970, strikes, including those by teachers, rose from 15 to 412 per year.[41] It was not until the 1980s that public employee strikes declined dramatically.[42]

The final step in enacting collective bargaining legislation to spur public sector union growth was action by politicians. Politicians, especially Democrats with links to organized labor, were quicker to act in places where private sector unionism was strong but worried about declining membership. Indeed, by the late 1950s, the AFL-CIO had come to see expansion into the public sector as the best new hunting ground and made Democratic politicians aware of their views. As political scientist John Alquist points out, "Private sector workers (and voters) were willing to support collective bargaining rights in the public sector because, at the time they were implemented, many private sector workers already enjoyed these rights themselves."[43] And there was a broad sense of solidarity between workers in both sectors.

For their part, Democrats saw the mobilization of public employees into unions as a means of consolidating a new constituency. And conceding new labor rights seemed less politically risky than it had a decade before. Organized labor's radicalism of the 1940s had largely been pacified. The Labor Management Relations Act of 1947 (also known as the Taft-Hartley Act) had allowed the southern states to pass right-to-work laws, reduced the number of strikes, and banned secondary boycotts. The CIO had purged communist-dominated unions and then merged with the more conservative AFL in 1955. And the private sector now had 25 years of experience with collective bargaining under the Wagner Act. Integrating government workers into such a regime seemed harmless. Groups such as the American Bar Association endorsed the idea.[44]

A mayor, a governor, and a president took the first steps. Together they provided examples that were soon emulated. In 1958, New York Mayor Robert Wagner, son of the senator behind the 1935 federal law, issued an executive order generally known as "the little Wagner Act." Mayor Wagner used the measure to mobilize the public sector workforce behind him and finally break the back of the Tammany Hall political machine. His order gave city employees bargaining rights and provided their unions with exclusive representation.[45] The election of Democrat Gaylord Nelson as governor of Wisconsin in 1958, after nearly a quarter century of Republican control, facilitated the passage of the first state-wide collective bargaining law, the Municipal Employees Relations Act, on September 22, 1959.[46] Lastly, in mid-January 1962, President John F. Kennedy issued Executive Order 10988 giving federal workers the right to organize and for some to bargain collectively. These three precedents established a paradigm that set off a wave of local union activity across the nation's states and cities.

Kennedy had been elected by the narrowest of margins in 1960 and had made a number of promises to organized labor on the campaign trail in return for its support. Upon his election, he named Arthur Goldberg his secretary of labor, as his first step in rewarding labor for its help during the campaign. Goldberg had been an attorney for the United Steel Workers of America. But labor wanted more. It had strongly supported a collective bargaining bill for federal employees sponsored by George Rhodes (D-PA) and Olin Johnston (D-SC) in the 1950s. But the measure had failed to gain traction in the face of the Eisenhower administration's opposition. Kennedy shared some of his predecessors' concerns about the legislation percolating in Congress—especially the possibility that it would give labor too much power. The top brass of the defense agencies were particularly concerned. To head off legislative action, he decided upon an executive order. The order, initially drafted by Cyrus Vance, the general counsel of the Defense Department, was significantly weaker than the Rhodes-Johnston bill. Goldberg, with the help of Ida Klaus and Daniel Patrick Moynihan, then stepped in, getting Kennedy to appoint him chairman of the Task Force on Employee-Management Relations in the Federal Service. After nearly half a year of interagency battles, Goldberg emerged with a stronger order, albeit one that still fell well short of labor's hopes.[47] After Theodore Sorensen drafted the final document, the president signed it on January 17, 1962.

Despite private disappointment, labor publicly endorsed it. ALF-CIO President George Meany called it "a Wagner Act for public employees." Within a few years of the order, the largest union of federal workers, the American Federation of Government Employees (AFGE), increased fourfold. By the end of the decade, nearly 850,000 federal employees were covered by collective bargaining agreements.

Between 1965 and 1970, 22 states followed the lead of Wagner, Nelson, and Kennedy. In many cases, the consequences of the new legislation were almost immediate. In New York State, for example, one year after the passage of the Taylor Law in 1967, 360,000 state and local government employees had been unionized.[48] This was on top of the roughly 340,000 workers (mostly in New York City) already covered by collective bargaining contracts.[49] According to the *New York Times*, the law had an "almost revolutionary effect."[50] Other states and cities experienced similar explosions in the number of public sector union members.

A 1968 Supreme Court ruling that state workers could invoke federal labor laws without violating the prerogatives of state governments intensified the impact of these laws.[51] By 1972, nearly half of the states (23) had public employee collective bargaining laws in state or local government or both. Of these, only seven were mandatory laws extending the full range of bargaining rights to all public employees on wages, hours, and conditions. The other states exempted some employees from coverage by bargained contracts, ruled some subjects out of bounds, or merely authorized rather than required bargaining.[52] Seventeen states with no collective bargaining laws on the books allowed the practice by the end of the 1970s. By 1970, the AFSCME had negotiated more than 1,000 collective bargaining agreements, which was nearly double the number in 1964.[53] Ultimately, in states with union-friendly laws, government worker organizing flourished; in states without such laws, it did not.

This rapid surge in the number of states with collective bargaining laws and the consequent increase in the number and size of public sector unions, especially teachers' unions, led to another push for federal legislation. Led by Albert Shanker of the AFT and James Harris of the NEA, the teachers' unions in 1975 pressed for a national statute that would grant collective bargaining rights to all teachers throughout the country.[54] The National Association of School Boards strongly opposed the legislation. A few bills were considered in US Senate and House committees but failed to garner enough support to become law. After this and other efforts to secure a national collective bargaining law for public employees, such as bringing public employees under the National Labor Relations Act, fizzled in the mid-1970s, the government labor movement was confined to slightly expanding and consolidating the gains made in the states.

LEGISLATIVE COALITIONS IN THE STATES

While these examples suggest a clear Democratic Party power play to gain the support of the budding government unions, the reality is more complicated. Indeed, in many states where the legal measures encouraging the unions went the furthest, large numbers of Republicans voted for them. In other cases, it was Democrats, especially those affiliated with political machines, who were the primary opponents of collective bargaining legislation. In most cases, bipartisan support was required for the new labor legislation in the public sector.

Take Wisconsin. In 1959, Democrats had gained control of the governorship and held a majority in the assembly for the first time since 1933. But Republicans still dominated the State Senate (20 to 12). The 1959 law signed by Gaylord Nelson applied only to local government employees and teachers. In 1967, Republicans controlled the governorship (Warren P. Knowles), the assembly (53 to 47), and the State Senate (21 to 12) and passed a collective bargaining law for state employees. In sum, the history of Wisconsin's government labor law in this period was a complex bipartisan affair.

Despite being an industrialized northern state with strong unions in the private sector, Illinois did not adopt a statewide collective bargaining law until 1983. The main reason for the delay was the opposition of Mayor Richard Daley and the Chicago Democratic machine. Daley mobilized a group of Cook County state legislators to forge an alliance with rural Republicans to block collective bargaining legislation in Springfield. However, after Daley's death in 1976, Jane Bryne ran for mayor as the antiestablishment candidate in 1979 and promised to support a collective bargaining measure. Yet once comfortably ensconced in city hall, she found patronage politics congenial. Harold Washington's election as mayor in 1983 with the support of the local AFSCME finally did the trick. Washington and his allies viewed the Chicago patronage operation as a means of perpetuating white dominance of city hall. They saw collective bargaining legislation as a means of weakening the machine, which had been unfriendly to the majority of blacks. With solid support in both chambers of the state legislature, collective bargaining measures (H.B. 1530 and S.B. 536) were pushed past the tepid opposition of Republican Governor Jim Thompson.

In many cases, support for new measures in public sector labor relations came from liberal Republicans seeking "labor peace" in light of the wave of strikes by government workers in the 1960s—even though more strike activity was on the way after the collective bargaining laws were passed. Some may also have believed that collective bargaining in the public sector was the same thing as in the private sector. Indeed, many liberal Republicans in the northern and midwestern states had worked for large corporations and had sat across the bargaining table from unions in the private sector. Examples included Ohio (Jim Rhodes), New Hampshire (Meldrim Thompson), and Pennsylvania (Raymond Shafer). Political scientist Nicol Rae found that labor management relations were one of the areas of greatest difference between liberal Republicans from the Northeast and the Great Lakes region and the rest of the GOP, which was much more hostile to unionism.[55]

In 1968 in California, the Democratic-controlled state legislature passed the Meyers-Milias-Brown Act, which was signed by Republican Governor Ronald Reagan. It extended collective bargaining rights to local government workers. Reagan was, after all, a former union leader: the head of the Screen Actors Guild. As he became more conservative over the course of the 1960s, Reagan did not adopt the hard-edged anti-unionism sometimes found on the Right. In general, he reacted moderately, like other governors of the period, to increasing public sector labor activity. Indeed, Reagan's friend and ally, Nevada Governor Paul Laxalt, signed a similar measure the same year.

California teachers (Educational Employment Relations Act), state employees (State Employer-Employee Relations Act), and state university professors (Higher Education Employer-Employee Relations Act) were granted collective bargaining rights in 1976, 1978, and 1979, respectively, under Democratic Governor Jerry Brown. Brown's moves follow more closely the model of the Democratic Party solidifying its alliance with public employees.

On the other side of the country, three days after a major transit workers' strike in New York City, Governor Nelson Rockefeller appointed a blue-ribbon panel to "make legislative proposals for protecting the public against the disruption of vital public services by illegal strikes, while at the same time protecting the rights of public employees." The panel, chaired by George W. Taylor, an industrial relations professor and labor arbitrator, issued a report whose recommendations would form the core of the 1967 Public Employees' Fair Employment Act, which became known as the Taylor Law. Rockefeller brought his private sector experience to bear, believing that institutional mechanisms were necessary to resolve differences between labor and management. He wanted a partner he could deal with to avoid future strikes.[56]

RETHINKING THE TRADITIONAL STORY

The rise of public sector unionism challenges the conventional wisdom that organized labor in American politics has been declining for the last half century.[57] Political scientist Margaret Levi sums up that wisdom: "The era of Big Business, Big Government, and Big Labor has given way to Giant Corporation, Reduced Government, and Weak Labor."[58] Because union power, especially in the private sector, hinges on the number of members (union density), the decline as a percentage of the nonagricultural workforce is a key indicator that organized labor is weaker. Unions' diminished political power was evident by 1978 when Democratic President Jimmy Carter and solid Democratic majorities in the House and Senate failed to pass a bill to strengthen collective bargaining rights.[59] More recently, the inability of a Democratic president (Barack Obama) and large Democratic majorities in the 111th Congress to pass organized labor's highest legislative priority, the Employee Free Choice Act, is indicative of unions' political impotence.

There is much evidence to support this view. In 1955, organized labor represented about one-third of the nonagricultural workforce. Today, it represents only 11.3 percent.[60] And sheer numbers are of cardinal importance for unions in the private sector when it comes to pressuring management, whether at the bargaining table or on the picket line. Many analysts argue that insofar as labor is an important determinant of policy liberalism, declining membership has had harmful consequences for American politics.[61] The prospects for a liberal economic agenda have dimmed as Democrats and labor have suffered losses while Republicans and business have profited. Facing a weakened opposition, a powerful conservative movement emerged in the 1970s. By injecting energy into the Republican Party, it helped elect Ronald Reagan in 1980, spurred the 1994 Republican takeover of the House of Representatives for the first time in 40 years, and finally propelled the GOP to its highest point in postwar national politics in 2004.[62]

The reasons for the decline of private sector unionism are the subject of considerable debate.[63] At least seven factors are cited to explain the decline of organized labor:[64] (1) the disappearance of manufacturing jobs due to automation and outsourcing, itself enabled by globalization; (2) the purge of Communists and left-wing unions during the early Cold War, which deprived the labor movement of many of its best organizers; (3) the failure of the Democratic Party to be a more consistently prolabor party; (4) the Taft-Hartley Act, which prohibited a variety of union strike practices and political activities and right-to-work legislation in half the states geographically, confining the labor movement;[65] (5) the inability of unions to better integrate black Americans and connect with the feminist, consumer, and environmental movements of the 1960s and 1970s;[66] (6) employers becoming increasingly sophisticated in blocking union drives;[67] and (7) an increasingly conservative American electorate with less favorable views of unions.[68] In sum, fewer jobs in labor-dominated industries due to global competition and technological innovation, a difficult legal and political climate, and antiunion employers have all served to turn private sector unionism into a rout.

Despite the considerable merits of this interpretation, its dominance has prevented analysts from studying public sector unions, which complicate the picture. In fact, as labor historian Joseph McCartin has persuasively argued, on each of the aforementioned points, the rise of public sector unionism cuts against the traditional view.[69] First, by ignoring public employee unions, scholars discount the most important area of growth in union membership in the last few decades. Second, getting rid of Communists and radicals, far from hampering public sector organizing, was a precondition for it. Legislators and governors could not, politically, have allowed communist-dominated unions to represent government employees. Third, while private sector labor's relationship with the Democrats has been called a "barren marriage," the marriage of public sector unions and the Democrats has been fecund. Without close collaboration with Democratic politicians, laws requiring collective bargaining for government workers would never have passed in the states and cities. It is fair to say that most observers have underestimated union political power, especially at the subnational level. Fourth, while labor law since

Taft-Hartley hasn't been kind to private sector labor, it has been generous to public sector labor. Fifth, public sector unions, representing as they
often did more women and minorities, were intimately involved in the
civil rights and feminist movements of the 1960s and 1970s. Sixth, even if
private sector employers became tougher, those in the public sector have
rarely ever adopted hardball tactics to block organizing drives. Seventh,
public opinion, while sometimes unkind to private sector unions, has never
had clear and distinct views on their public counterparts.[70] Ultimately,
because scholars have overlooked public employee unions, whose unique
attributes have helped sustain labor's power, we lack a full picture of the
role of unions in American politics.

A Revolutionary Period

The 1960s and 1970s were a turbulent time in American politics. The civil
rights, antiwar, feminist, consumer, and environmental movements put
new issues on the national policy agenda. As these movements waxed,
many have concluded that the labor movement waned. Union members
were portrayed as "beery, hawkish, ethnic slobs," who supported the
Vietnam War and opposed the rights being won by blacks, women, welfare
recipients, and the disabled.[71] But there was another "rights revolution" in
this period that has been ignored. That revolution occurred when public
employees gained the legal right to collectively bargain, provide exclusive
representation, and have government collect union dues.

It was a revolution with major consequences for American politics, as
governments across the country effectively created a powerful new interest group. As noted in chapter 1 to this book, public sector unions have
advantages over their private sector counterparts, as well as other interest groups, when it comes to making their views known to politicians.
And these advantages have allowed the unions to make their mark on the
amount, organization, and delivery of many public goods. As one com-
mentator remarked in the late 1970s, "the public-employee unions plunged
into municipal treasuries like a starved man whose only thought is to eat as
much as he can swallow."[72]

Looking at the government workers' rights revolution forces us to alter
the traditional story of the American labor movement. Ultimately, the
contrasting trajectories of public and private sector unions suggests that

the alignment of forces that made for powerful private sector unions no longer exists and that this makes those in the public sector appear even more anomalous. Therefore, championing organized labor today really means championing government employees. This is especially the case, as a revival of unions in the private sector is an increasingly remote possibility. As labor scholar Melvyn Dubofsky has recently remarked, "Given the current alignment of forces domestically and globally, I find it hard to conceive of any tactics or broader strategy through which the labor movement might re-establish its former size, place, and power."[73] This is especially true when we reflect on the fact that both private and public sector unions grew in distinct spurts rather than a slow, steady accumulation of members.[74] Unless, then, there is a dramatic change in workers' attitudes, government policy, or the global marketplace, a revival of private sector organized labor is unlikely. Unionizing government did not cause the decline of private sector unionism, nor is it likely to help spur a rebirth. What will remain is the far more problematic unionization of government workers who today have far more job protections than most workers, in most places, for most of human history.

ELECTING YOUR OWN BOSS

Karla Katz, the former president of New Jersey's Local 1034 of the Communications Workers of America (CWA), which represents thousands of state employees, was for a time the richly rewarded girlfriend of billionaire Governor Jon Corzine.[1] Her influence on Corzine became clear in 2006 when the impassioned governor spoke to a Trenton rally of roughly 10,000 public workers and shouted out: "We will fight for a fair contract!"[2] This is striking because at the time Governor Corzine was in the position of management, which is supposed to check the demands of government workers. Yet, the power of the public sector unions to drive election outcomes means that they can exercise influence on both sides of the bargaining table. Even Corzine—who spent more than $100 million of his own money on his campaigns for a US Senate seat in 2000 and the governorship in 2005—still looked to the unions' get-out-the-vote operations for support. And given the unions' influence among his fellow Democrats in the Garden State's legislature, Corzine was careful to stay in their good graces.

Such stories are not atypical. The powerful Speaker of the New York State Assembly, Sheldon Silver, once told the United Federation of Teachers at a rally that: "I and my colleagues in the Assembly majority will be your best friends ... in Albany."[3] Public sector unions have become potent political forces at every level of American government. In addition to furthering their causes through collective bargaining, they also shape public policy through their extensive electioneering efforts. In recent campaigns and elections, they were the energy driving the labor movement. They are among the largest donors of money to candidates, mostly Democrats but sometimes Republicans, at the state and national levels and make important independent expenditures on campaign advertisements[4] (Table 4.1). The unions provide the foot soldiers for registration and get-out-the-vote drives in key races. Unionized public employees also turn out to vote at much higher rates than average citizens and nonunionized workers, which is particularly important in local elections. It is through this "second bite at the apple" that public sector unions can have the biggest policy effects on the size, cost, and efficiency of state and local government. These have been reflected in pay scales, work rules, pension commitments, annual budgets, and bond ratings.[5] Consequently, in 2011–12, Republican governors in Wisconsin, Ohio, Indiana, Michigan, and elsewhere sought to enact reforms in their labor relations that would reduce the political power of public sector unions.

Table 4.1 Top 15 All-Time Donors, 1989–2012.

Rank	Organization	Amount	%Dem	%Rep
1	ActBlue	$55,745,059	99	0
2	AT&T	$47,571,779	44	55
3	**AFSCME**	$46,167,658	94	1
4	National Association of Realtors	$40,718,176	47	49
5	**SEIU**	$37,634,367	75	2
6	**NEA**	$37,051,378	82	5
7	Goldman Sachs	$35,790,579	60	39
8	American Association for Justice	$34,715,804	89	8
9	International Brotherhood of Electrical Workers	$34,292,471	97	2
10	**Laborer's Union**	$31,876,950	89	7
11	**AFT**	$31,681,366	91	0
12	Carpenters & Jointers Union	$30,769,258	86	9
13	**Communications Workers of America**	$30,192,447	94	0
14	Citi Group	$28,842,146	49	49
15	American Medical Association	$27,880,935	49	49

Public employee unions or unions with substantial numbers of public employees in their ranks are in bold.

Source: Center for Responsive Politics, https://www.opensecrets.org/overview/topcontribs.php.

At first glance, public sector unions appear to be just one of many types of organizations that participate in American politics. However, these unions differ significantly from other interest groups made up of individual citizens (such as the National Rifle Association or the Sierra Club) or groups composed of organizations (such as the Chamber of Commerce or the Motion Picture Association of America). Because their members' interests are so closely tied to government policy—indeed, their members carry out government policy on a day-to-day basis—these unions are more focused in their drive to influence policy than most other groups. Their members have bigger incentives to be active than the members of other interest groups. And they have immense political resources to deploy: in 25 US states (and hundreds of cities), statutes (or contracts negotiated under them) guarantee unions both members and revenue. The legal differences make them distinct from other interest groups seeking to get their way in American politics. Businesses', humanitarian associations', and environmental groups' interests may be shaped by government policy, but how it affects the daily lives of their members tends to be more distant and abstract.

Furthermore, in contrast to many other interest groups, public employee unions have large membership bases that are united by common workplaces and tight communications networks that facilitate political mobilization. Consider New Jersey. The two most powerful unions representing public employees in the Garden State are the New Jersey Education Association (NJEA) and the CWA. The former has some 195,000 members spread across the entire state, which includes teachers (123,825), support staff (46,940), and retired educators (24,925). The latter boasts of 40,000 state workers and 15,000 county and municipal workers.[6] Obviously, not all of these workers are politically active in union causes. Yet even if a modest percentage is engaged, that is a huge number of "boots on the ground" ready to volunteer for political combat. Few other organizations can match such a number of activists. Combine that with the $100 million or more that the NJEA collected in dues in 2012 and you've got a powerful political machine.[7] One of the state's former governors, Thomas Kean, put it as follows: "If you ask anyone in politics, from either party, to name the top two or three most influential groups on legislation in Trenton, they'll name the NJEA."[8]

Public employee unions are so active because government workers have a direct stake in many aspects of public policy. Their day-to-day lives are affected directly by what government does and how it does it. Most other citizens don't feel the impact of government policy in the same way. So, while taxpayers and businesses give fleeting attention to many issues, public sector unions have a powerful incentive to remain mobilized, informed, and prepared to invest major resources in politics. It perhaps is not surprising, then, that 10 percent of the delegates to the Democratic National Convention in 2008 were members of teachers' unions.[9] And over the past 30 years, the teachers' unions alone have given nearly $60 million to Democratic campaigns for federal office, which is about 30 percent more than any single corporation.[10] At the state level, political scientist Terry Moe found that from 2000 to 2009, the teachers' unions outspent all business groups combined in 36 of the 50 states.[11]

At the local level, where union members can constitute a larger slice of the electorate, they can be particularly potent. Take, for example, Michelle Rhee, the hard-charging schools chancellor of Washington, DC, who decided that with the district spending $28,000 per year per student, more money wasn't the best way to improve the capital's underperforming schools. Therefore, she closed failing schools, fired more than 200 teachers and principals, and advocated merit pay.[12] The teachers' unions fought her tooth and nail. Eventually they used their electoral muscle to get rid of Rhee's boss, Mayor Adrian Fenty, and replace him with a more pliant mayor, which led to her resignation. Elections have consequences.

The electoral power of teachers' unions is also evident in school board elections across the country. Terry Moe conducted a battery of studies on teachers' unions' effects on school board elections in California. School board elections are peculiar. They are often held when no other major offices, such as president or governor, are being contested. The concerned electorate is narrow, as only a third of registered voters have kids in school. And these elections are usually nonpartisan, so that candidates cannot be identified by party labels, which eliminates a key source of information for voters. Yet, they are a powerful test of the power of public employees to get their way in low-turnout local elections.

In these elections, Moe found that teachers were more involved in school board elections than any other social group and used those elections to advance their own interests in electing candidates that favored collective bargaining and the concerns of teachers. If the local teachers' union simply endorsed a candidate, that was often enough to make him or her a contender, and the endorsed candidates were often highly sympathetic to the union's policy positions. Moe found that in small school districts (fewer than 5,000 students), the unions were often the only players on the field. In large districts, they had more money and resources but also faced more competition from mayors and other groups seeking to influence education policy. In both cases, the unions were powerful. Therefore, it is not surprising to find many former teachers and union officials elected to school boards. This is because teachers vote at much higher rates than average citizens in the school districts in which they live because they have a material stake in the outcome.

Moe makes a powerful case that the self-interest of public sector workers, in this case teachers, motivates them to turn out to vote at very high levels compared to average citizens. In fact, with turnout for school board elections hovering at around 10 percent or less, teachers and allied staff often constituted over 40 percent of the electorate. Moe studied school board elections in selected Los Angeles County districts in 1997 and 1999. In the Charter Oak School District in 1997, only 7 percent of registered voters turned out to cast ballots, while 46 percent of teachers who lived in the district did.[13] In short, teachers' unions have more influence over school board elections across the country than any other group. And school boards play an important role in shaping education policy. It is another example of the two-bites-at-the-apple phenomenon unique to public sector unions, which, in this case, use their electoral power to get what they want.

Jake Rosenfeld also studied public employee union member turnout in national elections. He found that in 2008, "Public employees outvoted those in the private sector by 13 percentage points."[14] Meanwhile, in the midterm elections of 1998, public sector workers outvoted those in the private sector by 23 percentage points. This is not surprising because government workers tend to be more affluent and educated. However, Rosenfeld shows that unionization further increases the probability that government workers will vote. Presumably, this is because unions try to "educate" their members about how their self-interest is at stake in upcoming elections. Yet, unions' ability to boost turnout tends to be weaker in the public sector than the private sector. This is because public employees are more likely to be college educated and relatively affluent, factors that also make them more likely to vote even if they weren't unionized. But unionization still has the effect of increasing voter turnout for government employees.[15]

The key takeaway point is that local elections often have low turnout and public employees often constitute a very large percentage of voters. The phenomenon of high public sector worker turnout, driven in part by self-interest, combined with the apathy of average citizens, is very significant for public policy, especially at the local level.

Public sector unions also differ from most interest groups in their allegiance to a single party and a single agenda in debates about the role of government. They are focused on a few key issues relating to the government jobs of their members: higher salaries and better benefits, more government employment, and thus higher taxes and more government services. They consistently favor voter initiatives and referenda that increase taxation and government spending. And public sector unions give money, volunteers, and other support almost exclusively to candidates of the Democratic Party. This prompted then Kansas senator Bob Dole to lash out at teachers' unions in his 1996 acceptance speech of the Republican Party's presidential nomination. Dole said, "The teachers unions nominated Bill Clinton in 1992. They're funding his re-election now. And they, his most reliable supporters, know he will maintain the status quo. And to the teachers union, I say, when I am president, I will disregard your political power for the sake of the parents, the children, the schools and the nation."[16] Whatever the merits of Dole's polemic, it didn't attract many voters and he lost to Clinton by 8 percentage points in the popular vote and 379 to 159 in the Electoral College.

ELIMINATING THE FREE RIDER PROBLEM:
THE AGENCY SHOP

Any interest group must overcome the individual citizen's incentive to "free ride"—to let others pay the costs of an organization while enjoying the benefits that that organization provides.[17] For example, we all benefit from breathing clean air. Therefore, we all have some incentive to form an organization to promote air quality. However, those who let others rent the office space, hire the staff, and otherwise do the work will benefit from clean air without having to spend any of their own time or money.

To counteract this incentive, interest groups proffer some combination of solidarity ("we're all in this noble cause together"), ideology ("we must act on our beliefs"), and economic incentives ("we get these concrete benefits for joining").[18] Groups must then devote considerable resources to spreading their message, recruiting members, and getting money from them. That's the job of staff skilled at identifying people who care intensely enough about the issue at hand to donate their time and money. And all this effort must be sustained over time. Without continual exertion, most interest groups in America would have to close their doors.

In 25 American states, public sector unions operate without this imperative. State laws and local ordinances require all workers in a bargaining unit to join unions or at least pay something to support them.[19] Under the laws of these states, by a one-time majority vote, government employees can force all their colleagues as well as future workers to make a union their "exclusive representative." This is called a "certification" election. Once anointed the exclusive representative, future employees will have no choice but to join the union or pay agency fees. As a practical matter, it is very difficult, especially in the public sector, to decertify a union. So even if new employees are hired and are less enthusiastic about union representation, it is nearly impossible for them to secure another certification election. Once unionized, public employees are likely to remain so.

Two legal provisions confer this unique advantage on public sector unions. The first provision is the "agency shop," which stipulates that because a union represents all workers in collective bargaining, nonunion workers must pay "agency" fees to the union.[20] Often, these fees are very close to the amount paid by members as union dues. In some jurisdictions, nonunion workers may recoup some of their agency fees, on the grounds that they should pay only for collective bargaining services, not the union's other activities.[21]

However, exercising this "clawback"—sometimes called *Hudson* rights—is often laborious, and the amounts returned can be quite small.[22] In my own case, I pay roughly $1,100 in agency fees a year to the Professional Staff Congress of the City University of New York (PSC-CUNY), which represents CUNY professors and other employees. The PSC-CUNY sets the amount of agency fees to be equivalent to union dues. Each year, I receive a letter detailing the procedures to request a refund for any monies used for political purposes and not for collective bargaining. The "objector" must write a letter explaining himself or herself between May 1 and May 31 of the year in which they wish to opt out of paying for the union's political activities.[23] In 2013, I received a refund of $141.

How the percentages of union dues apportioned to politics and collective bargaining are made is shrouded in secrecy. If a union member objects to the calculations of the union, the "objector" must send another letter to the union's president within 35 days of receiving his or her reimbursement check. This means that the union is holding many of the cards and has an incentive to say that as much as possible of the dues is being used for collective bargaining and as little as possible is for political activity. As the Supreme Court noted in a recent case, *Knox v. SEIU*, it is hard to know what constitutes a "chargeable" expense for collective bargaining. As the court put it, "The SEIU's understanding of the breadth of chargeable expenses is so expansive that it is hard to place much reliance on its statistics. 'Lobbying the electorate,' which the SEIU claims is chargeable, is nothing more than another term for supporting political causes and candidates."[24] Yet there is a method to the madness: in determining *Hudson* rights, unions have an incentive to keep as much money as possible from nonmembers and spend as freely on politics as circumstances dictate. In addition, the smaller the refund, the less likely agency fee payers are to go through the trouble of securing it.

Employees who know that they will be charged fees comparable with dues have little incentive not to join the union—especially since members, for the same payments, also get tangible benefits, such as dental insurance or legal services. The few workers who refuse, usually Republicans or Independents, are those who are strongly opposed on principle. Yet there is evidence that these stubborn holdouts have many colleagues who would join them if the rules were not rigged. Indeed, the contrast is striking between agency shop states and the 23 other states whose right-to-work laws ban the practice. In nearly every state that permits agency fees, more than 90 percent of teachers belong to unions. In states that don't allow agency fees, only 68 percent of teachers are unionized. Moe has found that the presence of agency fees made it 20 percent more likely that teachers would join a union.[25] Results are similar for other public servants. For instance, in California 97 percent of eligible prison guards are members of the California Correctional Peace Officers Association.

Most public employees would, then, voluntarily join unions for the benefits they see as accruing from collective bargaining. Most members of unions do not need to be forced to pay dues. But some do. And most members do not object to seeing a portion of their dues underwrite the state and national organizations. Yet some do. While most union members are quite happy with their local union's collective bargaining activities, a significant slice of them do not like the political activities of the state and national federations. Consequently, most unions have adopted a "unitary" dues structure that funnels dues money from the individual worker to the local union to the state and then the national federation. Surveys of teachers suggest that many Republicans and Independents, while perfectly happy with their local unions, do not appreciate their locals' alliance with state and national unions, such as the National Education Association (NEA) and American Federation of Teachers (AFT).[26] Agency shop provisions and unitary dues structures prevent public sector union organizations at all levels from losing out on substantial sums of money. They also make one wonder why, if unions are so important to democracy and do so much for members, they must in effect force a percentage of their members to join.

All that said, public employees have, and should have, the constitutional right to join organizations that give them a voice and seek to represent their interests. Even in right-to-work states, many public employees still voluntarily join associations or unions. Indeed, it is possible to be a right-to-work state with collective bargaining laws whose unions have only voluntary members. Such states include Florida, North Dakota, Nebraska, and most recently Indiana and Michigan. Even in Virginia and Texas, where agency shops and collective bargaining with most or all government workers are prohibited, some workers still voluntarily join unions. And these unions are still politically active.[27] In the states with agency shop laws, however, all workers in unionized workplaces end up giving material support to unions, regardless of their personal wishes.

Most states that adopted right-to-work laws did so over a half century ago. Most of the states of the South and Southwest did so shortly after the passage of the Taft-Hartley Act of 1947. The law modified the Wagner Act of 1935, which had given a powerful boost to the labor movement. The 1940s were the most radical decade in organized labor, with strikes and work stoppages in the private sector hitting all-time highs.[28] Partly in response, a coalition of Republicans and southern Democrats in the United States formed to pass changes to the nation's labor law over President Truman's veto. One of the key provisions of Taft-Hartley, section 14b, was that it authorized individual states to prohibit agency or closed shops. The southern states were ideologically hostile to unions, wanted to attract northern industry, and were fearful that biracial unions would disrupt the racial status quo.[29] They quickly passed right-to-work laws.

The number of right-to-work states was largely set by the middle of the 1950s. This halted private sector organized labor's advance and confined unionism to the Northeast, Great Lakes states, and West Coast. Yet, in the wake of the Great Recession, two states, Indiana and Michigan, have joined the ranks of the right-to-work states. And other states such as Wisconsin and Pennsylvania have flirted with the idea. Interestingly, the politics of the new right-to-work laws have been initiatives of Republicans in the state legislature—many of whom arrived in office after the Tea Party election of 2010—rather than the governors of those states. Both Indiana's Mitch Daniels and Michigan's Rick Synder only reluctantly signed these bills into law. The Great Lakes states have suffered in competition with the faster-growing South.[30] In fact, today there are two auto industries in the United States: foreign automakers that have opened plants in the South and American manufacturers in Michigan that required a federal bailout.

Given the decline in private sector labor, even in the United Auto Workers' (UAW) homeland, the impact of the new right-to-work law in Michigan may be felt most strongly in the public sector. Michigan has one of the more heavily unionized public sector workforces in the nation, with 55 percent of public employees belonging to unions. Meanwhile, only 12 percent of private sector workers belong to unions in Michigan. Without forcing workers to pay agency fees, the decline in membership will likely be sharper and steeper in the public sector.

OPTING IN: THE DUES CHECK-OFF

The second legal provision that benefits public sector unions is the "dues check-off," where the government withholds a portion of public employees' salaries to pay union dues or agency fees. With a dues check-off, workers never actually see the money that goes into union coffers. Unions have long argued that this eliminates free-riding (workers benefiting from union representation without paying for it), but it also eliminates workers' choices about how to spend that portion of their pay. Paying union dues that can be used for politics or collective bargaining is thus the "default option." As Richard H. Thaler and Cass R. Sunstein have shown, such seemingly innocuous policy choices about the default option can have huge consequences.[31]

In the absence of a dues check-off, workers might, for example, elect to remodel their homes, take the kids to Disneyland, save for the future, or give to charity. Before recent changes in Wisconsin law ended the dues check-off for public employee unions, teachers there paid as much as $1,100 a year in union dues.[32] According to Joseph Tanner, city manager of Vallejo (a city of some 116,000 people northeast of San Francisco), in 2007, each of the city's 100 firefighters paid $230 a month in dues, and each of the 140 police officers paid $254 a month. Hence, unlike other interest groups, the firefighters' union had a guaranteed annual revenue stream of $276,000, and the police union was assured $426,720 a year. This funding base made both groups powerful forces in the politics of the city.[33] In 2008, Vallejo, faced with soaring public employee compensation costs and falling revenue, declared bankruptcy.

In addition to agency fees for nonunion members covered by union-negotiated contracts, it was possible for the unions to make "special assessments"—that is, further deductions from workers' paychecks for political purposes in instances where the union felt that it needed extra money to press its case. Again, nonunion members could exercise their Hudson rights and opt out of their special assessment. But that meant they had to try to get money back from the union that had already been deducted. In addition, because the deductions in these cases are usually small for the individual, say, $25 per worker, many overlook the deduction and forego the trouble of trying to get their money back. However, in *Knox v. SEIU*, the Supreme Court ruled that "opting out" was not sufficient protection for nonunion members whose money could be used to fund political speech with which they disagree. Instead, Justice Alito held that before special assessments are made, unions must send nonmembers a form that asks them to "opt in" before any deductions from their paychecks can be made.

Where they can rely on dues check-off, public sector unions do not spend much money on fundraising—a staffer or two is sufficient to process checks from the government. Resources are thus available for politics that equivalent groups would have to devote to identifying supporters and persuading them to give money.

Unlike other interest groups, public sector unions enjoy a uniquely reliable revenue stream to support their political activities. Unsurprisingly, some of the resulting political power has been mustered to preserve the dues check-off. Unions are right to consider any proposed reform as a threat to their interests. *Washington Post* columnist George Will wrote, "After Colorado in 2001 required public employees unions to have annual votes reauthorizing collection of dues, membership in the Colorado Association of Public Employees declined 70 percent. In 2005, Indiana stopped collecting dues from unionized public employees; in 2011, there are 90 percent fewer dues-paying members. In Utah, the end of automatic dues deductions for political activities in 2001 caused teachers' payments to fall 90 percent. After a similar law passed in 1992 in Washington State, the percentage of teachers making such contributions declined from 82 to 11."[34]

Even without dues check-off, unions can still be potent actors during campaign season. For instance, according to an analysis by the *Denver Post*, public employee unions were the biggest donors to political campaigns in the 2010 election cycle in the Centennial State. The unions gave extensively to groups that, under Colorado law, can spend unlimited amounts of money to influence elections and are part of a well-coordinated Democratic network.[35] Affiliates of the NEA, Service Employees International Union (SEIU), and American Federation of State, County and Municipal Employees (AFSCME) all donated a little more or a little less than $1 million each.

WISCONSIN AND OHIO

The advantages that public sector unions gain through agency shops and dues check-offs were on display in the highest-profile political battles over collective bargaining by government employees. In Wisconsin and Ohio, Republican-majority legislatures passed, and governors signed, legislation reforming government–labor relations. Among the specific provisions, the measures sought to restrict what could be on the negotiating table during collective bargaining for most public workers and eliminate government's collection of union dues.

In response, the public sector unions—throughout the United States, not just those in Wisconsin and Ohio—summoned vast resources in an effort to stop the legislation and, after that failed, to repeal it. In Ohio, opponents of the legal changes spent an impressive $42 million in a referendum campaign to overturn the newly minted law (SB5)[36] (Figure 4.1). They succeeded, having outspent supporters three to one and having fielded a stronger get-out-the-vote operation on Election Day. Most of the money to fuel this political muscle came from unions. Indeed, 98 percent of the anti-SB5 campaign cash in some reporting periods came from unions (both public sector and private sector), rather than from individuals. The teachers' unions alone gave over $9 million, which is half of what Governor John Kasich spent on his entire 2010 election campaign[37] (Figure 4.2). In contrast, the supporters of SB5 were a blend of individuals and business interests.

In Wisconsin, the unions and their allies first sought to stop the bill's passage by mounting massive protests in Madison and a major advertising campaign in which they outspent supporters for the "budget repair bill" $3.37 million to $2.26 million.[38] After the bill passed, opponents sued to stop its implementation. In connection with their legal strategy, they spent

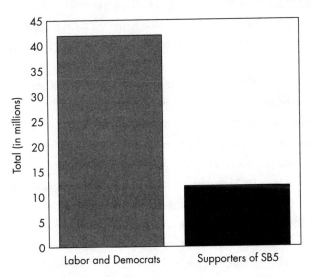

Figure 4.1 Money Raised for Issue 2 in Ohio.

Source: *Cleveland Plain Dealer*, Ohio Secretary of State.

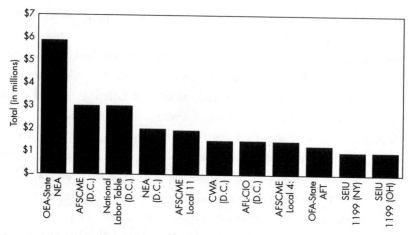

Figure 4.2 Union Spending: Ohio Issue 2.

Source: Ohio Secretary of State, http://thatherocom/2011/10/28/they-arent-ohio/.

another $1.5 million on a state supreme court election in hopes of improving the high court's reception of their case.[39] This approach failed: the incumbent, whom they correctly presumed would vote to uphold the law, won re-election, and the state's supreme court dismissed the suit. Unions then spent over $20 million trying to recall six state senators in order to retake control of the upper chamber[40] (Figure 4.3). (The amount that the unions spent on the six recall elections was more than half the amount spent on all state senate elections in 2010.) After the law's implementation, unions continued their electoral attack by enlisting 30,000 organizers to collect a million signatures supporting an election to recall Governor Walker.[41]

Wisconsin's public sector unions, led by the Wisconsin Education Association, forced a recall election of the governor and a number of state senators who had voted for the changes to state labor law. Under Wisconsin law, the Democratic Party had to hold an impromptu primary to select a candidate. The unions' favored candidate, Kathleen Falk, lost to Tom Barrett, the mayor of Milwaukee, who had lost narrowly to Walker in the governor's race in 2010. To win over the teachers' union, Barrett pledged to make it his number one policy priority to "invest in education," because "Education ... needs to be a top priority in Wisconsin." Walker raised a huge sum for the recall campaign and after a hard-fought battle prevailed, defeating Barrett by a greater percentage than he did in their first matchup.

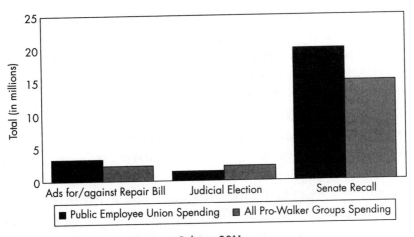

Figure 4.3 Spending in Wisconsin Politics, 2011.

Source: Campaign Media Analysis Group, Brennan Center-NYU Law, ABC News.

WHERE DOES THE MONEY GO?

As Wisconsin's and Ohio's recent histories vividly demonstrate, a large and secure revenue stream turns public employee unions into potent political organizations. Union political efforts take place at all three levels of government: federal, state, and local. Unions make direct donations to candidates and parties, fund issue ads in parallel campaigns, provide get-out-the-vote ground operations, run campaigns for and against ballot measures, and engage in extensive lobbying efforts. They overwhelmingly support Democratic candidates and consistently favor referenda that increase taxation and government spending. For example, the California Correctional Peace Officers Association (CCPOA) spent about $7 million on elections in the Golden State in 2010—out of an annual budget of approximately $30 million drawn from average member dues of some $80 per month per employee.[42] The CCPOA backed some 107 political candidates, 104 of whom won office. California State Senator Juan Vargas said, "I won by 22 votes and without CCPOA it wouldn't have been close .... They literally won this campaign for me."[43] In short, it is important to measure how much money public sector unions have for political action and precisely where that money is spent. In the first decade of the twenty-first century, the CCPOA political action committee (PAC) spent a whopping $30 million in hardball politics to move its agenda of tougher sentencing, more prison contraction, hiring more prison guards, and paying them better.[44]

Labor unions are required to divulge their revenue streams in financial reports that they must file with the US Department of Labor. In 2010, the national level of the AFSCME reported an income of $211,806,537; the NEA received $397,953,771; and the SEIU received $318,755,793.[45] There is another way to think about how much money they have. The NEA and the AFT have 4.5 million members combined. If teachers and support staff that are members of those unions pay, on average, $600 per year in union dues, that equals $2.7 billion in revenue. Of course, not all of that can be spent on politics but must pay for the costs of maintaining the union organization, including paying the staff and the rent, and the costs of collective bargaining.

Unions are not required to detail how they spend their income, making it difficult to assess how much of any given union's revenue it devotes to lobbying and electioneering. Some unions, however, have issued their own estimates of how much of their dues they spend on political activities that advance their interests. From such statements, one rough but reasonable rule of thumb is that public sector unions tend to spend about 20 percent of their dues on lobbying and electioneering. This estimate is derived from what unions say on disclosure forms to their members, what union leaders say publicly, and what various analysts have calculated.[46]

Using this estimate, we can arrive at some rough metrics by calculating the total number of union members and agency fee payers and the average paid by each worker. Consider all of California's public sector unions combined: they have about 1 million workers, with estimated annual average dues per person of $500.[47] If they spend 20 percent of those funds on politics, they have about $120 million to devote annually to influence federal, state, and local politics.

Where does that money go? Spending on lobbying is not easy to track at the federal level and even more difficult at the state and local levels. Furthermore, while there are good data on federal and state elections, most watchdog groups do not track local elections, where unions have the most at stake (because the majority of union members are employed by local governments). In addition, it is often hard to identify clearly the source of donations that have been funneled through PACs and similar organizations. Finally, government unions make many in-kind contributions, such as phone banks, office space, and volunteers, which are hard to quantify (and easily understated). For example, New York City's teachers union, the United Federation of Teachers, provides office space next door to its headquarters at 50 Broadway in lower Manhattan to the New York State Senate Democratic Campaign Committee.[48]

On the other hand, some forms of political spending can be quantified: unions are required to spell out the amounts they give directly to state and federal candidates, as well as money they spend on issue ads and expenses devoted to lobbying. The National Institute on Money in State Politics data show that in 2010, across all states, public sector unions spent about $150 million—up from $130 million in 2008 and $118 million in 2006. In 2010, unions gave Democratic candidates $86,641,325 and spent $53,663,888 on ballot measures; the rest (less than 10 percent of the total) went to Republicans and third-party candidates. This means that public sector unions were in the top five biggest-spending interest groups trying to influence politics at the state level.

Consider, too, the pattern of public sector union political spending on candidates and political parties. In 2008, not counting "independent expenditures" on issue ads, the NEA and AFT combined contributed $5.4 million to national campaigns, $61.8 million to state-level campaigns, and $37.5 million to local contests. Clearly, state and local elections are where the actions is.[49] However, even if one looks only at the national level and combines the political giving of the NEA and AFT, where they seem to give smaller amounts, they were the largest donor to candidates and parties from 1989 to 2012 (Table 4.2). If one adds AFSCME and SEIU to the mix, insofar as they are allies in favor of greater public employment and higher pay, benefits, and protections for government workers, public sector unions *blow away* the other big

Table 4.2 Top Five All-Time Donors, 1989–2012.

Rank	Organization	Amount	%Dem	%Rep
1	**NEA and AFT**	$68,732,744	86	3
2	ActBlue	$55,745,059	99	0
3	AT&T	$47,571,779	44	55
4	**AFSCME**	$46,167,658	94	1
5	National Association of Realtors	$40,718,176	47	49

Public employee unions or unions with substantial numbers of public employees in their ranks are in bold.
Source: Center for Responsive Politics, https://www.opensecrets.org/overview/topcontribs.php.

donors, which include AT&T, the National Association of Realtors, and Goldman Sachs (Table 4.3).

Turning to the state and local level, one recent study ranked the political power of teachers' unions in the various states. In the 2010 state election cycle, teachers' unions in more than half the states were among the top five highest-giving interest groups. In 20 states, surveys of education policy "insiders" found that most of them considered the teachers' unions "to be generally more influential, on average, than all other entities (including the state school board, state superintendent, governor, legislators, business interests, and advocacy groups)."[50] Terry Moe compared teachers' unions to other interest groups at the state level in the 2006 and 2008 elections.[51] He found that the teachers' unions were the top contributor to candidates and political parties in 40 percent of the states and either number one or number two in 60 percent. And in some cases where the teachers weren't number one in those election years, they were only slightly beaten out by the AFSCME or SEIU. Moe went further and compared the teachers' unions' political giving with *all* business associations by combining the latter into a single category. This included the small business associations, chambers of commerce, and international business groups. In 36 of the 50 states, from 2000 to 2009, the teachers' unions alone outspent all business associations *combined*.[52] It's not surprising that some have called them the most powerful force in the country.[53]

Table 4.3 Top 10 All-Time Donors, 1989–2012.

Rank	Organization	Amount	%Dem	%Rep
1	**AFSCME and SEIU**	$83,802,025	85	1
2	**NEA and AFT**	$68,732,744	86	3
3	ActBlue	$55,745,059	99	0
4	AT&T	$47,571,779	44	55
5	National Association of Realtors	$40,718,176	47	49
6	Goldman Sachs	$35,790,579	60	39
7	American Association for Justice	$34,715,804	89	8
8	International Brotherhood of Electrical Workers	$34,292,471	97	2
9	**Laborer's Union**	$31,876,950	89	7
10	Carpenters & Jointers Union	$30,769,258	86	9

Public employee unions or unions with substantial numbers of public employees in their ranks are in bold.
Source: Center for Responsive Politics, https://www.opensecrets.org/overview/topcontribs.php.

As this example attests, public sector union spending is highly uneven across the states, reflecting the difference between agency shop jurisdictions and those without these laws. Public sector unions were the third-largest spender in California's state elections ($45,730,777), after Meg Whitman, the Republican nominee, who self-financed her gubernatorial campaign, and electric utility companies, which spent $50,949,029.[54] Labor unions (mostly public but some private) spent $23,791,657 on independent expenditures during the campaign cycle—far more than any other group (Figure 4.4). California permits agency shops and has a strong public employee collective bargaining law.

In contrast, Texas prohibits collective bargaining in the public sector and is a right-to-work state. There, in 2010, public sector unions did not even rank in the top 15 largest contributors, and labor in general spent only $97,624 on political action (Figure 4.5). Florida is somewhere between California and Texas: it allows collective bargaining in government but forbids agency shops. There, public sector unions were the fourth-largest spenders ($11,362,386) after self-financing candidates, trial lawyers, and real estate and insurance groups. Florida labor's independent expenditures were a modest $1,638,101 (Figure 4.6).

The 2002 Florida gubernatorial election is an instructive example of the political clout that derives from abundant and secure sources of money. That year, Jeb Bush had finished his first term as governor and, along with

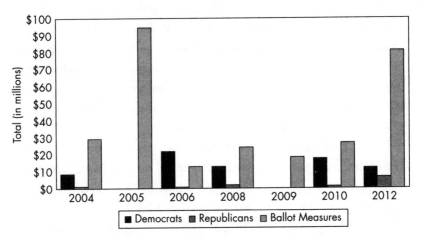

Figure 4.4 Public Sector Unions' Election Spending in California.

Source: National Institute on Money in State Politics, www.followthemoney.org.

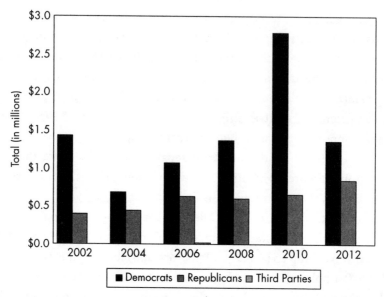

Figure 4.5 Public Sector Unions' Election Spending in Texas.
Source: National Institute on Money in State Politics, www.followthemoney.org.

the Republican legislature, had enacted an innovative education program, authorizing vouchers and creating new ways to hold teachers accountable for results. The Florida Education Association (FEA) responded by campaigning successfully to deny former US attorney general Janet Reno the Democratic gubernatorial nomination, winning it instead for the group's preferred candidate, political neophyte Bill McBride. In the general election, the FEA spent millions of dollars and its political operatives actually ran McBride's campaign. Not surprisingly, McBride's platform was to roll back Bush's education reforms. McBride lost. But the fact that he had, with no previous political experience, become a major-party candidate challenging a popular incumbent from one of the nation's great political dynasties is a testimony to the power of public sector unions—even in Florida, whose labor laws are not strongly pro-union.[55]

A look at the federal level provides another way to appreciate the scope and magnitude of government unions' political activity. Most public sector unions represent state and local workers. Therefore, state and local officials, not members of Congress, make most policies affecting them. Nonetheless, 6 of the top 15 biggest donors to federal political campaigns from 1989 to 2012, according to the Center for Responsive Politics, were government

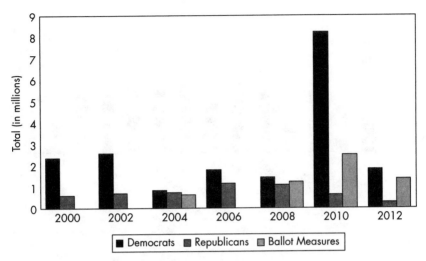

Figure 4.6 Public Sector Unions' Election Spending in Florida.

Source: National Institute on Money in State Politics, www.followthemoney.org.

workers' unions or unions with large numbers of public employees (see Table 4.1). The AFSCME was the third-largest donor, and the SEIU, half of whose 2.2 million members are public employees, was fifth on the list. The NEA ranked sixth, and the AFT eleventh. The Communications Workers of America, with about 20 percent of its membership made up of government workers, was thirteenth.[56] It is important to note that on most policies related to government spending and taxation, all these unions are allies, not competitors. In contrast, business groups' interests in tax and spending policy vary considerably and occasionally conflict.

At the federal level, as in individual states, public employee union political spending is closely aligned with the Democratic Party (Figure 4.7). Some 98 percent of AFSCME donations and 95 percent of SEIU donations went to Democrats, unlike other big contributors, such as AT&T, the National Association of Realtors, or Citigroup, which split their contributions nearly evenly between Republicans and Democrats. The partisanship of union contributions helps explain Democrats' advantage over Republicans in contributions from the biggest donors: $1.3 billion to $844 million over the last 20 years. In general, Democrats tend to be much more reliant on large donors, including unions, than their Republican opponents, who collect more in small individual donations. In the 2002 campaign cycle, 64 percent of individuals contributing less than $200

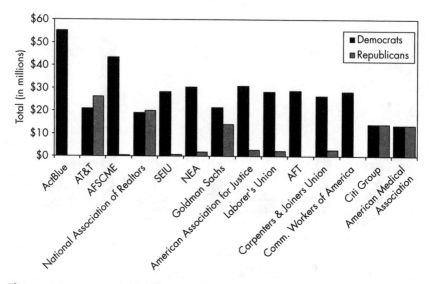

Figure 4.7 Top Donors by Party.

Source: Center for Responsive Politics, www.opensecrets.org.

to federal candidates, parties, or leadership PACs gave their money to Republicans. In contrast, those contributing $1 million or more gave 92 percent to Democrats.[57]

In addition to direct donations to candidates, public sector unions finance issue ads in parallel campaigns in federal elections. The SEIU tops the chart of independent spenders, with $70,479,179 over the last 20 years, followed by the National Rifle Association ($58,619,585), AFSCME ($53,447,240), and American Federation of Labor–Congress of Industrial Organizations (AFL-CIO) ($40,664,851).[58] These figures do not include further spending in parallel campaigns for state and local offices. Making an aggregate measure, the *Wall Street Journal* and the *New York Times* reported that the AFSCME spent $91 million during the 2010 election cycle, while the SEIU spent $44 million and the NEA $40 million.[59] This was more than the biggest Republican donors—the Chamber of Commerce and the Crossroads GPS PAC—combined.

Between elections, public sector unions also lobby federal, state, and local officials. The Center for Responsive Politics estimates that public sector unions spent $144 million from 1998 to 2011 on lobbying the federal government (Figure 4.8).

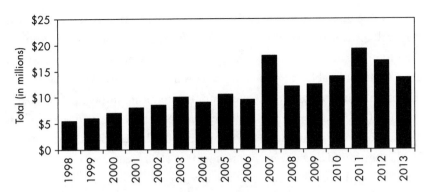

Figure 4.8 Annual Spending on Lobbying by Government Unions.

Source: Center for Responsive Politics, www.opensecrets.org.

The SEIU spent $60 million to help elect Barack Obama in 2008. Perhaps not surprisingly, Obama's most frequent visitor during his first six months in office was SEIU president Andy Stern. The political direc- tor of SEIU's Local 1199 in New York City was appointed to be the White House political director, and an SEIU lawyer was named to the National Labor Relations Board. Or consider New York City Mayor Bill de Blasio's relationship to the SEIU. The ties run deep. SEIU Local 1199 endorsed him in the hard-fought Democratic primary. De Blasio himself was a paid consultant for the SEIU when he launched his campaign for a city council seat in 2001. His first deputy mayor, Anthony Shorris, has long been an SEIU consultant—and Shorris's chief of staff also used to be an SEIU operative. Emma Wolfe, de Blasio's director of intergovernmen- tal affairs, was an SEIU organizer. Clearly, the de Blasio administration and the powerful healthcare workers' union are likely to see things simi- larly. These examples provide a sense of just how entwined public sector unions are with Democratic Party politics and how much influence they can exercise.

Some effort has been made to trace union effects on local elections. In urban elections, where turnout is often low, public employee unions can have an outsized impact.[60] In New York City's 2013 mayoral contest, all the Democratic Party's candidates went to great lengths to secure the endorsement of Michael Mulgrew, the president of the United Federation of Teachers (UFT), which has some 116,000 members.[61] And the UFT's agenda is public knowledge: stop closing poor-performing public schools, prevent the use of existing facilities for charter schools, and overturn mayoral control of the school system. Although he wasn't endorsed by the union during the primary, the eventual mayor-elect Bill de Blasio has gone to considerable lengths to ingratiate himself to the UFT. However, one recent study suggests that such endorsements are important. It looked at union (public and private) endorsements of candidates and their effect. The authors examined elections in America's 150 largest cities from 1990 to 2012. They found that union endorsements led to a greater vote share for the candidate endorsed. Not surprisingly, challengers, rather than incumbents, benefited more from the union endorsements. The analysts also found evidence that candidates backed by unions were apt to pursue union-friendly fiscal policies once in office.[62]

Public sector unions can find the most sympathetic ear in government when they have one of their own run for office. There are more than a few state legislators, city council members, and mayors who started their careers as union members. The CCPOA has had a few of its past members end up in the state legislature and on city councils, especially in towns with prisons.[63] Former Los Angeles mayor Antonio Villaraigosa cut his teeth as an organizer for the teachers' union. The current majority leader of the Connecticut State Assembly, Joe Aresimowicz, is the education director for AFSCME Council 4.[64]

Analysts and activists have focused too narrowly on the effects of unions' collective bargaining on government policy. It may well be that public sector unions have achieved more of their goals—increased wages and benefits, more government employment, and more government spending—by their work in the political arena than at the bargaining table. Automatic members and reliable money for political activity are the key advantages that public sector unions have over other interest groups, which underscores the importance of the agency shop and the dues check-off to their ability to defend their interests.

Even if agency shop provisions were eliminated, public employees' First Amendment rights would remain intact. They could still band together to press for better pay, benefits, and working conditions—as they do in right to work states. But like other interest groups, they would have to persuade people to join voluntarily and would have to solve the free-rider problem for themselves, rather than counting on the government to do it for them.

GOVERNMENT UNIONS AND THE CALIFORNIA
STATE LEGISLATURE

Moving from the general to the particular, it is helpful to consider an important case of union electioneering activity: the California state legislature. The Democratic Party dominates the Golden State's legislature. In the past half century, the Republican Party has had majorities on only one occasion in each of the two houses of the state legislature. The GOP's state senate majority lasted for two years, while the one in the assembly lasted less than a year. California's Democrats are closely allied with public employee unions in the state. As *Sacramento Bee* columnist Dan Walters has gone so far as to say, "public employee unions wield immense—even hegemonic—influence" over the Democratic majorities in the state legislature.[65] In fact, a number of California legislators are themselves former public employee union members. The control exercised by public employee unions was brought home to many when a 2010 video went viral. It showed an official of the SEIU in a legislative chamber telling elected officials: "We helped to get you into office, and we got a good memory .... Come November, if you don't back our program, we'll get you out of office."[66] While Walters and other commentators have often remarked on the power wielded by public sector unions in the state legislature, it is worth taking a closer look at their role in helping California's representatives get elected.

Electoral rules help reinforce connections between Democrats and the unions. California's gerrymandered legislative districts foster little meaningful competition between the political parties. What electoral competition there is in California takes place within the parties at the nomination stage. Whoever wins the primary contest in a so-called safe district usually walks away with the general election. Without party labels to guide voters, candidates turn to endorsements. Within the Democratic Party, the endorsement of the public sector unions looms above all others in importance. The unions offer both money and manpower to candidates they support. According to the *Los Angeles Times*, the California Teachers Association, the state affiliate of the NEA, "has deep pockets, a militia of more than 300,000 members to call on and a track record of making or breaking political careers."[67]

Public employee unions are among the most active groups in California's electoral process. They are among the leaders in direct donations to candidates and make significant independent expenditures on behalf of their favorite sons and daughters. As Table 4.4 indicates, public sector unions are regularly among the top three donors to legislative candidates. In many of the years when the unions were the number two donor, they were only outpaced by general trade unions. In combination, public and private labor unions outspent the next-largest contributor to candidates by two to one (Figures 4.9, 4.10, 4.11, and 4.12).

Furthermore, while other groups move up and down the donor rankings, depending presumably on the issues at stake in a given election year, public sector unions remain consistently at the top of the heap. Bear in mind that these figures only reflect the direct donation of public employee unions to candidates' campaign coffers. They do not include the independent expenditures the unions also make on behalf of candidates.

Table 4.4 Public Sector Union Contributions to California Legislative Candidates.

Year	Institution	Public Union Donations	Industry Rank
2012	Assembly	$5,600,000	NA
	Senate	$2,000,000	NA
2010	Assembly	$4,600,000	2
	Senate	$1,400,000	2
2008	Assembly	$5,400,000	2
	Senate	$2,100,000	2
2006	Assembly	$5,200,000	1
	Senate	$1,700,000	3
2004	Assembly	$4,600,000	1
	Senate	$1,600,000	2
2002	Assembly	$4,600,000	1
	Senate	$2,500,000	1
2000	Assembly	$6,500,000	1
	Senate	$3,600,000	1
1998	Assembly	$4,500,000	1
	Senate	$2,700,000	1

Note: Candidate committees and party committees were excluded from industry rankings.
Source: National Institute on Money in State Politics.

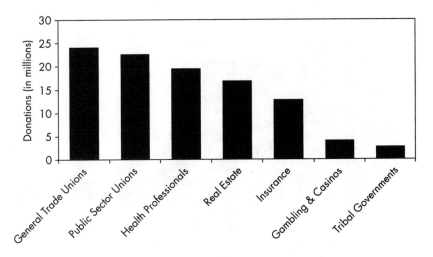

Figure 4.9 Donations to Assembly Candidates, 2008.

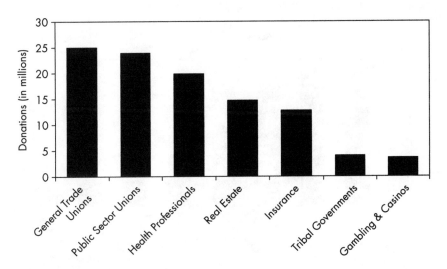

Figure 4.10 Donations to Assembly Candidates, 2012.

Public sector unions donate overwhelmingly to Democratic candidates (Tables 4.5 and 4.6). In 2002, the unions gave 90 percent of their donations to Democrats and 5 percent to Republicans. On the other hand, the finance, insurance, and real estate industries combined split their contributions nearly evenly between the parties, giving 53 percent of their contributions to Democrats and 45 percent to Republicans.

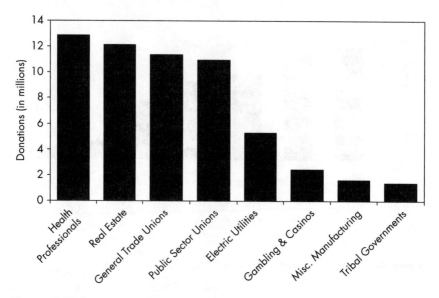

Figure 4.11 Donations to State Senate, 2008.

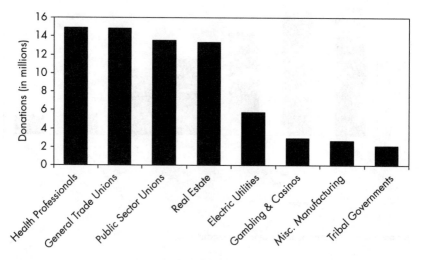

Figure 4.12 Donations to State Senate, 2012.

Beyond these aggregate figures, it is instructive to consider a few examples. Consider the saga of the state's charter school cap in 1998. California had a legal cap of 100 charter schools for the entire state. The teachers' unions were adamantly opposed to raising the cap and allowing more charter schools. Democrats in the state legislature, following the teachers'

Table 4.5 Public Sector Unions Spending in California by Party.

Year	Democrats	Republicans	Percent to Democrats	Percent to Republicans
2000	$10,800,000	$1,900,000	85	15
2002	$19,500,000	$1,200,000	90	6
2004	$8,600,000	$1,200,000	22	3
2006	$21,500,000	$800,000	61	2
2008	$12,600,000	$1,700,000	33	5
2010	$17,600,000	$1,100,000	38	2
2012	$12,200,000	$700,000	13	1

Note: Third parties excluded.
Source: National Institute for Money in State Politics.

Table 4.6 Finance, Insurance, and Real Estate Spending in California by Party.

Year	Democrats	Republicans	Percent to Democrats	Percent to Republicans
2000	$10,400,000	$8,900,000	54	46
2002	$29,000,000	$24,700,000	53	45
2004	$12,000,000	$12,900,000	20	24
2006	$27,600,000	$40,300,000	30	44
2008	$10,000,000	$19,200,000	20	38
2010	$12,900,000	$17,800,000	20	27
2012	$10,300,000	$4,600,000	13	6

Note: Third parties excluded.
Source: National Institute for Money in State Politics.

union line, refused to raise the cap. Reed Hastings, a Silicon Valley entrepreneur who founded Netflix, financed a ballot measure to lift the charter cap with $15 million of his own money.

The California Teachers' Association (CTA) was opposed to Hastings's move, as it would have to spend far more than $15 million to defeat the measure, which would severely cut into the funds it had to spend on candidates in the general election. In a series of private meetings, the CTA got Hastings to back off. It agreed to raise the cap by 100 schools the following year. Of course, neither Hastings nor the CTA had the legal authority to change California law. Only voters or the legislature could do that. Yet the union and businessman brokered the deal nonetheless. Democrats were happy to raise the cap once the CTA blessed the idea. The legislature dutifully produced a bill conforming to the CTA's private agreement with Hastings and passed it into law.

In sum, the Democratic Party handily controls all of California's electoral institutions. And the biggest contributors to that party in terms of direct donations, independent expenditures, and campaign foot soldiers are public employee unions. The unions' influence in the legislature combined with their record of success in the Golden State's direct democracy process makes for a powerful one-two punch.

GOVERNMENT UNIONS AND OFF-CYCLE ELECTIONS

The public sector unions are often most effective using their electioneering and lobbying resources in obscure aspects of the American electoral system. The opportunities to do this are most plentiful in local elections, which are a vital part of American democracy. There are some 19,522 all-purpose municipal governments in the United States. They spent $478 billion in 2012 and employed 2.4 million people.[68] There are also some 13,051 school districts that are an enormously important part of local democracy. There are some 4.3 million full-time teachers employed in America's schools, which is 40 percent of all local government employment. Over 40 percent of school districts' budgets are made up of teachers' salaries. Therefore, changes in teacher pay have a big impact on total government spending in the United States. Part of what shapes policy at the local level is when elections are held, who votes, and what groups are the most active during campaign season.

Local elections present opportunities for public sector unions to exercise their power. Why? Because as a long tradition of political science scholarship has shown, voter turnout for such elections tends to be much lower. While presidential elections have seen turnout of around 60 percent of eligible voters in recent years, turnout of 20 percent, 10 percent, and even less is common for local elections. The vast majority of Americans are accustomed to elections occurring every two even-numbered years. That is when candidates for president, senator, and representative, as well as most governorships and state legislative seats, are on the ballot. However, many elections—especially in cities—do not follow this pattern. The timing of elections in nearly 80 percent of American cities is different from presidential and congressional elections, and more than half of all American school board elections are held separately from state and national elections. One political scientist has estimated that there is one election per week occurring somewhere in the United States.[69] And holding the election "off cycle"—meaning during odd years or not in November—further depresses turnout. One group of scholars found that cities that held their municipal elections off cycle had turnout rates 36 percent lower than cities that held their elections in presidential years.[70] Therefore, the weight of the union and its members at the ballot box increases as the size of the electorate shrinks. And the unions' get-out-the-vote efforts have a bigger bang for the buck when voter turnout is 20 percent or less.

Consider New York City's mayoral elections, which are held in November on odd years. In 2013, only 24 percent or about 1 million of the Big Apple's 4.3 million registered voters showed up at the polls. Bill de Blasio won the election with 752,604 votes in a city of 8.4 million souls. Some 42 percent of voters belonged to a union household when only 22 percent of all workers in the city belong to unions—and only 14 percent of workers in the private sector belong to a union, while 72 percent of public sector workers are unionized.[71] In short, a large slice of the electorate, perhaps more than one-quarter, was composed of public employees and their family members. That was in America's biggest city, where political competition is often intense. In smaller places, with even lower turnout, public employees and their families can constitute an even larger share of the electorate.

Political scientist Sarah Anzia has conducted a battery of studies to test the theory that organized groups, specifically public sector unions, exploit the low turnout of off-cycle elections to secure policy outcomes they care about, namely, better pay and benefits for government employees.[72] Anzia examined how firefighters' and police unions exploit off-cycle municipal elections in California to secure better pay and benefits and thereby increase the costs of city government.[73] California cities employ 1.2 million full-time workers, two-thirds of whom belong to unions. But unionization rates are much higher for firefighters (84 percent belong to unions) and police officers (83 percent belong to unions). Firefighters are noted for being very well organized, politically active, and insulated from competing interests in urban politics.[74] Police unions are less well organized and often confront opposing groups in the political process.[75] So one should expect that firefighters' unions would fare better than police unions in winning things for their members, which is exactly what Anzia found. In cities with off-cycle elections, where public employee union members constituted a higher portion of the electorate, Anzia found that firefighters secured a $13,000 pay premium, when she included overtime and bonuses as well as base pay. Both firefighters' minimum and maximum salaries were higher in cities with off-cycle elections. The firefighters also received greater health and pension benefits. Anzia's findings for police officers were similar, although the pay and benefit premiums created by the one-two punch of off-cycle elections and unionization was smaller. Consequently, California cities with off-cycle elections, which privilege the protective service unions, tend to spend far more for those government services than cities that held on-cycle elections. Anzia estimated that off-cycle cities spend, on average, 33 percent more on employee salaries and 40 percent more per capita on employee benefits, controlling for a host of demographic factors. Consequently, off-cycle cities' operating expenses are about 15 percent higher, and these cities spend about 5 percent more then on-cycle cities on employee compensation. In sum, the municipal unions in the Golden State run up the score in obscure elections with low turnout, which makes the officials who win office in those elections more responsive to them, and that translates into policy outcomes the unions care about.

Anzia also studied school board elections, in which teachers' unions are often the single dominant interest group, and found that because the teachers' unions mobilize while average voters stay home, school board members who win office in off-cycle elections are more responsive to them.[76] Consequently, "districts with off-cycle elections pay experienced teachers over 3 percent more than districts that hold on-cycle elections." Furthermore, "the [pay] premium increases with teacher seniority, consistent with the claim ... that teacher unions are more responsive to senior teachers than beginning teachers .... Teachers with bachelor's degrees and no experience receive 1.5 percent more, teachers with master's degrees and 10 years of experience 3.8 percent more, and maximally qualified teachers 4.2 percent more in districts with off-cycle elections."[77] Former AFT president Albert Shanker put the matter bluntly: "If teachers control both sides of the bargaining table in a substantial number of school districts, we should find many teachers with huge salaries, greatly reduced class sizes, longer holidays and vacations than ever before—you name it."[78] And in considerable measure that is what has happened. Over the last three decades the teacher–student ratio has fallen to an all-time low of 15:1, the number of "contact hours" between teachers and students on a daily basis has been reduced, and salaries would be much higher if so many more teachers had not been hired.

WHAT DOES ALL THE MONEY BUY?

Many people believe that with so much money sloshing around American elections, public sector unions must be buying a lot of influence on issues that they care about. However, political scientists have had a hard time determining empirically how campaign contributions affect the behavior of legislators. Contrary to the popular belief that money buys votes in the US Congress, for example, many scholars have concluded that campaign donations have little influence on representatives' voting behavior.[79] Usually members' voting behavior can be better explained by looking at the character of their district, the political party to which they belong, or their personal ideological beliefs. In many cases, campaign money tends to go to candidates who already support the donors' positions. Rarely do interest groups give to candidates with the objective of changing their minds. Campaign cash also tends to closely follow incumbents and leaders in the polls. Nonetheless, this is an area of considerable dispute.[80]

Some scholars believe that campaign contributions may affect the amount of effort members of Congress devote to certain bills and to setting the legislative agenda.[81] Others also contend that campaign contributions can influence legislators' behavior at the crucial early stages in the legislative process, rather than at the later stage of roll call votes.[82] Exercising influence long before matters come to a vote can be hugely important—as it is in the early stages in which earmarks are crafted and the obscure details of legislation decided. Indeed, this perspective helps explain why the vast majority of monies raised by candidates, especially incumbent legislators, come from individuals and interest groups that stand to win or lose based on legislative action. The basic question is, if donors were not getting something for their investment, why would they continue to give away their money?

At the level of state legislatures, political scientist Lynda W. Powell has found that it is in large, populous states where legislators are highly paid and there are professionalized leaders for whom donations are especially influential.[83] Her findings suggest that the question is not *whether* campaign contributions have an influence on public policy— she contends that they do—but rather *where* and *when* in the legislative process they do. The issue is that campaign contributions may be very consequential at some times and in some places in the legislative process and virtually invisible—at least to scholars' statistical analyses—in others. This influence is often exercised on seemingly narrow matters of interest only to the donor groups involved. Yet, it is often the case that the devil is in the details and those details can have hugely important consequences for the groups concerned. Such details can affect whether a company gets a government contract, a tax incentive, or some regulatory advantage over a competitor. For a public employee union, they might shape the nature of civil service rules to provide more job protections, change the pension formula, or reconfigure the criteria by which certain categories of workers can qualify for disability. Therefore, spending a lot of campaign cash to win seemingly small legislative victories makes eminent sense from the point of view of most interest groups.

Furthermore, scholars have long held that campaign contributions work in tandem with lobbying efforts to form pay-to-play relationships between interest groups and legislators. Groups must donate to campaigns and parties to open the door to legislators' offices, where they will then be able to lobby and advance their interests. (Lobbying by public employee unions is discussed in chapter 6). In an analysis of the link between donating and lobbying at the federal level, one group of scholars found, "Although groups that have both a lobbyist and a PAC account for only one-fifth of all groups in our sample, these groups account for fully 70 percent of all interest group expenditures and 86 percent of all PAC contributions. Groups that do not have PACs also tend to spend little on lobbying, or are legally prohibited from contributing."[84] Another group of scholars examined the politics of health policy in the states. They found that while only 14 percent of organizations both lobby and have a PAC, these groups donate 76 percent of the money given by PACs.[85] Examining local politics, two scholars also found that local officials respond to interest groups in proportion to their resources, activity, and size, which in many cases meant that business groups were less powerful than many surmise.[86] Such findings suggest that there is something to the common-sense notion that extensive campaign contributions and powerful lobbying operations work hand-in-glove. And like other groups that are so active in state and local politics, public sector unions can and do exercise significant policy influence.

Many press accounts, anecdotal stories, and case studies bear out the notion of the powerful one-two punch of campaign donations and lobbying by public sector unions. For example, Cari Lynn Hennessey studied the politics of a proposed living wage ordinance for big-box retailers in Chicago in 2006.[87] Mayor Richard Daley strongly opposed the measure, which he claimed would hurt the city's economic development. Yet, a seemingly veto-proof majority of 35 council members defied the mayor and voted for it anyway. Hennessey argues that it was the threat by a coalition of labor unions—mostly public but some private sector unions—to spend huge sums to unseat aldermen who voted against the measure that pushed many to support it. The unions also partnered with a group of local community organizers to launch rallies, phone banks, and press events and to directly lobby members on the city council. Yet, there was a break in the ranks after Mayor Daley vetoed the bill, as three council members refused to vote to override the mayor, so the measure never became law. Yet those who feared the unions had good reason to do so. In the next election cycle, the unions were the biggest spenders, outpacing the big-box stores and Mayor Daley. Consequently, a number of aldermen who opposed the ordinance were unseated by candidates backed by the unions or had to raise and spend huge sums to hold on to their seats.

POLITICS AND COLLECTIVE BARGAINING

To a large extent, public employee unions' electioneering activities are meant to supplement collective bargaining. What can't be won through legally mandated negotiations can still be pursued in politics. It's the second bite at the apple. Yet, like all groups in American politics, unions never fully get their way. At the national level they are confronted with intense competition from other groups on many issues—and those groups are occasionally prepared to outspend the unions. As one descends to the state and local level, however, the competition begins to thin out and union election activities become more and more influential and pronounced. In some state capitals and cities, they have a unique arsenal of campaign resources that few other groups can match. Such electoral influence is especially evident in the direct democracy procedures of initiative and referenda campaigns. That is the subject of the next chapter.

THE DISTORTION OF DIRECT DEMOCRACY

Of all 50 states, California has the most robust tradition of making laws through a direct vote of citizens. Such direct democracy methods bypass the normal checks and balances of the legislative process and, in theory, hand power directly to citizens in the voting booth. However, in practice, direct democracy has opened up new avenues for the influence of interest groups. In 1988, for example, the California Teachers Association (CTA) put Proposition 98 on the ballot that would require the state to spend 40 percent of its budget annually on public education. The union then launched a massive campaign to secure its passage. This was a huge political victory. How often does any interest group get a state government to devote 40 percent of revenues to the policy area of most concern to it?

California is not alone in using direct democracy. In more than half of the states, laws can also be made through the direct vote of citizens. These ballot measures could be about any kind of public policy and trump the normal give and take required by American legislative institutions. The hope was that the direct democracy techniques of initiatives and referendums would reduce the influence of special interests on public policy. That hope has largely been in vain, as the initiative process in many places has become a new battleground for those very same interests.[1]

Public sector unions have been especially apt to engage direct democracy electoral processes when they have been challenged by business groups or policy entrepreneurs or have been unable to get their way in the legislature. Facing the prospect of dramatic construction of collective bargaining rights, Ohio's public employee unions quickly secured enough signatures to get the repeal of the newly minted law on the ballot and then launched a vigorous campaign to get voters to overturn it. Sometimes unions try to get what they want through the referendum process. In California in 2012, Governor Jerry Brown teamed up with the state's public employee unions, led by the CTA, to win passage of a set of tax increases to stave off budget cuts to education and other public services, such as universities, parks, and healthcare. However, the unions sometimes lose. In 2012, Michigan's unions placed a referendum on the ballot that would have enshrined collective bargaining as a state constitutional right. But voters rejected it at the ballot box. Finally, unions often engage in the direct democracy process to fight measures they don't like. And they are often very successful. For instance, in 2012, teachers' unions fought off proposals to eliminate teacher tenure in Idaho and South Dakota by launching expensive media campaigns and organizing drives to get voters to the polls who would vote against the measures.

Besides contributing money to candidates and parties and mobilizing get-out-the-vote operations to influence elections at all levels, public sector unions also engage extensively in direct democracy campaigns in states and localities that permit them. They take sides in campaigns for state constitutional amendments, initiatives, and referenda presented to voters at the ballot box. They have on occasion spent millions on television and radio ads and mounted larger voter mobilization drives to champion or defeat measures affecting their interests. With a large number of members and a tight communications network between the union organization and workers, they can constitute a disproportionate share of the electorate in these ballot contests. Of course, all of this is perfectly legal, but it pushes direct democracy processes further away from citizens' preferences and closer to those of the unions.[2] To get a closer look at public sector unions' activity in this area of American politics, this chapter takes a deep dive into the initiative process of California, the state that has made the most extensive use of direct democracy techniques.

Why a case study of California? First of all, the use of direct democracy techniques is far more extensive in the Golden State than anywhere else in America. There are more policies decided by initiative and more campaigns to study than elsewhere. Other strong union states, such as New York or New Jersey, rarely use ballot initiatives in comparison with California. Second, public sector unions are particularly strong in the state. State statutes supplemented by local ordinances provide for collective bargaining, agency shops, and dues check-offs along with other union security provisions that favor the unionization of government workers, such that 57 percent of the government workforce belongs to unions. For these reasons, California offers the best laboratory to study the role of public sector unions in initiative campaigns than anywhere else.

The results are illuminating. They reveal that public sector unions are extremely effective at blocking reforms they oppose and have a solid track record of winning on issues they support. All told, public sector unions have played a big role in pushing for higher taxes and thwarting reform— all in an effort to maintain a status quo that favors their interests at the expense of the public's interest in an effective, efficient government that is responsive to its preferences. Although it seems like a somewhat banal point, the power to thwart change can sometimes be even more important than the power to enact it. Yet public employee unions' power is often reflected in their ability to defend a status quo that privileges them.

Direct Democracy in California

Public sector unions play an outsized role in California's politics. In the Golden State's direct democracy process, public sector unions have been quite successful at blocking reforms that they deemed anathema to their interests. How have California's public sector unions exploited their unique arsenal of political resources in the state's direct democracy processes? For starters, they took a position on 40 percent of the 178 ballot initiatives over the last 30 years. Voters ratified nearly half of the measures they supported, while 75 percent of the measures the unions opposed were defeated. Public sector unions consistently side with the liberal position on ballot issues of concern to them. They backed only a handful of conservative initiatives, and among those they opposed, 66 percent were either conservative or didn't fit neatly on the left–right spectrum.

Looking more closely at the handful of ballot measures that were most important to the unions reveals that when the chips are down, they almost always win. In these big battles, they often outspend and outmobilize their opponents by huge margins. Many of these fights have been over education policy, with the teachers' unions being the central actor. The unions' victories include Proposition 98 in 1988, which mandated that 40 percent of the state's general fund be spent annually on K–12 education and community colleges. That measure has greatly constricted the state's fiscal flexibility, reduced the efficacy of public education, and helped make California's teachers the most expensive in the country. In opposition, the teachers' unions twice defeated proposals for school vouchers and other proposals to bring more accountability to the state's public schools.

When one combines the effectiveness of public sector unions in the initiative process with their powerful influence in the state legislature, it becomes evident that they are arguably the single most powerful political force in the Golden State.[3] Indeed, the unions in California have three avenues to promote their policy goals and defend their privileges: the initiative process, the state legislature, and in collective bargaining. Given their extensive political resources, they can usually find a way to use one of these venues to either get their way or defend their interests. The trouble is that what is good for California's public employee unions is not necessarily synonymous with what is good for the Golden State as a whole. While special interests hijacking government and using multiple means to do so is intrinsic to politics, public sector unions do this in their own special way.

The sheer size of the Golden State means that, for better or worse, what happens there has huge ripple effects. Twelve percent of the nation's population (37 million people) lives there. The state is the ninth-largest economy in the world. It had the second-largest budget in the country (after the federal government) and the largest budget deficit ($16 billion) of any state in fiscal year 2012. It also has the most progressive income tax system in the nation (with the second-highest top marginal rate), has a pension system with some $500 billion in liabilities that is less than 80 percent funded (the minimum percentage at which experts agree is fiscally sustainable), and boasts some of the most powerful public sector unions in the country (57 percent of state and local workers belong to unions). California has also been a harbinger of political changes that are later visited on other states and cities.

Two ballot measures made the fall 2012 campaign especially intense. One was a set of tax increases (Proposition 30) pushed by Governor Jerry Brown and the state's main public sector unions.[4] Its passage has helped temporarily stave off deep cuts, improved the budget picture, and reduced the pressure to undertake more significant reform.[5] Working in the opposite direction was a measure (Proposition 32) that, had it passed, would have prohibited direct donations to California political candidates from unions and corporations and, more significantly for the unions, prohibited deducting money directly from members' paychecks and funneling that money to political activism.[6]

In California, elected officials don't really like to debate whether to change or maintain the status quo. With a largely dysfunctional state legislature, direct democracy techniques have become the favored means in California for enacting significant policy change. Originally implemented in the Progressive era to get around a corrupt legislature dominated by railroad interests—called "the Octopus"—direct democracy in the Golden State has not worked out the way its proponents expected. They hoped that it would make politicians more accountable and incite greater citizen participation in politics. It was not to be. The initiative process in California has not become a tribune of the people. Instead, it has become yet another venue for special interests to do battle.[7]

Public sector unionism in California today manifests itself in three forms: the teachers' unions, those in the protective services (police officers, firefighters, highway patrol, and corrections officers), and the Service Employees International Union (SEIU), which represents a potpourri of workers, including noninstructional school staff, prison staff, home health-care workers, and many others. Consider one example of the power of public sector unions. According to the California Fair Political Practices Commission, the 335,000-member California Teachers Association alone spent more than $210 million in the first decade of the twenty-first century on political campaigning—more than any other organization in the state. And as policy analyst Troy Senik notes in *City Journal*, "The CTA outspent the pharmaceutical industry, the oil industry, and the tobacco industry *combined*."[8] California is one of the states where the teachers' unions alone outspent all business associations combined between 2000 and 2009.[9]

How have public employee unions used direct democracy to advance their policy goals or block things deemed anathema to their interests? Public sector unions in California have been more effective in blocking changes they oppose than winning things they want.[10] And many of the things they've managed to stymie are reforms that might well have improved the performance of California's institutions. Yet, some of the instances where they did get their way have had negative consequences for the state's fiscal health. All told, when the unions care most, they win.

Prior to 2012, the only tax initiatives passed in the last 30 years lowered rather than raised taxes. Efforts to increase income or sales taxes have failed miserably. In 2012, however, the governor campaigned hard for the measure and framed his proposal as being tied to the fate of education. He thus enlisted the support of the teachers' unions, one of the most powerful political forces in the state, which gave the measure a better-than-usual chance of approval. "Paycheck protection" measures that would eliminate dues check-off have also been on the ballot in California. The public sector unions have twice led the campaign to defeat them. After outspending supporters of the measure five to one, they defeated it a third time in 2012.[11]

California's Troubles

Governing California in the last decade has been an enormous challenge. The Golden State has been compared to Greece and regularly referred to as "dysfunctional" and even as a "failed" state.[12] For much of the first decade of the twenty-first century, the state was in near-permanent crisis. It regularly ran budget deficits and papered them over with accounting gimmicks to satisfy the constitutional requirement of a balanced budget. The state's nonpartisan Legislative Analyst—the equivalent of the Congressional Budget Office—estimates the state will face similar structural deficits for years to come. Governor Brown has colorfully described the state's budget process as a "pretzel palace of incredible complexity."

Other signs point to problem. Four cities—Vallejo, Stockton, Mammoth Lakes, and San Bernardino—have declared bankruptcy. The state's three largest public employee retirement plans—CalPERS, CalSTRS, and UCRS—cover 2.6 million workers and have unfunded liabilities of over $500 billion, according to the Stanford Institute of

Public Policy Research.[13] Today, California's A-bond rating competes with Illinois for the worst in the country. Between 2000 and 2010, its economy grew by 17 percent compared with 26 percent in Texas, where many of its companies have fled.[14] Population growth was flat in the first decade of the twenty-first century for the first time in the state's history.

The state's political establishment is paralyzed by these colossal problems. The incapacity of California government to manage its own affairs is a long, complicated story, with many contributing factors and blame widely distributed. Among the guilty parties are the direct democracy procedures instituted in the Progressive era, supermajority requirements for passing revenue bills in the legislature, party polarization, and voters who want extensive services and low taxes. There is no single culprit.

Into this mess stepped a septuagenarian, Jerry Brown. He has called for pension reform, spending cuts, and new tax revenues. Few of his proposals, however, touch the deeper problems in the state's finances, which stem from the benefits for existing government employees and retirees, Medicaid, the prison system, and the tax structure.[15] Because changing the pension scheme was anathema to public employee unions—the most powerful special interest in the state—Brown's plan was scuttled in the legislature. The state legislature then tried to produce its own plan to show that it was fiscally responsible before the tax increase was placed before voters.[16] As for taxing and spending, Brown and the legislature have sought budget cuts in areas with limited political clout, such as the universities, parks, the court system, and welfare recipients. In addition, they have cut aid to local governments, who in turn must reduce public services. None of these cuts address the structural drivers of California's fiscal problems.

To address the budget crunch, Governor Brown sought to raise more revenue rather than undertake structural reforms. But he ran into a roadblock in the legislature. The feeble but antitax Republican Party had just enough votes to block the necessary supermajority for a tax increase, which prevented Brown and the Democrats in the state legislature from muscling through a bill to raise revenue. Therefore, the governor took his case to the people directly. His team was forced to hit the street and collect approximately 800,000 signatures to put a measure before voters in November.[17] Therefore, a battle over yet another tax increase to cover the structural budget problems for at best a few years took place in the fall of

2012. The governor and his allies prevailed and California's budget picture has brightened for now.

Brown's initial plan temporarily increased sales taxes slightly for four years and income taxes on the affluent for five years. The governor optimistically estimates that the imposts would yield additional revenue of some $7 billion a year. However, Brown ran into opposition from public employee unions, who wanted to tax the rich more and eliminate the sales tax increase. In March of 2012, the governor reached a deal with the unions. Their merged proposal became Proposition 30, which reduces the sales tax increase a smidge to 7.5 percent. Although billed as a "millionaire's tax," it creates two new brackets and imposes a 10.3 percent tax rate on income over $250,000 but less than $300,000; an 11.3 percent tax rate on taxable income over $300,000 but less than $500,000; a 12.3 percent tax rate on taxable income over $500,000 but less than $1,000,000; and a 13.3 percent tax rate on income over $1 million (Table 5.1).

The unions then backed the revenue raiser promoted by the governor. Both framed the measure as a way to repair the overall budget and benefit the public schools. Governor Brown argued that the increased tax burden must be borne for the sake of the state's children. As he put it: "This is not about any other issue. It's not about the environment, it's not about pensions, it's not about parks. It's about one simple question: Shall those who've been blessed beyond imagination give back 1 or 2 or 3 percent for the next seven years, or shall we take billions out of our schools and

Table 5.1 Proposition 30: Brown's Tax Plan.

Income Taxes			
Tax Bracket	Current Rate	Proposed Rate	Percent Increase
$250–$300K	9.30%	10.30%	10%
$300–$500K	9.30%	11.30%	18%
$500K–$1 million	9.30%	12.30%	24%
$1 million and up	10.30%	13.30%	23%
Sales Tax			
Tax Bracket	Current Rate	Proposed Rate	Percent Increase
NA	7.25%	7.50%	3.45%

colleges to the detriment of the kids standing behind us and the future of our state?"[18]

Yet, this being California, that wasn't the end of the story. Two other tax measures had also made it onto the ballot. The higher profile of the two was the brainchild of Molly Munger, a well-to-do civil rights lawyer. (She is the daughter of Charles Munger, Warren Buffett's partner at Berkshire Hathaway.) Her bill promised to raise more money—estimated at some $10 billion a year over 12 years—by raising income taxes across the board, not just those of the affluent.[19] Finally, it would've earmarked most of the new revenue for public education rather than address the current budget crisis.

These competing initiatives provided for a vigorous campaign in the fall of 2012. Some business and taxpayer groups opposed both outright. Governor Brown and the unions fought hard for their tax increase, which voters approved. Munger self-financed the campaign for her measure, which voters rejected.

UNIONS AND THE BALLOT

The late 1970s were when the seeds for the current crisis were planted. As school spending rose in the wake of *Serrano v. Priest* (first decided in 1971 and reaffirmed in 1976)—an important state supreme court decision regarding the equity of education financing—localities increasingly sought new revenues through higher property taxes. This contributed significantly to the Tax Revolt and the passage, in 1978, of Proposition 13, which capped property tax increases at 2.5 percent, required a two-thirds majority in the legislature for any tax increases, and sought to slow the growth of local governments.[20] Proposition 13 had huge consequences for the state's public finances, affecting both how much revenue was collected and, more importantly, where that money went. It also revived interest in direct democracy in California. In the 1960s, only 9 initiatives qualified for the ballot; in the 1970s, the number increased to 22; and then in the 1980s, it more than doubled to 46. In the last decade, 74 initiatives were placed before voters.[21]

This was also the period during which public employees were granted collective bargaining rights and began to unionize. In 1968, Governor Ronald Reagan signed the Meyers-Milias-Brown Act, permitting collective bargaining and unionization in local governments. Building on that step, Governor Jerry Brown extended collective bargaining rights to nearly all public employees in the state. He signed the Public Educational Employer-Employee Relations Act in 1976 (K–12 school teachers) and the Dillas Act in 1978 (state workers) and capped it off in 1979 with the Higher Educational Employer-Employee Relations Act (university employees). The result was a huge wave of unionization among government employees in the 1980s.

Therefore, 1980 is a fitting year to begin our analysis of public employee unions' role in the initiative process. It was only really after that point that they became a formidable presence in state politics. By the early 1980s, they had real assets: money, manpower, organization, and legal protections. In the ballot process, as elsewhere, public sector unions can use their power in two ways: to press for policies that advance their cause or to block those they deem antithetical to it.

Using a database of propositions placed before voters, I examined 178 initiatives from 1980 until 2010.[22] Of those, 73 were voted into law and 105 were rejected (a 41 percent passage rate). The measures were then categorized as "liberal," "conservative," or "other."[23] "Liberal" initiatives were those that either raised labor or environmental standards or increased public spending or taxes. "Conservative" initiatives went in the opposite direction in those areas or emphasized "social" issues such as blocking illegal immigration, halting affirmative action, or banning gay marriage. Issues not easily categorized as liberal or conservative—such as gaming on Indian reservations or electoral reforms—were coded "other." All told, there were 93 liberal, 39 conservative, and 45 other total initiatives. A total of 32 liberal initiatives passed and 61 failed (a passage rate of 34 percent), while 20 conservative measures passed and 19 failed (a 51 percent passage rate). Liberal measures were thus slightly below and conservative measures slightly above the overall passage rate. These figures suggest that liberals are more likely to propose and be successful at getting measures on the ballot than conservatives in California. But conservatives are more likely to see voters enact their initiatives than are liberals. Conservatives have succeeded in passing measures that limit taxes, get tough on crime, define marriage, eliminate bilingual education, and place restrictions on illegal immigrants.

Next, the measures were categorized by whether public sector unions were in favor, opposed, or neutral.[24] To determine the unions' position, the state voter guides were used. They contain the arguments for and against a measure and are signed by supporters and opponents with their organizational affiliation.[25] Therefore, the ballot guides provide a substantial public record of whether the unions were for or against a measure. Unions took a position on 74 of the 178 measures (or 42 percent) and were in favor of 30 measures and opposed to 44 (Figure 5.1). Of those they opposed, 11 passed and 33 were voted down. The unions were able to block around 75 percent of the initiatives that they opposed, 17 of which were conservative, 15 liberal, and 12 neither.

Of those they favored, 14 passed and 16 were rejected, for a passage rate of 47 percent. Public employee unions supported only four conservative initiatives. They also backed 23 liberal initiatives and three that didn't fit into a left–right alignment. Although there are only a few cases, the passage rate for measures the unions supported was higher than the overall passage rate. The rejection rate for measures the unions opposed was, however, much higher than the overall rejection rate. Ultimately, the unions were more successful on defense (trying to stop conservative initiatives) than on offense (trying to win things they want).

From this aggregate analysis it seems that while there have been more liberal ballot measures over the past 30 years, public employee unions have

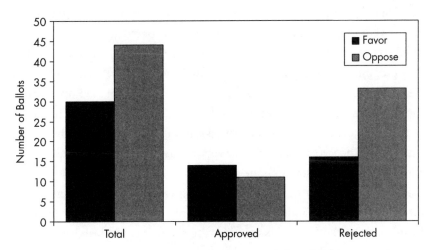

Figure 5.1 Public Sector Unions and Ballot Initiatives, 1980–2010.

made use of direct democracy about 40 percent of the time. For a number of reasons, direct democracy should be an attractive venue for public employee unions because they would appear to have a considerable number of advantages over other interest groups. Due to their common workplace, they have a membership base that is easy to mobilize for signature drives and get-out-the-vote operations. They have a steady and stable revenue stream, as monies are deducted directly from members' paychecks by government and funneled into union coffers. Their members tend to have higher levels of education than most citizens, which political scientists have found correlates with more avid electoral participation. Finally, in low-turnout contests, which ballot measures can be, union members can constitute a higher proportion of the electorate.

However, a more qualitative and particularistic treatment of key measures reveals that California's public employee unions have fared extremely well in direct democracy campaigns. To see this requires closer inspection of the measures that were really important to public employee unions. In fact, some of the individual measures that unions have either favored or opposed have had huge consequences for California.

Big-Ticket Ballots

Concentrating on the big ballot battles is instructive of unions' power in California's direct democracy. One can isolate the 15 propositions that stand out as particularly important to public employee unions (Table 5.2).[26] These were major battles on which the unions spent huge sums of money in efforts to persuade the electorate and mobilize their members. When they pull out all the stops, they almost always win. Of the major initiatives, the unions opposed nine and supported six. Voters enacted only one of the key measures, ending bilingual education in 1998, over union opposition. On the other hand, voters ratified four of the six measures the unions supported. The two defeats were by very narrow margins. One would have allowed school districts to issue their own bonds if approved by a simple majority of voters rather than the existing two-thirds requirement. The other would have established campaign contribution and spending limits. In sum, out of the 15 ballots most dear to them over the last 30 years, the unions only lost three times. An impressive record.

Table 5.2 Most Important Measures for Public Sector Unions, 1980–2012.

Year	Proposition	Yes%	No%	Union Position	Short Description
1986	Prop 61	34.1	65.9	Oppose	Cap on public employee salaries
1988	Prop 98	50.7	49.3	Support	General fund financing—school funding
1992	Prop 162	51.0	49.0	Support	Public employee retirement systems
1993	Prop 174	30.4	69.6	Oppose	State education vouchers usable for public or private schools
1996	Prop 212	49.2	50.8	Support	Campaign contributions and spending limits. Restricts lobbyists
1998	Prop 8	36.9	63.1	Oppose	Create fund for reduction in class sizes. Requires teacher testing
1998	Prop 226	46.7	53.3	Oppose	Union members' permission required to use dues for politics
1998	Prop 227	60.9	39.1	Oppose	Ending bilingual education
2000	Prop 38	29.3	70.7	Oppose	Authorizes state payments of $4,000 per pupil for private and religious schools
2000	Prop 39	53.3	46.7	Support	Authorizes bonds for construction of school facilities if approved by 55% vote
2000	Prop 26	48.7	51.3	Support	Authorizes school districts to issue bonds if approved by majority of voters
2002	Prop 49	56.6	43.4	Support	Increases funds for after-school programs and low-income schools
2005	Prop 74	45.0	55.2	Oppose	Extends period before tenure from two to five years for public school teachers
2005	Prop 75	47.0	53.5	Oppose	Prohibits public employee unions from using dues for political purposes
2005	Prop 76	38.0	62.3	Oppose	Sets limits on state spending, relaxes education spending requirements
2012	Prop 30	55.4	44.6	Support	Increase sales and income taxes

Education issues are clearly central to the teachers' unions in California and were among the largest and most controversial ballot measures. Indeed, 10 of the 15 most important measures touched on education issues. On defense, six of the nine measures the unions opposed were education related. Led by the California Teachers Association (CTA), they managed to block proposals for school vouchers (twice), teacher evaluation and testing, new requirements for teacher tenure, and a relaxation of education spending requirements. On offense, four of the six measures they supported were designed to funnel more money into the schools. On all of these propositions, the unions spent substantial sums (Figure 5.2). Indeed, on some of them, they almost entirely underwrote the campaign. In most of these campaigns, the teachers' unions and their allies significantly outspent their rivals. While a few of the votes were close, in most of the cases the union position won an overwhelming majority. No wonder former Governor Pete Wilson described the CTA as a "relentless political machine."[27]

The most important of all these education-related measures was Proposition 98 in 1988. It required that 40 percent of the state's general fund be spent annually on K–12 education and community colleges. That year the CTA spent $4.5 million, a very large sum in those days, to promote it. The CTA's victory, by a slim margin, was one of the most significant pieces of legislation in the last 30 years of California history. It also demonstrated the teachers' unions' power. As political scientist Terry Moe asked,

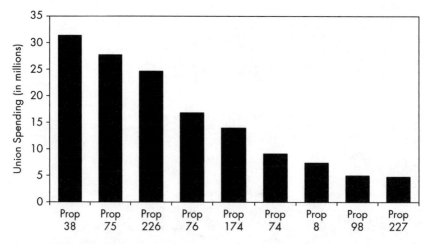

Figure 5.2 Public Sector Union Spending on Education Initiatives.

Source: National Institute for Money in State Politics.

"How often is a special interest group able to commandeer 40 percent of a state's entire budget for its own realm of policy?" The consequences were a severe constriction of the state's fiscal flexibility. By guaranteeing such lavish funding, Proposition 98 also reduced accountability, as school districts have had to worry less about the most efficient allocation of resources. Finally, by using its influence on local school boards, the CTA channeled much of the new monies—about $450 million a year—into increasing teacher pay.[28] The Golden State now boasts of the highest average teacher salaries in the country.

In opposition, the teachers' unions have also vehemently opposed voucher plans, which they see as a threat to their survival. They don't want any children (and the dollars attached to them) exiting a public school for a private school. School vouchers have made it onto the ballot twice in California: Proposition 174 in 1993 and Proposition 38 in 2000. In both instances, the teachers' unions single-handedly bankrolled the opposition campaign.[29] In 1993, the CTA spent $12.5 million on the opposition campaign, outspending supporters eight to one. In addition, it persuaded March Fong Eu, the secretary of state, to significantly change the proposition's title from Parental Choice to Education Vouchers.[30] According to Myron Lieberman, the more controversial title dropped Proposition 174 ten points in the polls, where it had initially been well received by voters.[31] In the 2000 ballot fight, the teachers' unions spent some $21 million. In both cases, many other interest groups in California—such as the National Association for the Advancement of Colored People (NAACP), the Parent Teacher Association (PTA), and the American Civil Liberties Union (ACLU)—publicly opposed school vouchers. Yet, when the rubber met the road, they spent almost nothing to defeat vouchers at the ballot box.

The teachers' unions have also blocked efforts to impose greater accountability measures on California's public schools. In 1998, the CTA spent nearly $7 million to defeat Proposition 8. The measure would have allowed the use of student performance as a criterion for teacher evaluation and required teachers to take credentialing tests in their fields. In 2005, Governor Schwarzenegger in his supposed "Year of Reform" proposed a measure aimed at teacher "tenure" in K–12 education that would have extended the apprentice period for teachers from two to five years. Another measure would have set limits on state spending and relaxed the education spending requirements imposed by Proposition 98. The CTA alone spent $57 million, mortgaging its Sacramento headquarters to fight these and another measure.

Looking at other issues on the list that public employee unions supported or opposed, one can see that they are arguably the most effective interest group at getting their way. The unions outspent their opponents handily on many issues. In 2005, the unions and their allies spent $54 million to defeat Proposition 75, a paycheck protection measure that would have prohibited unions from deducting monies from workers' paychecks to use for politics. Its supporters mustered a measly $5.8 million. Governor Schwarzenegger's state spending cap elicited zero support, while its opponents, led by the unions, shelled out $28 million. If one includes the paycheck protection measure of that year, all public sector unions combined spent a whopping $90 million in opposition, according to the National Institute on Money in State Politics. Supporters of the measures didn't even come close.

A brief glance at initiatives that were important to business suggests that the campaigns (for and against) tended to spend far less and be much more evenly matched. So while there are other major ballot issue financing groups besides the public sector unions, their interests and attention level vary considerably with the issue at stake. In contrast, the role of the unions is concentrated and thus outsized. This finding comports with reporting by the *Wall Street Journal*, which found that organized labor, led by the SEIU, spends far more on political activity than is generally thought.[32] In sum, the notion that public sector unions are regularly outspent by business interests (however defined) in California's direct democracy process is a myth.

Despite facing an uphill battle, Brown's initiative was approved by a majority of voters and voters rejected, for a third time, the paycheck protection measure to weaken public sector unions' political power. Governor Brown recognized the challenge he faced and therefore argued that his campaign needed to "generate the moral equivalent of war," because "people must understand that we have to make sacrifices if we want to have a future." Prior efforts to raise income and sales taxes all failed, sometimes miserably.[33] Wisely framed to "save the children" by tying it to school funding, Brown's tax hike pulled at the heart strings and enlisted powerful allies. After strong initial showings in the polls, when voters weren't abreast of the stakes, public support declined to a bare majority in midsummer.[34] However, because the governor and the unions framed the measure as tied to education spending and thus enlisted all the resources of the teachers' unions, they were able to generate enough voter support to pass the measure. As for paycheck protection, it failed by nearly identical margins (47 percent in favor to 53 percent opposed) twice before—most recently in 2005—and fared even worse this time around. In each case opponents of the measure vastly outspent and outmobilized its supporters. To combat the most recent measure, opponents, led by the unions, had outraised supporters two to one by mid-July.

CALIFORNIA AND AMERICA

All told, public employee unions have used the ballot process in California to stave off changes they opposed and occasionally won things very important to them. They exploit their inherent advantages over other interest groups in member turnout and get-out-the-vote operations. When they care about an item on the ballot, they are often the biggest spender— sometimes virtually the only one—on the campaign.

The power of unions to block change in California and in 26 other states that practice direct democracy has been enormously important to preventing experimentation with different modes of public service delivery. The enormity of ballot politics in the Golden State is striking, but the patterns of union influence are similar across the country. Teachers' unions have spent a fortune to defeat proposals for vouchers and measures to change the nature of teacher tenure. In combination with the teachers, other government unions have sought to block attempts to make public sector unions more like other interest groups in the way they collect money— that is, first securing the consent of their members. The unions have also opposed ballot measures to cap government spending and property taxes. So the unions are deeply involved in state governments' taxing and spending authority, which affects the way state and local government as a whole operates. Lots of other groups benefit from bigger government, but few have as direct a material stake in it as public sector unions. So while other groups like construction firms and trial lawyers are often involved in ballot politics, the biggest players are consistently unions representing public employees.

Consider a few examples. In 2009, both Washington State and Maine had spending caps on the ballot. In both cases the public sector unions provided between one-third and one-half of the total funding opposing the measures. When it comes to reducing or redirecting tax revenue, the unions can be counted on to lead the opposition as well. In 2008 in Massachusetts, the unions led the charge against a proposal to end the state's income tax. In 2006, Washington State voted on whether to repeal its estate tax, the campaign against which was underwritten by the state's public employee unions.

The result of public sector unions' activity in direct democracy has been to stymie efforts to reform America's education, taxation, and spending priorities. Whether or not those reform efforts were wise is obviously the subject of disagreement, but public employees have a vested, material interest in making sure that many things are not tried—in California or anywhere else. The notion that direct democracy would eliminate special interest influence has been converted into an area where the unions can quite consistently block policy experiment. The states' capacity to serve as laboratories of democracy is diminished.

6

GOVERNMENT LOBBIES ITSELF

Barbara Walters: "So you're going to be a very large and an increasingly larger political force?"
Albert Shanker: "There's no question about it."

—TODAY Show, February 26, 1975

In an early episode of the Netflix series "House of Cards," the antihero and Majority Whip of the House of Representatives Frank Underwood (played by Kevin Spacey) battles the teachers' unions. Conflict over an education reform bill sparks to a national teacher strike, which leads to a top teacher union lobbyist punching the majority whip in his office. In the run-up to that scene, union lobbyists possess remarkable access to key policymakers and are even involved in crafting the bill's language. Indeed, they are the only constituency the elected officials seem to be concerned about. "House of Cards" might be fictional and highly dramatized, but it provides a window into the world of public union lobbying.

In addition to trying to influence government through collective bargaining and electioneering, public employee unions also try to shape policy by lobbying legislators and regulators. Like other interest groups, public sector unions seek to advance their members' interests, encourage political participation, educate and mobilize voters, and monitor governmental activity. Between elections, the unions employ familiar tactics to exercise influence. They hire a coterie of lawyers and old political hands in Washington, DC, state capitals, and other big cities. The American federal and constitutional system provides multiple points of lobbyist access to policymakers. Consequently, the unions engage in this activity at all levels of government and even in states and localities where they do not enjoy collective bargaining rights. In fact, they are especially dependent on political activity in such jurisdictions.

Granted, the measurement of union lobbying influence on policy outcomes is difficult, as it is for other groups. A long tradition of scholarship holds that governments at all levels of American politics are more responsive to groups representing business, the professions, and white men than groups representing women, minorities, and the poor.[1] However, most of the research dwells on group membership and activity than on their real influence—in part because the latter is notoriously hard to isolate and observe.[2] If it were the case that financial and membership resources translated automatically into policy influence, both public sector unions and business groups would be very powerful indeed. However, many scholars have pointed out that extensive resources do not always translate into lobbying victories, in the sense that groups get what they want enacted. In short, a lot is going on under the label "lobbying," and it's hard to assess its efficacy.

This chapter examines what government employees' unions do and what benefits they actually secure through the lobbying. One of its conclusions is that while the unions have been highly effective lobbyists, the gains that they make tend to be small and incremental. In fact, much of their energy is devoted to blocking policies that might harm their interests, which is true for business groups as well. Another is that public sector unions have an advantage over business groups because they are more likely to present a unified front across several issues. The business community is often divided, and different firms work against each other. A third is that government unions are more likely to form coalitions with citizen and business groups than other interests, which gives them more power than the competition. A final point is that public employee unions rarely act as counterweights to business, whose lobbying power is often overestimated.

As we shall see, public sector unions maintain unique advantages and positions of privilege. Former California state senate president Gloria

Romero, a Democrat, describes public employee unions' behind-the-scenes influence as follows:

> There is no aspect of state government operations or public policy that is untouched by the power of public-sector unions and their allies in Sacramento .... From enacting legislation to writing a state budget to confirming state board and commission appointees, labor's presence is omnipresent. It also includes ghostwriting eleventh-hour legislative changes to push ballot-qualified citizen initiatives to a more obscure ballot position so that their backed initiatives will be seen by voters first. Their influence extends beyond the Legislature, and includes clout with how the state's legal counsel writes ballot summaries and titles.[3]

This account diverges sharply from the popular impression that interests favoring the privileged few over the disadvantaged many dominate lobbying. Later, I will offer reasons to reconsider claims that public sector unions counterbalance business interests and that business dominates state and local politics.[4] Even when public sector unions confront business interests directly, they usually do so when the issues are highly ideological and often partisan. In such instances, the electoral incentives created by their particular constituency are more likely to drive legislators' responses than the lobbying efforts of either side. Therefore, public sector unions can make small incremental gains over time on low-profile matters but may have more trouble winning high-profile fights over legislation. And the record suggests that this pattern was operative from the 1980s until the Great Recession. After 2008, the activities of public sector unions began to receive much more scrutiny.

Just because there are many other players on the field does not mean they are all competing in the same game. Public sector unions have been effective at winning policy language important mainly to them. It is often the case that public employee unions, like other groups, lobby for small detailed changes in legislation that receive little or no press coverage and are only of interest to insiders and experts. And they are not always adversarial to business interests, as one might assume. Public employee unions often form coalitions with other groups, which sometimes include elements of the business community. Lobbying is not, in most cases, a zero-sum game between labor and business.

PUBLIC SECTOR UNIONS AND THE INTEREST GROUP LANDSCAPE

Today, almost every segment in American society has at least one interest group representing them, or claiming to, in state capitols and Washington, DC. The most active participants are citizen groups, trade associations, business corporations, professional associations, labor unions, think tanks, and intergovernmental groups. Kay Scholzman and John Tierney's 1986 study found that the interest group universe was composed of 30 percent business groups, 26 percent trade associations, and 18 percent citizen groups.[5] More recent scholarship finds a slightly different balance, suggesting that citizen groups are more prolific and influential than was previously recognized.[6] And while business groups constituted a plurality of all groups, many observers have argued that it is wrong to treat "business" as a monolithic interest. Very often businesses have competing or parallel objectives with each other. Indeed, one scholar found that business "groups" are often single firms acting alone rather than business lobbying coming from the Chamber of Commerce, which combines a multiplicity of businesses under a single umbrella.[7] Public sector unions, on the other hand, often behave in a more monolithic fashion in the lobbying arena.

When it comes to lobbying in state capitols, government workers' unions have lots of competition. From 1975 to 1990, the average number of interest groups registered to lobby state legislatures increased from 175 to 587. The total number of registered lobbyists doubled from 15,000 to nearly 30,000 in 1990.[8] Today, there are about 40,000 lobbyists working in state capitols across the country. The total number of interest groups has quintupled over the last half century. And over a billion dollars is spent annually.[9] The amount of money spent varies greatly by state. In big states, the sums are quite large. In California, interest groups spend more than $250 million a year on lobbying. In New York, they spend over $200 million annually. In 2011, public sector unions spent a total of about $15 million out of the total $220 million spent. Unions representing public employees were 5 of the top 10 spenders (out of a total of 2,786).[10] Other states, especially those in the South and West, see interest groups spending between $1 million and $50 million on lobbying.[11] Of course, one must take into account the size and cost of doing business in each state.

As interest groups, public sector unions are what political scientists call "membership groups" in that they rely on financial contributions from individuals and do not represent larger entities. However, they are different from other membership groups because they represent government workers and existing law solves their collective action problems by strongly incentivizing workers to join the unions and often deducting dues directly from their paycheck. The fact is that public sector unions are, to a large extent, interest groups created by government itself.

As lobbyists, what do public sector unions do? Like other interest groups, they perform a variety of tasks:

1. Influence public policy
2. Represent the views of their members
3. Provide information to government officials
4. Provide information to the public
5. Help set the governmental agenda
6. Monitor the government
7. Create vehicles for worker participation

Lobbying by interest groups occurs in many places: on the phone, by email, on the streets of the nation's capital and throughout state capitols and city halls, and in the hallways outside committee and subcommittee hearings. Therefore, it is hard for scholars to directly observe and measure its effects. In addition, there are all the unofficial lobbyists—consultants and other political operators—who enjoy strong ties to legislators and often work in the same direction as the registered lobbyists.

Furthermore, many lobbying efforts are not intended to persuade policymakers to change long-standing positions. Rather, lobbying sometimes aims to stiffen legislators' spines—whether they are on the fence on an issue, have taken no position, or are even opposed to a group's interests. In fact, there may only be a few issues on which legislators lack information a lobbyist can provide and are still persuadable. So the popular notion that lobbying changes legislators' minds rarely occurs in reality.

In the lobbying game, public sector unions can employ two basic strategies: (1) an "insider" strategy that includes access to key decision makers and recourse to the courts and (2) an "outsider" strategy that

involves appealing to the public through issue ads and organizing rallies. Public sector unions are uniquely equipped to engage in the latter, since their members work for government and they often maintain
visible headquarters near well-trafficked statehouses and city halls.
Obviously, both insider and outsider strategies are often pursued simultaneously. Indeed, according to Gary Andres, the majority staff director
of the US House Energy and Commerce Committee, lobbying is starting to look less like an insider's educational quest and more like an election campaign.[12]

Nor is there a clear distinction between campaign contributions and
lobbying. Usually campaign contributions lead to lobbyists' access to
politicians. And if it is true that campaign contributions are the principal means of buying access to legislators, then public sector unions at the
state and local level should have more access to politicians than almost
any other group. They also enjoy access to policymakers through the collective bargaining process where ideas can be floated and tested. So when
some legislators "shake the tree," meaning they raise an issue in a committee hearing or some other visible arena, interest groups know to donate to
their campaign if they want access to members—and public sector unions
are often first in line.

Although unions (public and private) receive attention as special interests in the media, they are a small slice of the total interest group community in Washington, DC. According to a team of political scientists, unions
constitute just 6 percent of that community. And even that figure over-
states it, as there are really just six unions that are active on the Potomac—
the most prominent of which are public employee unions (National
Education Association [NEA], American Federation of State, County and
Municipal Employees [AFSCME], and Service Employees International
Union [SEIU]—50 percent of whose membership are government workers). While these unions' political operations are well financed and professional—a glance at the headquarters of the NEA or the SEIU broadcasts
the power of these two unions—they are spread thin, as they are active on
many issues. Industry groups simply have more money and manpower to
devote to pressuring lawmakers about things that they care about.

Yet, they are rarely pitted against each other in head-to-head battles.
And while labor unions compose a smaller slice of the interest group community, they often act in a unified manner, which political scientist Robert

Dahl argued was the most important criterion of an interest's political effectiveness.[13] Business, on the other hand, is rarely unified. In addition, at the state and local level, public sector unions constitute a larger slice of the interest group universe than they do in the crowded corridors of Washington, DC. Indeed, they often outpace nearly every other interest on the scene. And it is at the state and local level where most policies with the most importance to public sector unions are decided.

Public employee unions can also punch above their weight by forming coalitions with citizen and business groups that find themselves on the same side of a given question. In the lobbying game, such behavior is common. Many interest groups make strange but content bedfellows. Yet, in contrast to private sector unions and other interest groups, public sector unions are particularly apt to build coalitions. In the private sector, the union strength required to win things for their members hinges on the solidarity of the workers to take economic action—strikes, job actions, and so on. In the public sector, a major source of power is the union's ability to build coalitions. This is because of their more fundamentally political nature. Sometimes they even fund other groups with which they then "partner."

For example, the California Correctional Peace Officers Association (CCPOA) has been very effective at creating a united lobbying front in the Golden State with groups representing crime victims—such as the Crime Victims Bureau, Crime Victims United of California, Parents of Murdered Children, and Citizens Against Homicide.[14] The emotional appeal of the victims offers political cover to the economic interests of the correction officers. Sometimes the CCPOA has even gone so far as to financially underwrite victims' advocacy groups. And many representatives of victims' groups have been appointed to state boards and commissions related to crime and punishment, which then provides another channel of influence for the CCPOA. To cap it off, the CCPOA spent $3.5 million to retain top lobbying talent in the first decade of the twenty-first century.[15]

Public sector unions liaise with other interest groups because political activity is a complement to collective bargaining.[16] To maximize their political power, public sector unions need allies, who require them to work for a broader agenda. Hence, unions have made themselves indispensable to the liberal coalition that supports the Democratic Party and issues having little to do with union members' job-related interests, such as gun control, abortion, gay marriage, and so on. By teaming up with the National Association for the Advancement of Colored People (NAACP), the American Civil Liberties Union (ACLU), trial lawyers, and other groups, government unions gain leverage and amass chits they can later call in. Given such power, one teachers' union representative noted that "the perception is that if we're not going to play, that it will affect the outcome. We are sought after to be on coalitions."[17]

Lobbyists' agenda and the public's agenda are usually quite different. When the issues are technical and receive little public scrutiny, lobbying looms larger. The public agenda, however, is focused on a few big pieces of legislation. When interest groups lobby on highly salient public agenda items, usually backed by a president or a governor, those battles are more likely to be decided by what legislators believe their constituents want, which they infer from election outcomes and polling results. Because these issues often turn on ideological questions about the size of government, the media covers them. Citizens can more easily form judgments and hold legislators accountable. Many groups mobilize on either side. Lobbying is likely to matter less, and voters' preferences, more in politicians' calculations.

When the lobbying agenda and the public agenda are one and the same, the battles are especially intense. Take the battle over Act 10 in Wisconsin, which sought to alter the rules of public sector collective bargaining. More than 80 groups registered with the state to lobby on the bill. Lobbyists and their organizations on both sides of the issue spent some 22,300 hours working on the measure, or 13 times more than what was spent on the next-most-lobbied measure in 2011. Unions reported spending more than any other group on lobbying that spring. The Wisconsin American Federation of Labor–Congress of Industrial Organizations (AFL-CIO), the teachers' unions, and the two state AFSCME affiliates spent a combined $6.3 million.[18] This is far from the norm.

The lobbying agenda tends to focus more on smaller issues and regulatory matters, many of which require a lot of technical knowledge. It is mostly concerned with intricate matters of concern to various professions, industries, and businesses. Most of the time, union lobbying occurs in back rooms on issues such as pension accounting, arbitration rules, collective bargaining procedures, and other minutiae. Average citizens would find it nearly impossible to participate in the technical details of these debates—if they were even aware that they were going on.

Public sector unions tend to concentrate their lobbying efforts on members of Congress, state legislators, and city council members from both parties (although mostly Democrats) who sit on committees dealing with budgets and rule-making agencies. For instance, the United Federation of Teachers has some 30 in-house lobbyists to stay on top of the New York City Council.[19] At the federal level, the Center for Responsive Politics lists over 100 registered lobbyists for public sector unions. About one-third of these lobbyists have worked on Capitol Hill, at federal agencies, or at other government-related jobs in the nation's capital. Such experience makes them savvy operators for their clients. While business retains many more registered lobbyists, it is not nearly as unified on as many issues as public employee unions are. For the unions, this means that fewer lobbyists can carry more weight.

THE GOALS OF PUBLIC SECTOR UNIONS

To understand public employee unions' lobbying agenda, it is helpful to think of a set of concentric circles. At the core are the bread-and-butter occupational interests of the union's membership. This includes the things that affect workers' lives on a day-to-day basis: salary, benefits, job protections, and working conditions. At the second level are broader issues affecting workers more generally, including issues such as labor law, healthcare policy, and the minimum wage. At the outer edge are broad liberal causes that unions support—sometimes half-heartedly—in order to forge alliances and good will with other progressive groups. These often include many social issues, such as civil rights, abortion, and prayer in schools.

Many business interest groups struggle to get legislators and their harried staffs to pay attention to their concerns—especially when those issues are small-bore and technical. Public union lobbyists are less likely to want for attention because the day-to-day execution of public services depends on them. They are effectively *government lobbying itself.* The importance of education, police and fire protection, transportation, and so forth to the political careers of elected officials, especially at the state and local level, are hard to overstate. Service delivery is what state and local government is all about and where citizens are more likely to engage their elected representatives. Therefore, public sector unions naturally have an easier time getting these issues on elected officials' radar screens.

Furthermore, any policy change offers a mix of tangible and symbolic benefits.[20] Public sector unions are especially well placed in this regard. They can secure material goods while still providing the public with assurances about how the schools, public safety, and other government services are improving. They can argue that they favor protecting and expanding public services that every citizen wants. Teachers' unions claim to promote better education, police unions endorse lower crime, corrections officers want to lock up criminals, and sanitation workers favor clean streets.[21] There is little societal disagreement that these goals are worthwhile. Yet, the debates over how best to achieve them—about cost, implementation, feasibility, and unintended consequences—are often too complicated and too technical for average citizens to participate in. That opaqueness allows them to work for details of a policy favoring them while assuring the broader public that they share commensurate goals. The unions can thus take credit for broadly approved actions of government while obscuring benefits that accrue to them.[22]

How much time and energy unions spend lobbying on issues often depends on the views held by their leadership. Union leaders tend to be more liberal than those of the rank and file. For example, more than a few school teachers are Republicans. While they strongly support their local union when it concentrates on bread-and-butter issues in collective bargaining, they dislike the national teachers' union with which their local union affiliates.[23]

Consider Jerry Wurf, the longtime leader of the AFSCME. Wurf became executive director of New York City's District Council 37 in 1959 and was then elected AFSCME International president in 1964. He served as the union's president for 17 years until his death in 1981. During his career, Wurf was deeply engaged in political issues that went far beyond the prosaic concerns of New York's municipal employees, including campaigns for civil liberties, women's rights, antinuclear and peace movements, and the Democratic Party.[24] He was in Memphis with Martin Luther King Jr. to support the striking sanitation workers of AFSCME Local 1733 in 1968, when King was killed.

Transfer Seeking

The larger cause of American liberalism aside, public sector unions are basically transfer-seeking groups. They are not part of the productive economy. Rather, they seek to capture a larger slice of society's existing wealth. In many people's minds, however, transfer-seeking interest groups and productive companies are doing the same thing: pursuing their own self-interest. And that's true in a narrow sense.

However, there is a big difference. Productive investment makes society wealthier by increasing the size of the economic pie. Transfer-seeking groups, on the other hand, simply move resources around. As Jonathan Rauch of the Brookings Institution has pointed out, transfer seeking creates a double drag on the economy. First, transferring resources is inefficient because some time, energy, and money are always sucked up in the process. Second, by forcing other groups to mobilize and invest in political action, for example, to block an unfavorable piece of legislation or regulatory rule, transfer-seeking groups reduce the amount of time, energy, and money that could be invested in the private economy.[25]

The transfers of wealth that public sector unions seek include pension and health benefit increases, changes to collective bargaining procedures that favor them, and the exclusion of their potential competitors. These things cost society money. For example, a pension sweetener lowering the retirement age for a certain category of workers while expanding their benefits will have to be paid by taxpayers in the future. Increasing coverage of public employees' health plans or reducing the amount they must pay for them are also means of transferring monies in the budget to public employees at the expense of others. A change in collective bargaining or arbitration procedures may give unions an advantage in securing higher salaries for their members, which is covered by other citizens' tax dollars or higher interest rates. Excluding competitors means blocking privatized services (think sanitation, prisons, etc.), limiting the number of charter schools allowed in a state, and so on.

As in physics, in politics, any action creates a reaction. So when public sector unions seek transfers, other groups mobilize to stop them. However, this action–reaction cycle saps resources from society, since those other groups and the people who fund them could be spending their money elsewhere. For instance, rather than fight the teachers' unions over the charter schools allowed in New York State (currently 460 under state law), education reformers could dedicate hundreds of thousands of dollars they receive in donations from wealthy individuals to resources for students.[26] Instead, they must try to counteract the nearly $4 to $6 million a year that New York's teacher unions spend on lobbying in Albany.[27]

Of course, public sector unions also mobilize to block change that they believe would harm their members' interests. By defending the status quo, they significantly raise the political and monetary costs of legislating in many policy areas. For instance, public pension reform, privatization or contracting out of services, and education reform are all areas where unions force their opponents to mobilize huge resources—resources that could go to other things. If the unions had fewer resources at their disposal, countermobilization efforts would not need to be nearly as large. Such countermobilization efforts reduce the amount of money and manpower available for programs that benefit people who are far less well off than public sector union members—especially today, when inequality is rising.

Whether the objective is winning new benefits or fighting off unwanted change, the problem is that the system of transfer seeking imposes many costs. Some are visible to voters, others less so. As Rauch puts it, the "benefits from lobbying—subsidy checks, tax breaks, favorable regulations, court awards, and so on—are highly visible; but the costs—the waste, the inefficiency, the rigidities, the complexities, the policy incoherence as subsidies and deals redistribute money in every direction at once—are diffuse and often invisible."[28] These are the hard-to-detect and hard-to-measure costs of what political scientist Paul C. Light has called "government thickening"—a process as readily apparent at the state as at the federal level that Light studied.[29] Thickening refers, in part, to the growing number of procedural rules and bureaucratic steps required before government can act. The consequence is another cost: government's inability to adapt and innovate. Instead, it calcifies.

This is not to malign the motives of public sector unions or their leaders. The union leadership is charged with advancing their members' interests by all legal means. Indeed, they are legally bound to equally represent all workers in a bargaining unit. Most union leaders consider what they are doing noble and believe they are serving the larger cause of social justice; otherwise, they would probably look for other employment. Their critics see them as self-interested and self-serving. However, motives don't really matter. What matters are the negative effects of transfer-seeking. Watching a transfer-seeking duel, the average citizen could get the impression that government is an employment program for lawyers and lobbyists.

Lobbying and Public Policy

What do interest groups in general—and public sector unions in particular—get from lobbying? If the news media are to be believed, the answer is a lot. And there are many powerful cases of unions exercising influence. For instance, the NEA helped get President Jimmy Carter to support the creation of a cabinet-level Department of Education in 1979. Congress was unenthusiastic about the idea, and many Democrats opposed it. Yet, historian Gareth Davies argues that "Carter would not have fought for the bill, and most likely would not even have endorsed it, had it not been for the unprecedented influence that the NEA enjoyed within his White House."[30] The NEA had toiled on Carter's behalf during the battle for the Democratic Party's presidential nomination in 1976. It also donated $400,000 to his general election campaign and mobilized teachers to vote in key states, such as Ohio, Pennsylvania, and Florida, when Carter's 30-point lead in the polls over Gerald Ford disappeared. The NEA's political action committee also contributed to the campaigns of 300 congressional candidates in 1976 and 350 in 1978, effectively endorsing a majority of the 96th Congress. After Carter's election, between three and six full-time NEA lobbyists worked with Connecticut Senator Abraham Ribicoff's staff to craft a bill creating a Department of Education. The NEA team determined the timing of the committee hearings, indicated who should be called as witnesses, rounded up bill cosponsors, funded ads, organized grassroots pressure, and told the White House which members needed pressuring by the president and vice president.[31] The NEA wanted a federal Department of Education, and with Carter's leadership, the union got its wish. The NEA then promptly endorsed Carter's renomination to head off Massachusetts Senator Edward Kennedy's potential primary competition. The 311 NEA delegates at the Democratic National Convention constituted the largest bloc in support of Carter. Political scientist Byron Shafer has pointed out that in the 1980 presidential contest, the NEA became the Carter campaign in many parts of the country.[32]

For an example at the state level, consider the lobbying resources of the New Jersey Education Association (NJEA). It collects about $100 million in dues each year. This pays for a substantial lobbying and research staff with offices in a big building next to the state capitol on State Street in Trenton. Consequently, stories like the following are not uncommon: In the early 1990s, state Education Commissioner Saul Cooperman was discussing an education bill with then-Senate president Carmen A. Orechio. Orechio agreed that the measure had significant merits. Yet, she said she couldn't vote for it. When asked why, according to Cooperman, Orechio posed this rhetorical question: "Look, I'm in a swing district. Can you give $10,000 to my campaign and give me five knowledgeable people to help with my campaign?" When Cooperman said he couldn't, Orechio responded: "The NJEA can."[33]

However, according to many political scientists, most interest groups don't get much for their efforts most of the time. But this is because "lobbying" is an umbrella term that covers myriad activities. Some groups are actively trying to change policy in their favor, which is what the general public thinks of as lobbying. Others, however, are actively trying to prevent change to existing policy. And still others are just trying to figure out what is likely to happen next and how it could affect them.[34] One must also bear in mind the conceptual distinction between lobbying and electioneering, even if in practice the two resemble each other. At any given time, what public sector unions "get" from policymakers may be due more to their electoral pressures than the lobbying efforts—and vice versa. Sometimes what is called "lobbying" by the media is really electioneering, and vice-versa. Separating the independent influence of these two closely linked activities is difficult.

The American political system is famous for its status quo bias. The design of the nation's government institutions—separation of powers and federalism with multiple veto points—makes enacting change hard and blocking it easier. Therefore, entrenched constituencies can often prevent big shifts in existing public policy. This is especially likely when the policy in question benefits a narrow slice of the population that is mobilized to defend its privileges and the costs of the policy are broadly diffused.[35] One team of political scientists argues that the single best predictor of lobbying success is not how much money and resources a group has but whether or not it is trying to protect the status quo. If it is, the group is likely to be quite successful.[36] Consequently, many policy areas are characterized by slow, incremental change, which consumes the attention of stakeholders and insiders but remains largely out of the public eye.[37]

That most run-of-the-mill lobbying gains are relatively modest is an enormously important and often underappreciated point. It is why policy change tends to be incremental. There is generally a balance of forces that have produced particular outcomes in a given policy area. Once policy is more or less settled, groups aren't likely to lose all that much, nor are they likely to make sweeping gains. The power of business, the professions, or public sector unions is already baked into the status quo—which, given American institutions, is hard to change.

Therefore, interest groups are usually only able to make big policy changes during specific windows of time.[38] These usually coincide with the mobilization of new groups. For instance, some of the biggest salary and benefits gains for public employees occurred shortly after collective bargaining statutes and ordinances were passed in the states and cities (see chapter 7). Unions of public workers mobilized, bringing new actors and organizations into the political system. They used their newfound political power to extract benefits from government, namely, more jobs and more money. After a certain point, however, a new status quo emerged and the gains the unions could make became smaller. New professional communities of policymakers, bureaucrats, lawyers, and lobbyists emerged. Therefore, public sector unions' power in the lobbying arena probably peaked in many places in the 1970s and 1980s, with a few latecomers in the 1990s. After their initial burst onto the scene, the unions settled into a pattern of slowly ratcheting up existing gains and preventing the roll-back of attained benefits.

Public Sector Unions versus Business

Despite occasional stories of government union influence, many citizens and scholars believe interest group activity reflects an upper-class bias.[39] As a consequence, some also believe that public sector unions can act as a counterweight to business interests. It is true, and altogether unsurprising, that materially well-off people are more likely to join interest groups and donate money. Wealthy individuals have more flexible work schedules and more disposable income. Therefore, groups representing business and the professions are much more numerous and better financed than organizations representing minorities, consumers, or the disadvantaged.[40] However, these facts alone can't predict the lobbying efficacy of business, the professions, or other upper-class interest groups. They are only inputs into the system, not output.

Many people fear that if business groups deployed their massive resources in unison, they would run roughshod over citizen preferences and make government subservient to them. We would live in an oligarchy with a democratic veneer. However, such a fear is probably overblown— at least there is little conclusive evidence to support it. The relationships between economic inequality, interest group activity, and policy outcomes are not well understood. A 2004 American Political Science Association Task Force on Inequality and American Democracy concluded, "We know little about the connections between changing economic inequality and changes in political behavior, governing institutions, and public policy."[41] More recent scholarship has spawned serious debate but little consensus about these connections.[42]

In addition, there are reasons to think that some observers overestimate the power of business and the wealthy in American politics. The policy preferences of wealthy Americans aren't that different from Americans in general, and those preferences have been remarkably stable over time.[43] Compared to other industrialized nations' business communities, the US one is known for its fragmentation. Indeed, much lobbying in cities, state capitols, and Washington, DC pits different elements of the business community and the professions against each other.[44] As one scholar has remarked, when companies "are feuding and atomized, their political impact tends to be inconsistent, at times contradictory, and thus neutralized."[45] In short, business has trouble acting as a unified front. Whether it does so, how often, and to what effect are the subjects of ongoing debate.[46] Businesses are often focused on limited objectives standing to benefit a single industry. The construction industry focuses on housing policy. Airlines concentrate on matters affecting landing rights at airports. Most business lobbyists spend far less time on the big headline-grabbing issues of tax or trade policy than on "private goods" important to them exclusively.[47]

Nor is it clear that when business unites its forces, it becomes an unstoppable juggernaut. Political scientist Mark A. Smith argues that even when business is unified on an issue, that unity does not increase the direct political influence of business.[48] This is because business is only likely to be unified on issues on which the public supports (or opposes) and expresses its preferences through elections. Public agenda items—especially ideological ones about the size of government, taxing and spending, and budgetary decisions—tend to unite business, but their high saliency forces legislators to pay more attention to public opinion than to the business community. In other words, business unity often follows rather than leads the political conversation. It is likely, then, to be least influential when it is unified. On big, divisive agenda items, public opinion and election outcomes are what drive policy.

Business political activity is also likely to face a great deal of public skepticism and even outright criticism, which may lead business groups to try to conduct their affairs as far from the prying eyes of the press as possible. Political scientist Jeffrey Berry points out that most of the time business finds itself in the position of reacting to critical press coverage driven by citizen groups concerned with consumer or environmental issues. Berry found that in a single year, two-thirds of network news stories involving corporations were about how corporations responded to accusations of bad behavior.[49] Such coverage helps explain why when business is unified on highly public, salient, and ideological issues, its influence declines. The coverage is often adversarial, which turns off many citizens. Business's preference for an under-the-radar approach is a far different strategy than that used by unions who frequently seek press attention.[50]

Then there is the information problem: in order to invest sensibly in political action, a business firm needs to know the kinds of returns it can expect on that investment. This sounds easy enough. Yet in reality, it is enormously complicated, especially the further the firm tries to see into the future. Bigger firms must also spread their political resources across the many issues affecting them. And for larger firms, changes improving matters for one product may hurt another. Furthermore, business is less likely to take the initiative to promote policies and more likely to react to threats from competitors in the political system.[51]

Business is attentive only sporadically to public sector labor relations— and it is easily outspent in campaigns by unions. Conversely, unions pay little attention to many of the microconcerns of businesses. Such informational asymmetries give the unions a big advantage in their policy domains. For instance, big business has little immediate stake in the management of police and fire departments. To the extent that businesses care about such things, they feel the same as almost every citizen save criminals and arsonists: they want to catch crooks and prevent fires. They want crime rates to stay low and fires to not damage much property. And they don't want those services to overextend the cities' financial resources. Yet, like average citizens, business leaders have a hard time detecting when the protective services have become too expensive. That gives the unions representing them a large margin for maneuvering before drawing the attention of local business elites.

Take prison system lobbying. In states like California and New York, correction officers' unions are powerful forces. They push for greater prison construction and against the closing or consolidation of prisons, since either option would reduce employment for guards. More controversially, they have lobbied for longer sentences for criminals (which increases the number of inmates and in turn the number of prison guards needed). In the first decade of the twenty-first century, the CCPOA—with 30,000 dues-paying members—spent $10 million on state politics, either in direct contributions to politicians or in spending on ballot initiatives. They pushed hard for the enactment of a controversial "three strikes" sentencing law, which took the power away from judges to determine sentences for convicts and prescribed mandatory minimum sentences. Their hope was that it would increase the prison population and the need for more corrections officers. In a 2010 speech, Supreme Court Justice Anthony Kennedy called the correctional officers' union sponsorship of the three-strikes law "sick!"[52] By 2009, the Golden State's prison system was so overcrowded that it was forced to release 40,000 inmates.

Sociologist Joshua Page studied the union and found that it was the dominant interest group in California's penal policy conversation.[53] It achieved this success in large measure by partnering with groups representing the victims of crimes. The CCPOA also found allies among construction firms that built the new prisons. It completely stymied the one business group trying to break into the corrections business: private prison companies. Other than the private prison operators, business has invested few resources in the policy battles over California's penal system. The CCPOA has staked out its own policy fiefdom to the detriment of taxpayers, criminals, and government managers.

Or consider education policy. Occasionally business groups get involved in school board elections, especially in big cities where they worry about the human capital of future employees. Yet, their engagement is episodic. The teachers' unions, on the other hand, care almost exclusively about education policy. In some cases they are the only influencers in school board elections, where turnout can be as low as 10 percent of the electorate. And even when parental, community, and other groups get involved, they are usually easily outgunned by the teachers.[54]

Furthermore, business and public sector unions generally have different interests when it comes to issues like tax rates—with unions favoring higher rates and business favoring lower ones. But on particulars, businesses can often be found on either side of the tax issue. (Public sector unions, however, are almost never on the side of lower rates.) As with most complex policy matters, few have just two sides. Most issues are like a game of three-dimensional chess. Therefore, while public sector unions tend to be unified, they can still be divided and prioritize different aspects of different pieces of legislation. And this is doubly true for business.

Cities are where public sector unions are most politically active. This is important because the unions' ability to mobilize their members for electoral participation gives them an outsized influence. They are helped by voter turnout rates in cities, which are often dismal. For instance, observers have remarked that Maria Elena Durazo, the head of the Los Angeles County Federation of Labor, which coordinates 300 locals, is the "single most influential individual" in L.A. politics.[55] In the ecosystem of urban politics, business—especially real estate—is active. Yet business is only sporadically attentive, and they don't spend a lot of time and money on many issues of concern to unions. On many issues, such as pensions, the unions have little organized opposition. All of the pressure on state legislators—at least until the Great Recession of 2008–11—came from the side promoting the expansion of benefits.[56]

The most vocal groups in urban politics are the unions' allies—not their adversaries. Think of civil rights groups and minority interest groups. Their interests often converge, not only because the unions often donate substantial sums to groups such as the NAACP and because members of their leadership serve on their boards, but also because in big cities minorities form a large slice of the public employee base. For instance, in New York City, roughly a third of blacks belong to unions (public and private), while only about a quarter of whites do.[57] And in 2013, blacks (28 percent) and Hispanics (19 percent) constituted 47 percent of the mayoral electorate. All told, 42 percent of the 1,027,000 New York City voters in the 2013 mayoral election reported that they belonged to a union household.[58] That is nearly half of the electorate, which was only 25 percent of registered voters and 18 percent of eligible voters.

Finally, public sector unions are often allies with big-business interests. For instance, the CCPOA was able to enlist big construction firms as allies in its quest for tough law-and-order policies because the firms would win the business of building the new prisons. Then there are the billions of dollars in pension funds that financial firms want to manage in exchange for millions in fees and commissions every year.[59] State and municipal bond issues provide another entry point for alliances between money managers and unions. The money managers earn fees and commissions from the sale of bonds on the market. The unions support bonding practices because they help pay for government services in the here and now. Government employee unions have also forged alliances with "affordable housing" advocates and real estate developers. By supporting construction and zoning changes, the unions can get real estate interests to cooperate on policy areas of importance to them. All told, the argument that public sector unions will act as a counterweight to "big business" in some generalized sense does not withstand scrutiny.

1199 SEIU AND NEW YORK'S HEALTHCARE POLITICS

To test the logic of some of the aforementioned points, it is helpful to look at a case study of a single union that straddles the public/private sector divide. 1199SEIU Health and Hospital Workers East is one of the most powerful players in New York State politics today, especially in the healthcare sector. Tracing its trajectory shows the benefits and the limits of a powerful union-lobbying operation. While most of its members are nominally private sector workers—employed by nonprofit hospitals—they are largely dependent on government, in particular Medicare and especially Medicaid. Therefore, much of the health policy in New York State is a three-way struggle involving workers (represented by 1199), employers (nonprofit and teaching hospitals), and the state government. Given the size of New York State's Medicaid program—the largest in the country—and its weight in the state budget, in times of fiscal stress it sets up conflict between the government on one side and the union and the hospitals on the other.

In the 1990s, 1199SEIU made a watershed decision. Rather than continue to fight hospitals for better pay and benefits, the union, under the highly effective leadership of Dennis Rivera, created an alliance with the Greater New York Hospital Association (GNYHA) and its powerful collective bargaining operation, the League of Voluntary Hospitals and Homes. The essence of the deal was that while state law prevented New York's nonprofit hospitals from lobbying in Albany, the union was free to do so. Therefore, 1199 offered to lobby on its own behalf, as well as on behalf of the hospitals. Both sides decided that they had, as Kenneth Raske, the head of GNYHA, put it, "a common enemy," and that "government [held] the key to all our problems."

Both sides' bottom line was that the hospitals needed more revenue if they were to offer the workers a better deal.[60] At the beginning of the twenty-first century, some 60 percent of revenues in the hospitals and 85 percent in the nursing homes came from Medicare and Medicaid funds. Medicaid in particular has grown incredibly fast in New York, doubling in size in the 1980s and then again in the 1990s. New York today spends more on Medicaid than Texas and Florida combined—partly a consequence of the political effectiveness of the SEIU–GNYHA alliance. As historians Leon Fink and Brian Greenberg put it, "The solution, both sides concluded, required a *political* strategy more than a *collective-bargaining* strategy."[61] That political strategy was to expand the eligibility rules and increase money spent on Medicaid.

To realize that strategy, the union built the most extensive and sophisticated political operation of any interest group in Albany. By 2007, it had a staff of more than 50 professionals and a member-driven political action fund with annual revenues of more than $5 million. It was led by Jennifer Cunningham, who joined SEIU 1199 in 1999 after cutting her teeth in the political affairs office of Victor Gotbaum's AFSCME District Council 37 in New York City, which is the largest union of municipal workers in Gotham. Cunningham had also been a staffer for Sheldon Silver, the powerful Democratic speaker of the New York State Assembly. Of the change in 1199SEIU's political tactics, she said, "[We took] the existing [union] culture of giving to political candidates and ramp[ed] it up to a whole new level."[62] She combined fundraising and political advertising with a sophisticated voter and legislator lobbying operation. She created a political powerhouse on the basis of the 125,000 members who voluntarily contributed $5.5 million in special assessments of $5 to $10 on top of their union dues. Cunningham attributed the union's political success to "the ability to mobilize voters around a public policy issue, sophistication of materials, and frankly, a boatload of cash." It became one of the premier get-out-the-vote operations in the state.[63] It spent a striking $7 million to influence the state legislature in 2012.[64]

There had been occasional conflict between 1199 and Democratic Governor Mario Cuomo over Medicaid spending in the 1980s. Matters came to a head after the election of Republican George Pataki in 1994. Pataki's efforts to cut Medicaid to eliminate yawning budget deficits provoked a major response from the union. 1199 President Rivera bused demonstrators from New York City to Albany and unleashed a $1 million advertising blitz that significantly hurt Pataki's approval rating in the polls.[65] Pataki backed off and withdrew his proposal.

To help alleviate pressure on New York's massive Medicaid program, Rivera also lobbied then-vice president Al Gore to redirect an additional $1.25 billion in Medicaid monies to the Empire State in 1997.[66] And Cunningham kept up the pressure on the governor, becoming famous for giving Pataki administration officials previews of the ads SEIU planned to air against them in an effort to unnerve them. The New York Post dubbed her "the most powerful woman in Albany."[67]

Eventually, both Pataki and Republican Senate Majority Leader Joseph Bruno would become allies of 1199SEIU—thanks in part to extensive contributions from the biggest political action committee in the state. Pataki's re-election campaign in 2002 was even endorsed by the traditionally left-wing union.[68] To explain this apparent change of allegiances, then secretary-treasurer and now president of the union George Gresham has said, "One motto in this union is, 'We have no permanent friends; we have permanent interests.'"[69]

In 2007, when Governor Elliot Spitzer announced plans to cut Medicaid spending by $1.3 billion, Cunningham launched a $12 million ad campaign to beat back the plan. She was also an informal campaign adviser to future governor Andrew Cuomo in the run-up to his 2010 election. She advised Cuomo on major decisions, such as the timing of his entrance into the race and whom he should hire as campaign staff.[70] Perhaps not surprisingly, the Cuomo administration spared Medicaid, and by extension 1199SEIU, from budget cuts during the Great Recession and reshaped the program in ways that some observers believed benefited the union.[71] Instead, Cuomo filled the budget gap by reneging on a campaign promise and raising income taxes on high earners.

The story of 1199 shows how cozy the relations between union lobbyists, governors, and state legislators can become. Yet, the union and its defenders argue that the expansion of Medicaid in New York State has provided health insurance to far more people than would have otherwise been covered and improved the salaries and working conditions of nonprofit hospital workers. Critics, on the other hand, argue that the expansion has come at the expense of other programs and priorities. Furthermore, while it benefits a small number of new Medicaid recipients and 1199 members, it does little for the middle class and is financed by some of the highest income taxes in the nation.

Lobbying on Pensions

In most places in America, pensions are not subjects of collective bargaining. Therefore, the only way for government worker unions to increase this type of compensation for their members is through political activity. This is especially important because so much of public employee compensation in state and local government is back-loaded into retirement. And the sums of money in public pension funds are huge. For example, California has two giant funds: CalPERS, the sixth-largest pension fund in the world, which administers a $260 billion investment portfolio for 1.7 million workers (past and present), and CalSTRS, which handles $166 billion for teachers. It is in this area that one finds the closest links between public sector unions and business interests. Indeed, the financial services industry is incentivized to back union benefit expansion, insofar as it would increase the chances of getting a cut of the investment action and collecting fees from the government.

From the 1980s until the Great Recession, the politics of public sector pensions in most states and cities were relatively stable—and conducive to increasingly generous benefit schemes. The old politics of pensions could be described as follows: In order to maintain political alliances with public employee unions, Democrats favored more generous benefits. Republicans tended to go along with legislative changes—in some cases they also had ties to unions, but mostly because there was little pressure to oppose expansion. The issues were technical; the public was uninformed and uninterested. Problems seemed far off in the future. The unions had the political playing field to themselves—as there were no groups actively seeking to counter them. Raising red flags about pension costs paid few political dividends for the GOP. Using a dataset of state legislators' votes on hundreds of pension bills passed between 1999 and 2011, political scientists Sarah Anzia and Terry Moe found that until 2008, Democrats and Republicans consistently voted in favor of benefit expansion.[72]

All that changed in 2008. The recession revealed both the lavishness of many pension plans and the extent to which they were underfunded. In the new politics of pensions, the Democrats are divided. Many of those holding office, especially mayors and governors, are concerned about how pensions are squeezing everything else in their budgets. They are open to reform, and sometimes they are leading it. Other Democrats—especially those who serve in city councils and state legislatures and retain close ties to public sector unions—remain opposed to reducing the generosity of pensions. Republicans are facing pressure to behave more like conservatives on this issue. Think tanks, business leaders, and Tea Party groups are calling on them to restrain the growth of government spending. Republicans have switched from quietly going along with expansion to calling for retrenchment. In short, this is a classic area where an interest group-dominated policy subsystem is broken up and the alignment of forces changed by a crisis—in this case the Great Recession.

Before the recession, however, public employee unions were the most powerful lobbying presence on the field. Take the extraordinary example of California's major expansion of public employee benefits in 1999 and 2001. The SEIU, CCPOA, and the California Teachers Association all strongly backed the election of Democrat Gray Davis for governor in 1998. Davis came into office with solid Democratic majorities in both the state senate and assembly. Davis then signed Senate Bill (SB) 400, which increased state workers' retirement benefits by lowering the retirement age, rejiggering the benefit formula, and in some cases, both. The bill also granted a 6 percent boost in benefits to those who had already retired and increased survivor benefits.

According to Steve Malanga of the Manhattan Institute, the executive board of CalPERS, unlike most pension funds, became "an outright lobbyist for higher member benefits" in its efforts to pass SB 400.[73] Government workers choose six of the board's 13 members and high-ranking labor officials have occupied those seats in recent years. Two more members are statewide elected officials (California's treasurer and controller), and the governor appoints another two. After Gray Davis had been elected governor and Phil Angelides state treasurer in 1999, both with strong support from public sector unions, the New York Times noted that the CalPERS board was wearing the "union label."[74]

In fact, it was the CalPERS board that developed and lobbied for SB 400. It argued that the state should retroactively place all post-1991 state employees in the older and more expensive plan than the one created in a 1991 reform. They also sought to lower the retirement age for all state workers and offer additional sweeteners for police and firefighters. Those in the protective services would, under the proposal, be able to retire at age 50 with 90 percent of their final salaries. Other government workers could retire at age 55 with 50 to 60 percent of their final salaries. To pay for these lavish promises, CalPERS would later have to make more risky investments in equities.

The CalPERS board went on to essentially write the legislation and lobbied hard for its passage. It downplayed the fiscal dangers such a generous proposal for public workers could entail for taxpayers. In fact, the board claimed that the state could offer such great benefit plans at no cost. The state's retirement fund, CalPERS, where the unions exercise considerable influence, claimed that "no increase over current employer contributions is needed for these benefit improvements."[75] The Golden State's annual required contribution would remain constant, despite a massive benefit increase. Concerns about the possibility of stock market declines were waved away. The California state legislature quickly passed the legislation and Governor Davis signed it.

In years to come, the result would be nearly disastrous. First, recessions in 2002 and 2008 forced the state government to massively increase taxpayer contributions, taking away funds from other priorities. When the pension fund earned far lower returns than were projected, the state (i.e., taxpayers) was forced to contribute some $27 billion to make up the difference. Second, it encouraged local governments to match the state's offer to public workers, all the while believing that CalPERS would cover the cost, which meant that they sweetened the deal without a sure means of paying for it. Finally, the pension increase has been one of the biggest drivers of California's recent budget crunch, which only a large tax increase has helped alleviate. Current Governor Jerry Brown sought to reform the pension system to little avail. Even his modest proposals have been rejected by the union-friendly state legislators in Sacramento, and his proposal to add two new members with financial bona fides to the CalPERS board was rejected.

Similar lobbying efforts that downplay the costs of changes to pension schemes came to light in New York. For nearly a decade, the state legislature in Albany relied on an actuary, Jonathan Schwartz, to determine the costs of changes to its pension systems. All the while Schwartz was on the payroll of a host of public sector unions—most notably AFSCME District Council 37—but also unions representing teachers, firefighters, detectives, corrections officers, and bridge and tunnel officers. When asked how many unions he worked for, Schwartz replied, "How many are there?" Over nearly 10 years he provided actuarial estimates on hundreds of bills affecting New York City's pension system for public employees. In nearly every case, he said the proposed changes would have no cost, or limited cost, to the city.[76] His underestimates cost the city some $500 million.

When queried about his accounting methods, he described them as "a step above voodoo."[77] Asked to elaborate, he explained that "back in my days as a city actuary, I would go to that part of the range that would make things look as expensive as possible. As consultant for the unions, I go to the part of the range that makes things as cheap as possible, but I never knowingly go out of the range." Schwartz also quipped that "the Legislature knows full well I'm being paid by the unions. If they choose not to disclose that, that's on them, not me." This sort of inside job, over nearly a decade, is a striking example of the coziness of many state lawmakers and public sector unions.

The results have been good for New York's public employees, who saw the size of their pensions increase. It has not been so good for the health of the state or New York City's public finances. The Empire State contributed $368 million to its pension system in 2001 and $6.6 billion in 2011.[78] State workers only contribute 3 percent of their incomes to the funds, which is one of the smallest employee contribution rates in the country. The Big Apple now has a $69 billion pension liability. And those costs have become a larger and larger share of the city's budget, crowding out other services. In 2002, the city spent $2 billion on pension contributions. In 2014, it will spend $8.2 billion.

Sometimes things in the Empire State spilled over into outright corruption, as financial interests sought to access pension fund managers. For instance, Alan Hevesi—who served as state comptroller of New York State from 2003 to 2006—admitted that he accepted nearly $1 million in gifts from California businessman Elliott Broidy, a founder of Markstone Capital Partners. Hevesi violated his fiduciary duty to act solely in the interests of pensioners by endorsing $250 million in fund investments in Broidy's outfit.[79] While public pension plans are much better managed today than they were 20 years ago, the opportunities for corruption are rife.

COUNTERWEIGHTS

Public sector unions are important lobbying presences at city hall, at state capitols, and in Washington, DC. They are active on a wide array of issues and often form coalitions with other groups—most often liberal groups but sometimes business and financial interests as well. They provide lawmakers with information relevant to the state of public employment, compensation, and pension and health benefits.

Contrary to liberal polemics, or perhaps hopes, public employee unions—unlike their private sector cousins—rarely directly confront business or act as counterweights to it. It is only on highly ideologically charged issues related to the size and scope of government activity— where lobbying is likely to count for less and public opinion and election results for more—that the two square off. More often, the two cooperate. In fact, there may be more cooperation than conflict between the two.

Furthermore, many argue that because businesses, nonprofits, and others in American society lobby government in hopes of improving their lot, why shouldn't public employee unions? In fact, groups representing public employee unions can, should, and will continue to be involved in the political process. They are too essential to it not to. However, whether they need the sort of assistance from government in the form of dues check-off, forced membership, and access to policymakers through collective bargaining is another question.

THE PRICE OF GOVERNMENT
WORK

Pam and Maria are administrative assistants. Both are pretty good at their jobs and have roughly the same levels of education and years of experience. But Pam earns about $4,000 more a year than Maria—and also has greater job security, more paid vacation days, a pension plan, and health insurance. Maria's hold on her job is more tenuous and she lacks a pension plan and health coverage. What explains the difference? Pam works in a government agency and Maria for a small business. Government work appears the better deal. However, junior associates at big law firms pull in $200,000 a year, while senior government lawyers toil for $100,000. And while managers of large government agencies can sometimes make a quarter million dollars, corporate CEOs receive eight-figure pay packages. In that light, the private sector is clearly better.

It is these sorts of comparisons that make comparing compensation (wages and benefits) in the public and private sectors so fraught. Often missed in these discussions is the difficulty of making such comparisons. Police officers in Chicago cannot be compared to shopping mall security guards around suburban Winnetka. Some jobs in government have no counterpart in the private sector—and vice versa. One needs to make apples-to-apples comparisons. Yet even with all the sophisticated tools in the labor economist's kit, this exercise can be challenging.

There are two contentious debates over compensation for public servants. One is over what economists call "comparative pay": whether public employees earn more or less than private sector workers who do similar jobs with similar levels of education, experience, and other characteristics. In the language of economists, the question is whether one sector provides a compensation "premium" and the other a "penalty." The other issue is whether public sector unions' collective bargaining and political activities cause unionized workers to receive greater compensation relative to nonunionized government workers and thereby increase the costs of government beyond what is actually needed to produce the same quality of public services. These are complex issues and involve many variables. The data have their shortcomings and the statistical methods their limits. It's often a war of studies using different data, methodological assumptions, and mathematical models—enough to make many people's eyes glaze over.

However, these issues are very important. Compensation levels are now hotly debated among policymakers coping with fiscal distress and tight budgets.[1] If public sector workers are overpaid, then government belt tightening—such as reducing pensions for new workers, slowing salary increases, and so on—will have little impact on the attractiveness of public employment. Government will not have difficulty recruiting and retaining quality workers. And taxpayers will stop overpaying for the services they receive. On the other hand, if government employees are underpaid, the public workforce is likely not attracting the best workers already.[2] Further cuts to compensation would only make matters worse. Taxpayers will receive fewer and lower-quality services. These competing scenarios illustrate why the comparative pay of public and private sector workers has become a major issue, especially in the wake of the Great Recession.

The public compensation debate has also become entangled with partisan politics.[3] Some conservatives have taken to criticizing government workers as overpaid loafers. During his first campaign for a US Senate seat in Massachusetts in 2010, Republican Scott Brown made an issue of federal pay. And Representative Eric Cantor (R-VA), the former majority leader in the House of Representatives, has said that "Americans are fed up with public employee pay scales far exceeding that in the private sector."[4] Liberals have responded that conservatives are making "scapegoats" out of hard-working public servants. Jonathan Cohn of the *New Republic* has argued that government workers are "the new welfare queens"—referring to the Reagan-era critique used by Republicans to rally antigovernment conservatives.[5]

In addition, if public sector unions drive up wages and benefits for workers and thereby increase the costs of government for taxpayers, politicians may be tempted, especially in the current age of austerity, to try to rein them in.[6] And if public sector unions help compress wages in the public sector—that is, by limiting differences in pay between better or worse employees, or those at the top and bottom of the pay scale—then they may be discouraging highly skilled workers from government employment. Without top talent in its ranks, the public service would be less effective.

Finally, wrapped inside these technical debates among labor economists are issues of equity and efficiency. Fairness demands some workers not be paid more for the same job just because they are in the public or private sectors. And efficacy means that government pay should be no more than is necessary to attract competent workers. Any violation of these principles is unjust to both workers and taxpayers.

BACKGROUND

It's helpful to start with some basic facts about government workers. The federal government employs about 3 percent of all workers (excluding the military)—about 3 million people. State and local governments employ roughly 14 percent of American workers (17 million full-time workers). Roughly three-quarters of them work for local governments and one-quarter for state governments. More than half of local government workers are in education, either as teachers or as support staff. Public sector workers also tend to have more schooling and experience than those in the private sector. Some 52 percent of workers in the public sector have at least a college degree, while only 35 percent of private sector workers do. Fifty-one percent of workers in the public sector are over the age of 45, while only 44 percent in the private sector are. There are also more women in the public sector (57 percent) than in the private sector (42 percent). Public sector workers also tend to stay on the job longer than private sector workers. The former have a median tenure of eight years, compared to five for the latter. Teachers are the source of many of these demographic characteristics because they constitute the lion's share of the public workforce. Finally, some 37 percent of public sector workers are unionized, compared to just 7 percent of private sector workers—and in some states, such as New York, the percentage of government workers belonging to unions reaches nearly 70 percent.[7]

Wages for many jobs in the public sector are lower than wages in the private sector. However, pensions and health benefits are far more generous in the public sector. Some 76 percent of public sector works have an employer-sponsored pension plan, compared to only 43 percent of private sector workers.[8] And the types of pension plans offered in each sector are dramatically different. Some 80 percent of public sector workers have a defined benefit plan, compared to just about 20 percent of private sector employees. A defined benefit plan pays a fixed amount in retirement regardless of the market performance of the pension plan. Therefore, all the risk is borne by government and taxpayers and none by the pensioner. On the other hand, private sector workers with defined contribution plans shoulder almost all of the risk associated with the performance of their retirement plan. Finally, retiree healthcare plans are much more common and more generous in the public than in the private sector.

COMPARABLE PAY

If these facts are broadly agreed upon, there remains much dispute over whether similarly situated workers make more in the public than in the private sector or vice versa. One does not have to be a public choice economist to appreciate that there are good theoretical reasons to expect government to be a more generous employer than business. As Harvard public policy scholar John Donahue explains, the public sector labor market lacks attributes such as a profit-motivated hostility to excess costs and full managerial discretion to hire, fire, and discipline, which would generate optimal compensation levels.[9] Yet, demonstrating these theoretical claims empirically is hard to do.

Raw Bureau of Labor Statistics numbers show that for many jobs, government pay is higher, on average, than private sector pay. While polemical editorialists may cite such figures, they don't tell us very much. As noted earlier, government workers tend to have more education and experience and jobs in government tend to be more white collar and technical. Only once all those differences are factored into the analysis in a statistically rigorous way can we know with even a limited degree of confidence if there is a public sector compensation premium or a penalty. And for nearly a third of government jobs, by one estimate, there aren't private sector equivalents.[10]

However, even if a premium or a penalty can be established, most of the analyses will not tell us many things that we'd like to know. This is because there are many things that are hard to capture in the empirical studies due to the limits of the data and the statistical techniques. It's hard for labor economists to account for differences between workers' levels of motivation, intelligence, and other things relevant to compensation levels. For example, the resumes of workers in each sector may be quite similar but other less tangible attributes quite different. Both workers may have gone to good four-year colleges and spent a decade working similar jobs. But that doesn't tell us whether one has a drinking problem and is generally lazy and the other is a hard-driving fitness nut. This means that their pay—especially in government, where compensation is more loosely connected to performance and more closely tied to seniority and educational credentials—may not accurately reflect how good they are at their jobs. In short, it's really hard to say whether one is getting what one pays for. Bearing this in mind should induce a sense of moderation and humility about the claims one can make.

However, some studies have tried to get at some of these hard-to-observe aspects of worker productivity and hence genuine worth. A number of economists have used job-switching analyses: instead of just looking at pay for observably similar workers in the two sectors, they account for harder-to-observe performance characteristics by looking at how pay changes for the same worker who switches from the public to the private sector, or vice versa. The general finding of these studies is that when typical public employees leave government employment, they tend to receive a lower salary, along with much lower benefits, while those who shift into public jobs generally get pay increases.[11]

Not surprisingly, then, labor economists have been investigating these questions for nearly 40 years. And over the last few years a number of think tank analysts have engaged in a bitter dispute over whether public employees are "overpaid" or "underpaid" compared to their private sector counterparts. Some say the private sector pays better and that there is a "wage penalty" for government employment.[12] Others say that government is the more generous employer and that there is a "wage premia"—in other words, an advantage—for working in the public sector.[13]

Despite such disagreements, it's helpful to put on the table the few things that researchers agree upon. One is that there is much more "wage compression" in the public than in the private sector, which means that the pay of those at the top and the bottom of the salary scale are closer together. Another point of agreement is that the public sector offers better compensation to workers with low levels of education and skills than the private sector and that the private sector is more lucrative than government for workers with high levels of education and skills. For example, janitors and secretaries in the public sector receive an appreciably better deal than they would in the private economy. According to the Bureau of Labor Statistics, in 2008, the average annual salary for the roughly 330,000 office clerks who work in government was almost $27,000 in 2005, while the 2.7 million in the private sector received an average pay of just under $23,000. Nationwide, among the 108,000 janitors who work in government, the average salary was $23,700; the average salary of the 2 million janitors working in the private sector, meanwhile, was $19,800. At the other end of the labor market, private sector economists earned an average of $99,000 a year, compared to the $69,000 earned by their government colleagues. And accountants in the corporate world earned average annual salaries of $52,000, compared to $48,000 for their public sector counterparts.[14]

A final point of agreement is that, in the aggregate, wages tend to be lower in the public than in the private sector but that fringe benefits (in particular, pensions and retiree healthcare) are much more generous in public than private employment. Much public sector compensation is thus back-loaded into retirement. All told, public employees do better. For federal workers, the Congressional Budget Office found a 16 percent average compensation premium, and other studies found an even larger one. At the state level, economists Jason Richwine and Andrew Biggs also find that on average total compensation is higher, by about 15 percent, but varies greatly from state to state.[15] Where the analysts disagree is over how exactly to value pension and healthcare benefits in total compensation and the value of job security.[16]

Indeed, much of the dispute among the recent studies comes down to how to value fringe benefits and job security in the econometric models. If the model makes certain assumptions about the long-term value of pensions and healthcare and values job security highly, it will find a public compensation premium. If it is assumed that job security isn't worth as much (or is entirely unmeasurable, and therefore irrelevant to the equation), and if a different valuation of benefits is calculated, a public sector compensation penalty results.

The general consensus when looking at wages and salaries alone is that highly educated and experienced public sector workers are underpaid compared to their private sector counterparts, while the reverse is true for workers with low levels of education.[17] The wage penalty for working in government is estimated to be between 6 and 12 percent.[18] However, because wages and salary are only one component of compensation, other studies factor in the value of pension, health, and other benefits. This is particularly important because so much of public employee compensation occurs in retirement. And this is where the controversy lies. At issue is whether public sector benefits offset its generally lower wages. Almost all analysts agree that benefits are much higher for state and local workers than those in the private sector. Most then find overall parity between public and private sector compensation for comparable workers. A few find a slight public sector penalty. A few find a public sector premium, especially for federal workers.

Let's now turn to some of the peer-reviewed scholarly studies along with some of the recent ones by public policy institutes. Looking at the federal government, a majority of the studies find a public sector premium. Beginning with Sharon P. Smith's work 40 years ago, economists began to find a pay premium for federal employees.[19] But at the same time, official studies by the government concluded that federal workers suffered a wage penalty. In 1994, the Government Accounting Office tried to sort out why university professors and government analysts came to different conclusions without much luck.[20] Much hinged on whether the study compared categories of jobs or attributes of workers. In one of the more sophisticated studies, Brent Moulton found a public sector premium of about 3 percent but showed that the disparity was not across the board between public and private but differed greatly across categories of workers.[21]

In 2002, George Borjas examined state and local, as well as federal, wages relative to the private sector's wages from 1960 to 2000.[22] He found a relatively stable wage penalty (ranging from –5 to –10 percent) for public sector workers. Most of this penalty could be attributed to men, while women over this period went from receiving a premium for working for government to near parity with the private sector. However, the stability of public sector pay persisted even as income inequality grew rapidly in the private sector. Thus, while the private sector became more unequal, the public sector continued to compress wages. The consequence, Borjas held, was that the public sector became less attractive for highly skilled workers in the 1980s and 1990s. Fewer highly educated and talented workers entered and remained on government payrolls. Using Commerce Department data, he was able to look at workers who moved into or out of government employment, that is, the experiences of workers on either side of the public/private sector divide. This technique is much more accurate for making comparisons between different workers inside and outside government because it looks at *the same worker* in two different settings. Since the 1970s, Borjas found that workers at the high end of the labor market with lots of earning potential increasingly found the private sector more congenial. Fewer of them were likely to seek government employment, and those in its employ were more likely to quit for jobs in business and the professions. As he put it, "The substantial widening of wage inequality in the private sector and the relatively more stable wage distribution in the public sector created magnetic effects that altered the sorting of workers across sectors, with high-skill workers becoming more likely to end up in the private sector." We will return to some of the consequences of this "brain drain" in chapter 9.

Other studies have gone beyond just looking at the federal government. Lawrence Katz and Alan Krueger examined federal, state, and local employees.[23] They also found big differences at the high end (penalty) and at the low end (premium) of the labor market for state and local workers. Others found similar premia for low-skilled workers.[24] Examining three low-end job categories in Houston, Texas, two other scholars found pay premia for cleaners, bus drivers, and mechanics.[25] Comparing all 50 states, Jason Richwine and Andrew Biggs found large compensation premia in some states and small penalties in a handful.[26] William Evan and David Macpherson found similar results for state employees.[27]

In sum, state and local government workers tend to do quite well by low-end employees (bus drivers, trash collectors, secretaries) but suffer a penalty in relation to more highly credentialed (lawyers, accountants, engineers) private sector workers. Greater equality in compensation has thus persisted in the government workforce, while it has declined in the private sector. Therefore, looking at aggregate levels of compensation in the two sectors obscures big differences depending on education and experience.

Another group of studies looks at the attractiveness of public sector employment. Here the analyst measures demand for government work by looking at "job queues."[28] Most of the studies look at federal employment rather than state and local jobs.[29] For example, Alan Krueger analyzed the number of applications for federal versus private sector jobs. He found that, on average, federal jobs received 25 percent to 38 percent more qualified applicants than private sector positions.[30] If government employment paid more than the private sector, there should be excess demand for public sector jobs. One of these studies found that federal compensation exceeds the private sector by about 4 percent for men and 22 percent for women. Another found a 25 to 38 percent higher job application rate for government jobs than for those in the private sector. These findings suggest that federal jobs pay more than the private sector.

Finally, a study by the Center for Retirement Research at Boston College asked whether public sector workers ended up better off at the end of their careers than private sector workers. The researchers found that workers who spent nearly their entire career in public employ ended up better off financially than similarly situated workers—people with similar jobs and skills—who spent their entire careers in the private sector or worked for government for a short time. In fact, people who had only a brief spell in government employment during their careers ended up worse off at the point of retirement than workers who spent their whole careers in one sector or another.[31]

This conclusion is confirmed by some simple calculations. A number of "pension calculators" have sprouted up online. These allow users to enter basic data—age at retirement, number of years on the job, and their final average salary—and see what their monthly and yearly pension payment would be and how much a worker in the private sector would need in an annuity or savings account to generate an equal monthly income. The results are striking. An average public sector worker in New York, retiring at age 65 after 30 years of service and with a final average salary of $75,000, would receive a $45,000 annual pension or $3,750 a month. For a similarly situated worker in the private sector, he or she would need savings of $713,000 to generate similar monthly income for the rest of his or her life.[32] If the final salary were $100,000, the private sector worker would need nearly $1 million in savings to generate comparable income in retirement.[33] Given most Americans' savings rate, which bottomed out at 2 percent of personal disposable income in 2005, few have sums like that in the bank.[34]

Part of the disagreement among economists hinges on whether the Bureau of Labor Statistics' Employer Costs for Employer Compensation survey, which most of them rely on as their data set, understates public sector retiree compensation. Critics argue that it omits retiree healthcare entirely and it does not properly value public sector defined benefit plans relative to private sector defined contribution plans. Factoring in healthcare and using a different method to account for defined benefit plans boosts public sector compensation to at least parity if not greater.

The final source of disagreement concerns whether and how job security should be factored into the compensation studies.[35] Clearly, it has some value, as public employees in surveys say they care about it and unions consistently seek to shield their members from layoffs. But how to measure its monetary value is contentious. Some argue that to the extent that workers have greater job security—a major goal of collective bargaining—they should be more willing to accept lower wages or salaries. If one ascribes greater importance to that factor, then public sector workers do turn out to enjoy a substantial compensation premium. Ascribe it less weight and it is not enough to push public sector workers past parity with their private sector counterparts. Therefore, how job security should be measured and employed in labor economists' regression equations is the subject of considerable controversy.

Interestingly, the core issue of whether public sector workers really have greater job security than their private sector counterparts remains in dispute. There is some evidence to suggest that they do. Looking at workers over the 2000–10 period, which includes two recessions, working for government reduced the likelihood of being unemployed by 2 percentage points. In addition, if one looks at "quit rates"—the rate at which workers voluntarily leave their jobs—they are much higher in the private than in the public sector. This suggests that the security and protections afforded by public sector employment make it safer. One study found that "much of the observed difference in unemployment rates is attributable to the ability of unions to promote job security in the public sector."[36]

However, some have asked whether job security should be considered part of the work environment rather than part of compensation. These analysts argue that job security simply offsets the lousy working conditions that many public employees endure. Anyone with firsthand experience of government employment knows that it often occurs in dim offices with shopworn furniture and old computers, printers, and copiers prone to malfunction. In addition, job security is offset by the fact that salary adjustments and promotions are very slow for government workers. Yet, as regards other nonmonetary factors that affect employees' day-to-day lives, such as stress and danger, public employees are found to be better off than private sector employees. All told, there's no consensus on what weight to give job security in making a comparison between total compensation in the private and public sectors.

Three points in this discussion are worth highlighting. First, it is often more important to pay attention to particular areas of compensation premia or penalties rather than look to the aggregate percent differentials. The devil is in the details and the existing research does not point to a broad generalization that "government workers are overpaid (or underpaid)." The fact is that some states and localities may be paying more than necessary to attract talent and can afford to reduce compensation without turning off talented workers. Others, however, may not be paying enough. Furthermore, some governments' pay scales may be overly compressed and therefore unable to attract and retain top talent.

Second, debates today often turn on the nature of the data and how job security (something government employees tell pollsters that they value a great deal) and pension and health benefits are weighed in comparing total compensation. That is, even if skilled employees make less, they benefit from strong job protections and guaranteed retirement income. Those types of security are clearly very valuable but hard to quantify precisely. Yet, one thing is clear: workers who remain on the job for many years are the ones who really reap the benefits of generous pension and health plans. Therefore, such munificence is unlikely to serve as a powerful instrument for retaining younger workers. Teachers' compensation structure, which heavily favors older teachers, is a case in point.[37]

Third, the comparable pay of those government workers who lack counterparts in the private sector, such as police officers, firefighters, and corrections officers, is hard to capture. For example, in New York State, county police officers were paid an average salary of $121,000 a year in 2006. In that same year, according to the *Boston Globe*, 225 of the 2,338 Massachusetts State Police officers made more than the $140,535 annual salary earned by the state's governor. Four state troopers received more than $200,000, and 123 others were paid more than $150,000. While people whose jobs entail greater risk of life and limb certainly deserve higher pay, government's monopoly status—meaning they are sole providers of the service—combined with union power adds a substantial premium. And while police officers and firefighters can face dangerous situations, their jobs are probably less dangerous than those of fishermen and loggers. However, workers in public safety are often excluded from comparative pay studies because they lack a clear counterpart in the private sector.

UNIONIZATION AND COMPENSATION

Most analysts agree that public sector unions' collective bargaining activities and political power lead to more government spending.[38] From 1992 to 2009, public employees who belonged to unions earned a higher weekly salary than those who were not unionized.[39] In 1992, the median weekly salary for government workers belonging to unions was $579, while for nonunion workers it was $100 less. In 2009, local government workers belonging to unions earned, on average, $236 more than their nonunionized counterparts. State employees belonging to unions earned, on average, $139 more than nonunionized state workers. Those differences seem small, but stretched over the whole year and across thousands of employees, they add up fast.

Despite these interesting differences, most of the research on the impact of public sector unions and collective bargaining was conducted in the 1970s and 1980s, when unionization was increasing and government workers' unions were new players on the scene. Fewer economists studied these issues during the 1990s. Most of the early scholarship focused on city governments and particular categories of government workers, such as police officers, teachers, and firefighters. It explored the impact of public employee unions on government wage and salary expenditures, on employment, and on other metrics of government activity.[40] Recent conflict over public sector labor relations has sparked new interest in these questions. Putting the old scholarship together with the new, the overall finding is that government expenditures on wages and salaries tend to be higher (per capita and per worker) when employees are unionized.[41] And workers' earnings tend to be higher in unionized environments.[42]

These findings should hardly be surprising. Indeed, they confirm simple economic theory. The central purpose of unions is to extract "rents" (usually in the form of higher compensation) from their employers. That unionization increases workers' wages in the private sector is well documented. In the public sector, the unions can use both collective bargaining and politicking to achieve that end. And they succeed, at least in part, at increasing government expenditures on wages and salaries.[43] Economist Laura Feiveson studied whether large cities spent the funds they received in federal revenue-sharing programs on new employment (hiring more workers) or increased salary. She found that cities with collective bargaining and strong unions spent more than half of the transfer payments on increased wages, while cities in states without such laws spent a greater fraction of the funds on new employment.[44]

In fact, economists Richard Freeman and Eunice Han found that even in the states that prohibit teacher collective bargaining, teachers still joined unions—even without collective bargaining rights workers can still join unions—and they were able to secure better retirement plans, higher earnings, and fewer working days.[45] Freeman and Han found that as the percentage of teachers joining a union rose, the more powerful and organized the union became. Coupled with political activity, these unions could then force school districts into "meet and confer" arrangements. Such arrangements are similar to collective bargaining in places where state law or local ordinance doesn't legally mandate bargaining.

Consider, too, the scholarship on teachers' wages and their impact on government's priorities. There is a broad consensus that greater unionization increases pay for teachers.[46] However, some studies reveal that pay premia have been reduced or even eliminated because the union pushes the school district to hire more teachers, which forces the district to spread the salary budget across more teachers. Economist Michael Lovenheim found that teachers' unions had no effect on pay, but he did find that unions increased teacher employment by 5 percent in three midwestern states.[47] Therefore, depending on the unit of analysis, the pay premium has varied substantially. From the 1960s through the 1970s, when teachers' unions were just forming, state-level unionization data produced estimates of a 2 to 9 percent wage premium.[48] Studies examining school districts found that the boost could be as little as 1 percent to as much as 12 percent.[49] Another study using state-level data covering the 1970s found smaller wage increases.[50] Studies of school districts in the 1980s, when the unions were more mature, found a much larger effect on wages. One study found premia of 12 to 21 percent.[51]

Another line of inquiry, which has received sustained attention, seeks to estimate wage premiums that derive from membership in unions— public or private.[52] Overall, the wage premium literature shows that public employees performing the same job with similar characteristics (education, experience, etc.) tend to have higher earnings if they belong to a union.[53] Again, this shouldn't come as a surprise. The unions leverage their resources to extract from government more of one of the things their members care about: money.

Most of the existing studies examine how union membership relates to employees' pay. These analyses do not, for the most part, examine health-care, pensions, or other fringe benefits. The few studies that have tried to examine union impacts on benefits, however, have come to the conclusion that public sector unions have a much larger impact on benefits than wages—even though pension benefits are not subjects of collective bargaining in most jurisdictions.[54] This means that the prior studies focusing solely on wage premiums driven by union membership understate the advantage secured by unionization because they do not account for benefits—a big piece of total public sector compensation. In addition, public employee benefits are more valuable and costly than their private sector counterparts.[55] Therefore, it may be the case that the total compensation premium is higher for unionized public employees than unionized private sector employees.

Political scientists Sarah Anzia and Terry Moe recently found that wages, staffing, and payroll expenditures increased when the percentage of unionized workers went up. They took two cuts at this issue. First, they examined the period when public employees were first unionizing, which allowed them to see what happened to wages and salaries before and after unionization. Arguably, this is the best way to estimate the causal effect of unions on government finances. In this exercise, they follow prior scholarship but take some different approaches in their statistical methods. Previous longitudinal studies examined very short periods, while they look specifically at police and fire departments in cities with a population greater than 10,000 spanning the 1970s and 1980s. They estimate that the wage increase for municipal fire protection attributable to unionization was 3.9 percent. It seems that firefighters' unions increased their members' pay in a very short period of time following a union's certification. Cities also hired more firefighters after unionization and increased their overall payroll expenditures. They found that "a city whose fire employees organized for the first time could expect to spend nearly 11 percent more on fire protection salary and wages as a result."[56] The effects of police unionization were similar but smaller—albeit still statistically significant—than those of firefighters. Police officers' wages increased by 2.3 percent. Staffing levels increased by the same percentage, and these combined increases resulted in an average 3.7 percent increase in per capita payroll expenditures for city police. Of course, these results aren't very surprising.

To remain as current as possible, Anzia and Moe undertook another analysis using different data and methods and looking at the 1992–2010 period. By 1992, most cities inclined to adopt collective bargaining for their municipal employees had already done so. Therefore, rather than compare wages before and after unionization, Anzia and Moe compare cities' expenditures on salaries and health benefits for police and fire departments on the basis of whether or not the cities permit collective bargaining. To isolate the independent effect of collective bargaining, the authors control for the cities' political leanings, as more Democratic cities are more likely to have highly unionized workforces and more generous compensation. They also control for the private union membership rate, as some states are more union friendly than others, as well as differences by region.

They found that on average, municipal fire departments with collective bargaining spend about 9 percent more on employee salary and wages and about 25 percent more on health benefits per employee. Taking the average across cities, collective bargaining means that each firefighter costs an extra $1,507 a year. They conclude that "collective bargaining for fire protection employees has sizeable effects on compensation costs." Turning to municipal police departments, Anzia and Moe find similar outcomes.

When cities allow collective bargaining, they spend 10 percent more on salaries and wages and about 21 percent more on health benefits for police protection than do cities without collective bargaining. Taken together, the typical police officer is $1,200 more expensive in cities with collective bargaining than in those without it.[57] In sum, cities that adopted collective bargaining in the 1960s, 1970s, and 1980s have followed far different trajectories than those that did not—especially when it comes to the expansion of health benefits for their police officers and firefighters.

It should be noted that all of the studies reviewed here use simple measures of unionization rates or the presence of collective bargaining as proxies for union power. None of the statistical models tries to capture whether unions' political activities away from the bargaining table—such as the electioneering and lobbying activities discussed in prior chapters—also serve to boost compensation. There are strong reasons to believe that they do. As we have seen in previous chapters, unionization is likely to generate more politicking on behalf of workers' interests. However, data to empirically test this proposition are nearly nonexistent. The one analysis that has tried to capture political effects on compensation, again by Anzia and Moe, used whether unions endorsed candidates for office as a proxy for political activity and found that it did increase wages and benefits. While this analysis is provisional, the central finding chimes with what economic theory would predict.

As the aforementioned research indicates, unionization of government workers tends to increase wages and health benefits. Yet, while it is clearly the case that public sector employees enjoy more generous pension plans than their private sector counterparts and a greater percentage of them belong to unions, researchers currently disagree on whether public sector unions' collective bargaining or political activities increase the generosity of pensions and/or increase the likelihood that they will be underfunded.

Unionization and Benefits

Media reports are full of stories connecting government unions to underfunding of state and local pension and health commitments. Most American states and cities offer their employees defined benefit pensions and a variety of health plans that cover them, should they retire before Medicare eligibility, and provide various supplements to Medicare during retirement. These liabilities are huge. By one recent estimate, the total pension gap is $2.7 trillion or 17 percent of US gross domestic product.[58] The healthcare bill may be nearly as high as the pension tab, but it is even harder to estimate. When Detroit declared bankruptcy in 2013, it had $18.2 billion in long-term debts, $9.2 billion of which was unfunded retirement benefits ($5.7 billion for health benefits and $3.5 billion for pensions) for city workers. Some of these costs result from the fact that people are living longer, which requires public plans to pay out more.

However, some are also the result of major abuses—even if those abuses are within the letter of the law and current arrangements give workers incentives to game pension systems. Sometimes workers are promoted just before retirement or work excessive overtime hours to claim a higher final salary for pension benefit calculations. Other workers immediately become "disabled" upon retirement to collect extra monies. Conductors on the Long Island Railroad in New York were found to retire early and visit "disability mills" where doctors produced fake paperwork that qualified retirees for tens of thousands of dollars in additional payments. In one year, 97 percent of those who retired also qualified for disability, costing the federal government millions of dollars.[59] These practices are colloquially referred to as pension "spiking." Still others retire early to collect a pension and then take another government job and begin accruing another pension—a practice called "double dipping." California's Little Hoover Commission pointed to the egregious example of a fire chief who retired in 2009 on a pension of $241,000 and then was hired back as a consultant to the tune of $176,000 a year. New York City Schools Chancellor Carmen Fariña currently makes $412,193 a year—$212,614 in salary combined with a $199,579 Department of Education pension.[60]

Public employee unions and their allies defend the current pension system. They argue, rightly, that workers were promised these benefits when they signed up and are therefore owed these monies. They contend that good pensions also attract people to government work. In addition, they often claim that large pensions are far from the norm. According to the National Conference of State Legislatures, the average retirement benefit for public employees across the nation is only $22,600—a statistic often cited by unions and their allies. However, it must be noted that that figure includes many people who worked for state and local government long ago, when pension systems were far less generous, and people who worked for government for a short time. Including those workers brings down the average pension considerably. In contrast, today, municipal police officers and firefighters in California on average retire at age 54 after 25 years of service, earning $84,708 a year in pension benefits.[61]

As observers have pointed out, it is easier for politicians to offer benefit "sweeteners" to public servants than it is to raise their wages.[62] Wage increases appear in current budgets, while the bill for retirement benefits will come due on someone else's watch. In most places pensions are not bargained and increases can only be secured through political activity. But the unions can be politically very effective. Sometimes public sector unions are the key actors in winning cost-of-living adjustments well above rates of inflation. More than 20,000 retired public servants in California receive pensions of over $100,000 a year.[63]

Like salaries and wages, it appears reasonable to assume that public sector unions' push for more generous pensions for their members, as again, the unions' purpose is to advance the occupational interests of their memberships, which includes a more secure retirement. And the federal government does not insure public sector pensions, and most public employees do not participate in Social Security. Private sector defined benefit plans are backed by the Pension Benefit Guarantee Corporation (PBGC). The reason public pensions were excluded from PBGC coverage was that the Contracts Clause of the US Constitution, many state constitutions, and local ordinances protected public pensions and made them sacrosanct. Yet, Detroit and a handful of California cities are now testing the proposition of whether existing pension benefits can be cut during bankruptcy proceedings. For cities in or near bankruptcy, tinkering with pension payouts may become politically attractive, as the interests of a small number of pensioners are pitted against the interests of all city residents in seeing the city get back on its feet. Expanding pensions is attractive for politicians, until it isn't.

However, unlike salaries and wages and the generosity of the pensions—where unions' incentive to push for more are obvious—the motivations of public sector unions when it comes to the funding status of the plans aren't obvious. On the one hand, strong unions might want to protect the fiscal health of the pension funds that their members will rely on in retirement—especially since many employees will not have Social Security to fall back on. They would use their power to keep the funds solvent. In theory, strong unions might cause states to fund their plans well. The best example of this is New York State, which has the highest percentage of public sector workers in unions, while its pensions are among the best funded in the nation.

On the other hand, an equally plausible scenario is that strong unions might lead to underfunded pensions. Why? Stronger unions are likely to be more successful in getting politicians to agree to more generous pensions. Yet, more generous pensions increase budget pressures, which lead politicians to short the pension fund.[64] Furthermore, to the extent that unions and their political allies know that pensions are guaranteed—either by statute or state constitutional provisions—they can be confident that they will eventually be paid. Consequently, the best strategy for unions is to push for more generous pensions without expending much political capital to ensure the plans are well funded. The most obvious cases here are states such as Illinois, New Jersey, and California. In sum, unlike pay or benefit levels, funding status presents two theoretically plausible courses of action that union leaders might adopt, which makes this a complicated empirical question.

A study by Alicia Munnell and her colleagues at the Center for Retirement Research at Boston College found that public sector unions' collective bargaining activities *were not* a source of pension underfunding.[65] In her empirical analysis, the collective bargaining activities of public employee unions were not a statistically significant factor in explaining why some public pension plans were underfunded. She measures union strength simply by whether unions have collective bargaining rights. According to her, the reason pensions are underfunded is simply "a story of fiscal discipline." To have fiscal discipline, the government unit must have paid the full annual required contribution as defined by the Government Accounting Standards Board.

Yet, her empirical analysis of public sector unions' effect on public pensions hardly closes the case. First, it does not address whether union political power increases the generosity of public pensions. Second, regarding whether union strength causes underfunding, her statistical model makes it unlikely to capture union effects. She ultimately argues that pension underfunding is simply a result of states' "culture of fiscal discipline," which some states possess but others don't. Yet that just begs the question of what factors produce (or undermine) a culture of fiscal discipline.

Pointing in the opposite direction, an analysis by Anzia and Moe found that unionization increased the generosity of the pension and health benefits, as well as the degree to which the pension plans were underfunded. They used state-level estimates of public pension assets and liabilities as of June 2009 calculated by Robert Novy-Marx and Joshua Rauh.[66] Ultimately, they found that a 10 percent increase in union membership raised per capita pension liabilities by $1,412 or 20 percent of the state's gross product in 2009. Moving from the least to the most unionized state increased public pension liabilities per capita by nearly $10,000.

They also tested whether union power led to underfunding of pensions and found that it did. A shift from the least to the most unionized state increased unfunded liabilities by $4,369 or 10 percent of the state's gross product. This is an interesting finding because, as noted earlier, one reasonable hypothesis is that strong unions would want to ensure pensions are fully funded, since their members will depend on them in the future. If so, states with strong unions would have better-funded plans. However, because union leaders know that benefits are legally—and in some cases constitutionally—guaranteed, they have confidence that the benefits in the future will be paid. Union leaders adopt something of a "too big to fail" mentality. The sensible strategy for unions in this scenario is to push for more benefits and not waste resources trying to ensure plans are well funded. If plans start to run up against other budget priorities as the liabilities get larger, politicians will be tempted to shortchange them.

The most recent study, authored by analysts at the Beacon Hill Institute at Suffolk University, found that public sector unionization also increases unfunded pension liabilities. They found that "every percentage point increase in the unionization of public sector employees is associated with an additional $78 of state and local government debt per capita"—debt that is used to underwrite the pension and healthcare promises of public employees.[67] In addition, consonant with the Anzia and Moe analysis, states with stronger unions are more likely to fail to make their annual required contributions to their pension funds. The unions, in this analysis, do not appear to put pressure on states to fully fund their obligations. As the authors put it, "For each percentage point of the public sector workforce represented by unions," states are about 1 percent more likely to be rated as "very poorly managing their future liabilities" by the Pew Center on the States. In short, states where unions are weaker have better-managed plans.

THE GENERAL CONSENSUS

Once one puts aside popular press polemics, one discovers that comparative pay is a complicated subject where, nonetheless, there is a rough scholarly consensus on a number of important points. First, state and local public employees overall tend to make less in salary but more in benefits than their private sector counterparts. Second, the aggregate figures obscure the fact that public employees at the lower end of the job market do better than those in the private sector, while those at the high end fare worse. Those in the middle do about the same in both sectors. Third, federal employees appear to do better overall than comparable private sector employees—but this is complicated by the fact that so many federal jobs lack comparable positions in the private sector. Fourth, unionization of public employees increases their compensation, either by winning greater salaries or benefits or both.

Yet, there are still areas of considerable disagreement. One is over the value of job security—if and how it should be factored into the econometric models. Another involves whether or not unionization of government employees has increased the level of pension underfunding in state and local government.

Beyond all these aggregate measures comparing public and private sector employment, it is important to bear in mind that many big differences show up in localities. While public employees may not be overpaid overall, one can find big distortions inside certain job categories and within certain states and cities. There is a lot of variation across the states. These differences are often very relevant for policymakers and the public. For example, the *Los Angeles Times* found that 6,000 correctional officers in the Golden State earned more than $100,000 in 2006, many were paid more than double what prison guards in others states earn, and hundreds earned more than elected officials.[68] Such out-of-whack pay scales should be addressed.

Beyond issues of comparative pay, much evidence points to the common-sense conclusion that unionization and collective bargaining in the public sector have increased public employees' salaries and enhanced their benefit packages (pensions and healthcare) beyond what they otherwise would receive. This is what basic economic theory would predict. A new organization mobilizes and seeks to extract rents from government, at which it is at least partially successful. Given the resources of unions, both legal and political, it would be shocking if they didn't succeed at least in part.

Clearly, greater compensation is good for public workers. But it places a burden on the taxpayer that is, as we shall see in chapter 9, not evidently compensated for by greater productivity gains. Over the long term, pension underfunding has other negative fiscal consequences for states and localities. As their liabilities increase, many states issue questionable debt instruments like pension obligation bonds or encourage their pension funds to make more risky investments in equities to make up for shortfalls in government contributions.[69] Furthermore, increases in state debt, requiring higher interest payments, may be good for bankers and investors but are bad for everyone else. Those higher interest payments drain off taxpayer dollars that could be used for productive purposes or returned to citizens through tax cuts. One study has found that states with public sector collective bargaining laws have higher debt-to-state gross domestic product ratios and higher deficits than states without them.[70] In short, the introduction of unions and collective bargaining into government labor relations has increased costs to taxpayers, weakened state and local public finances, and exacerbated labor market inequities. Public sector unions increase the costs of government without providing commensurate benefits to the public.

SPENDING MORE, GETTING LESS

The introduction of collective bargaining and unionization into the public sector has increased the generosity of employees' salaries, pensions, and health benefits. Some analysts also find that public employee unions contribute to underfunding of public pension plans. Others, however, disagree such that a consensus has yet to emerge on this point. Yet, to the extent that unionization has contributed to increased salaries from which pensions are calculated, to politicians shorting pension funds, or to the inflated size of pensions and scope of healthcare offered to retired public workers, it has contributed to the biggest challenge confronting state and local public finances today. At bottom, public pension funds and healthcare plans are created and shaped by political choices made by governors and state legislatures, and mayors and city councils, which public employee unions try hard to influence.

State and local government finances are under severe pressure, not only from the widely discussed increases in Medicaid expenditures, but also, and even more so, from the exploding costs of public employees' salaries, pensions, and healthcare. Public sector compensation threatens to displace government spending on other goods and services on which citizens rely. For example, David Crane, a former economic advisor of California

Governor Arnold Schwarzenegger, warns that pension and healthcare obligations to his state's employees threaten to "crowd out funding for many programs vital to the overwhelming majority of Californians," including "higher education, transit, and parks."[1] All told, America's state and local governments face a sustained budget crunch driven partly by long-standing promises to their workers, whose implications have yet to be fully fathomed. This threat mirrors the more frequently discussed plight of the federal government, where retirement programs place major constraints on everything else government does.[2]

Tax dollars are scarce and government's priorities multiple—especially when austere budget conditions prevail. If government spends more on the salaries, pensions, and healthcare of its employees, it cannot spend more money on things like public transit, school buildings, park maintenance, and relief to the poor—unless it raises taxes, uses budget gimmicks, or takes on greater debt.[3] In other words, it shortchanges the basic functions Americans expect government to perform. This is especially true for middle- and lower-class Americans who depend more on public services. And rising costs of retiree benefits can even harm current public workers, who are called upon to pay more into pensions and healthcare systems, sometimes for less generous benefits. Some cities already spend more on retiree healthcare each year than on healthcare for current workers.

Not only is the budget crunch hitting average citizens, but also, ironically, it is coming back to bite public employees themselves. Their unions pushed for better pay and benefits, but now those costs are forcing layoffs and furloughs in many places. Detroit is the proverbial canary in the coalmine. New York City, for example, pays out more money annually to fund the benefits of retired police officers than the salaries of cops on active duty. Former Los Angeles mayor Richard Riordan and long-time *Los Angeles Times* journalist Tim Rutten have described the situation as one where "emergency response times are lengthening .... Libraries, parks and recreation facilities are shortening their hours or closing. Potholes go unfilled, sidewalks unrepaired and trees untrimmed. All that makes urban life rewarding and uplifting is under increasing pressure, in large part because of unaffordable public employee pension and health care costs."[4]

Over the next few years, it is likely to appear to average citizens that state and local governments are spending more but doing less—hardly a recipe for restoring trust in government. In fact, we may end up with smaller government that costs more and does less—not at all what conservatives or liberals have in mind. Furthermore, if America's state and local governments are going to undertake long-term investments in their workforces to increase productivity, in infrastructure to enhance economic efficiency, and in the health and safety of their citizens, they will need large reserves of public confidence. Government cannot be perceived as serving only insiders—whether those insiders are big businesses or public employee unions—and win citizens' trust. Taxpayers will begin to demand reform when changes in government liabilities translate into changes in government purposes. How politicians in our compound republic respond to these challenges will determine the civic health of the American polity.

In a powerful way, "budgeting is governing." Crafting a budget provides answers to the classic questions of politics—as political scientist Harold Laswell once put them—of who gets what, when, and how? In many ways budgeting is the heart of policymaking. Yet, with more budget items being set by past decisions, budgeting is increasingly disconnected from governing. The choices available to policymakers today are powerfully constrained by laws and collectively bargained contracts that passed years ago. Many budget items are essentially on autopilot. Today, federal, state, and local governments are budgeting more dollars but deciding less, as huge portions of budgets are fixed costs. Consequently, policymakers cannot set new goals when older, entrenched programs siphon off all the money. Crowding out thus affects government purpose and the capacity for self-government.[5]

Public employee unions are far from the sole cause of these problems. Elected officials deserve much of the blame, as many found sweetening public sector pensions to be good politics since it placated the unions but didn't show up in current budgets. Still other politicians decided not to make the annual required contributions to the plans sponsored by their cities and states because they wanted to use the monies to provide more services to citizens without increasing taxes or cutting other programs. These decisions were irresponsible. Voters also share some of the fault, as they consumed more services without holding their representatives accountable for making sure there was a way to pay for them.

Yet, to the extent that they pushed to increase the generosity of pension and healthcare plans for their members beyond what they would otherwise be, unions have contributed to the problem. They also now present the biggest obstacles to reformers trying to dial back those benefits. Through a politics of blocking, public sector unions force politicians to spend enormous political capital to address some of the causes of the current budget squeeze. For many lawmakers, pushing for reform of public employee retiree systems has few political upsides. They must alienate the unions, which can run ads and campaign against them, and they gain few kudos from the public. This is a persistent structural problem with public policies where the benefits are highly concentrated and the costs on society widely dispersed.[6] Public sector unions are mobilized to defend the benefits that have accrued to their members, while comparatively unorganized taxpayers see little benefit from taking on these issues.

THE CAUSES OF CROWDING OUT

What is driving the current budget crunch at all levels of American government is a series of past decisions that created formulas for how much retirees would receive in pension and healthcare benefits. Enacted and expanded when the economy was growing, it was often difficult for policymakers to foresee the long-term implications of their decisions. Even when they could see trouble ahead, it was of limited cause for concern, as politicians usually work within short time horizons and know that they would no longer be on the scene when problems emerged.

The Federal Case

While the focus of this book is on state and local government, the federal government is obviously facing a similar problem of crowding out, albeit not for the same reasons. Taking a brief look at the federal level, since it is more familiar and has received more press attention, helps illustrate the problem. Nicholas Eberstadt has recently documented how the federal government's purposes have been transformed as it has grown in size since the New Deal. Today, "U.S. government devotes more attention and resources to the public transfers of money, goods, and services to individual citizens than to any other objective." The principal cause of this change is the explosive growth in entitlement spending, that is, the costs of Social Security, Medicare and Medicaid, and other government transfers to individuals. The scale of these outlays is hard to wrap the mind around, totaling over $2 trillion (for all levels of government).

Many of the drivers of federal spending are essentially on autopilot because individuals are legally entitled to receive the benefits if they meet the eligibility criteria, and many more are set to meet those criteria as the baby boom generation retires. The direction of transfer payments tends to be from young to old, the employed to those not in the labor force, and workers to retirees. And they are politically very hard to reform.

Before the 1960s, the priorities of the federal government, as reflected in its spending priorities, were security, infrastructure investments, and limited public services that facilitated commerce and aided national unity. These priorities were evident in the portions of public spending devoted to defense, criminal justice, the postal service, national highways, and so on. That changed dramatically in the wake of the Great Society when Medicaid and Medicare were created and Social Security expanded. In 2010, almost 66 percent of all federal government spending was on transfers to individuals, with all of the other priorities taking up about one-third.[7]

The point of all this is that entitlement and other transfer spending will continue to squeeze other areas of government spending. For example, President Barack Obama's 2012 budget proposal, which includes spending and taxing projections for the next decade, avoids cuts to Social Security or Medicare, refuses to raise middle-class taxes, and therefore reduces discretionary spending (which covers everything else the government does except defense) to 1.7 percent of economic output by 2022, down from 3.1 percent in 2011.[8] The Senate Democrats recently passed a budget that reduces nondefense discretionary spending from 3.7 percent of gross domestic product today to 2.5 percent in a decade. "One way to think about this pattern," says *Wall Street Journal* columnist Gerald Seib, "is that it leaves wealthy retirees living in gated golf-course communities with benefits that are unscathed, while Head Start programs for kids, or research by scientists in university laboratories, for that matter, take a hit."[9]

In the nondefense discretionary spending category is everything from subsidies for higher education, low-income housing, and job training programs for the unemployed to financing for the Environmental Protection Agency (EPA), the Food and Drug Administration (FDA), and the Federal Emergency Management Agency (FEMA). As *New York Times* columnist Eduardo Porter has colorfully put it, "Without such spending, the government becomes little more than a heavily armed pension plan with a health insurer on the side."[10] As Dean of the Columbia Business School R. Glenn Hubbard told Porter, "Either we reform entitlements or we accept large tax increases or we crowd out everything else the government does." For states and localities, the squeeze on federal discretionary spending means far less assistance, which totaled $607 billion in 2011, and increased intergovernmental disputes.[11]

Drivers in the States

There is a parallel phenomenon taking place at the state and local level— albeit with different sources. Today, the US Census Bureau counts 89,527 units of government, of which 50 are states and 39,000 are general purpose local governments.[12] There is great diversity in the institutional arrangements of these governments and modes of financing them. Huge portions of state and local spending are mandated and partly subsidized by the federal government, most notably on health (Medicaid), education (schools), and transportation (highways). And those items, especially the expansion of Medicaid, will continue to strain local finances. But they are things pushed onto states and localities rather than burdens the states created for themselves.

That is not the case, however, when one turns to state and local pensions and healthcare plans for public employees, as well as bond payments on debt. In 2011, state and local government employed 16.4 million full-time workers. The majority of those workers are teachers, police officers, and firefighters (Figure 8.1). And it is the cost of compensating these employees (salaries, pension, healthcare, and other benefits) that menaces the fiscal continence of state and local government.[13]

In California, for example, state workers often retire at age 55 with pensions that exceed what they were paid during most of their working years. In New York City, firefighters and police officers may retire after 20 years of service at half pay. Those benefits quickly add up: in 2006, the annual pension benefit for a new retiree averaged just under $73,000 (and the full amount is exempt from state and local taxes). Per retiree, that is far more expensive than most pension plans were designed to sustain.

How, one might ask, were policymakers ever convinced to agree to such generous terms? As it turns out, many lawmakers found that

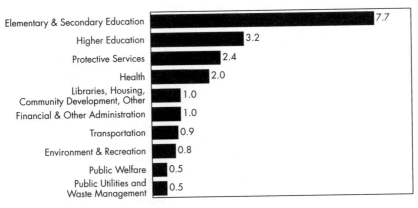

Figure 8.1 State and Local Jobs in Millions, 2012.
Source: U. S. Census Bureau.

increasing pensions was very good politics. They placated unions with future pension commitments and then turned around, borrowed the money appropriated for the pensions, and spent it paying for public services in the here and now. Politicians liked this scheme because they could satisfy the unions, provide generous public services without raising taxes to pay for them, and even sometimes get around balanced-budget requirements.

Unfortunately, the hit pension funds took recently in the stock market has exposed the massive underfunding that results from states and municipalities not paying for the public services they consume. In Illinois, for example, public sector unions have helped create a situation in which the state's pension funds report a liability of more than $100 billion, at least 50 percent of it unfunded. Yet many analysts believe the figure is much higher; without a steep economic recovery, the Prairie State is looking at insolvency. Indeed, finance professors Robert Novy-Marx and Joshua Rauh put the date of collapse at 2018; they also predict that six other states—Connecticut, Indiana, New Jersey, Hawaii, Louisiana, and Oklahoma—will see their pension funds dry up before the end of 2020.[14] What's more, according to the Pew Center on the States, 18 states face long-term pension liabilities in excess of $10 billion. In the case of California, like that of Illinois, the unfunded pension liability exceeds $50 billion. In fact, Pew estimates that, when retiree healthcare costs are added to pension obligations, the unfunded liabilities of the states total over $1 trillion.

In cities, the costs of employing workers have soared, taking an ever-larger slice of the budget. The city of Oakland has the highest crime rate in California but was recently forced to lay off more than 100 police officers. The monies saved were redirected to fund retirement benefits and to pay off bonds issued previously to cover pensions. Yet murders and robberies increased by 25 percent in 2012. Rather than cut further into public services, the city borrowed another $210 million to pay its pension obligations.[15] Chicago is facing a huge spike in the amount it must pay annually to fund its pension systems, which are severely underfunded to the tune of $19.5 billion—and one of the funds is set to run out of money by 2020. If the city is to meet state requirements of far larger contributions to the funds in 2015, which would mean an increase of $1 billion annually to cover past underpayments, it would have to raise property taxes by 150 percent.[16] Mayor Rahm Emanuel has ruled out that option. The conflict pits the city and the state, which are dominated by Democrats, against their union allies.

Other cities also face big increases in the costs of their public employees and retirees and are increasingly forced to make trade-offs between the two. In San Jose, the average cost of a full-time worker is $142,000 a year, up 85 percent in 10 years.[17] A sanitation worker in New York City now costs $144,000 annually, up from $79,000 a decade ago.[18] The increased cost is largely driven by the expense of pension and health benefits, not salary. Today, worker compensation costs at the local level tend to consume 70 to 80 percent of budgets.[19] To further complicate matters, state and local governments are struggling to raise revenues and are increasingly relying on more volatile sources.

To grasp states' and localities' budget plight, one must examine both the revenue and the spending sides of the coin (Figure 8.2). Although matters have certainly changed over the last century, state and local governments are still the primary interface for citizens. However, the revenue streams to fund these public services have been drying up or becoming more volatile in recent decades. In 2010, state and local government depended primarily on three sources of revenue: federal transfers (24.9 percent), fees and charges (16.4 percent), and taxes (50.7 percent). These units of government took in $1.3 trillion in tax revenue in 2010, down 1 percent from the previous year. And state and local government indebtedness increased 4.6 percent to $2.8 trillion. (Local governments are responsible

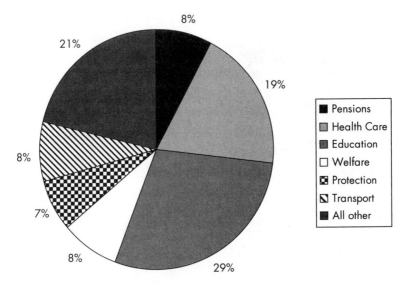

8%

21%

19%

8%

7%

8%

29%

Pensions
Health Care
Education
Welfare
Protection
Transport
All other

Figure 8.2 State and Local Spending, Fiscal Year 2012.
Source: U. S. Census Bureau.

for 60.7 percent of state and local government debt.) At the same time, state and local government spending increased by 4 percent from 2009 to $3.1 trillion in 2010.[20]

Sales taxes, on average, now make up about one-third of state tax revenue (Figure 8.3). But sales tax revenue has become more difficult to collect, as consumers purchase more lightly taxed services and many shop online. This has eroded the sales tax base.[21] Some states have responded by trying to increase sales tax rates—average rates across the states have increased from 3.5 percent in 1970 to 5.5 percent in 2000. Other revenue sources, such as taxes on goods such as gasoline, alcohol, and tobacco, have also slipped. Improved gas mileage has reduced fuel tax revenue. According to the State Fiscal Crisis Task Force, "Between 1960 and 2010, state and local motor fuel taxes declined relative to the economy by 60 percent." Consequently, states find it increasingly hard to fund transportation infrastructure, particularly highways and bridges.[22]

Finally, some states have raised income taxes on wealthy residents to offset the budget crunch. California did this most recently by referendum in 2012. The trouble with this strategy is that wealthy citizens' incomes tend to rely more heavily on the performance of the stock market. Consequently, when markets take a tumble, so do state revenues.[23] And while it may well

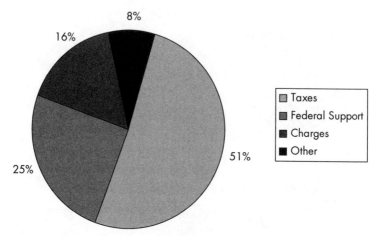

Figure 8.3 Sources of State and Local Government General Revenues, 2011.
Source: U. S. Census Bureau.

be overblown, it does raise the prospect of pushing out some wealthier residents and preventing others from moving to the state.

As revenues are increasingly hard to come by, public employee compensation squeezes state and local budgets. That compensation can be divided into salary and wages, pensions, and healthcare benefits. According to Elizabeth McNichol of the Center on Budget and Policy Priorities, compensation costs for all of these workers are, on average, 44 percent of state and local spending.[24] Some states are above that average, however. In Washington State, 60 percent of the budget goes to pay the salaries and benefits of the state's employees. This part of the budget is thus off limits to policymakers, since it is governed by union contracts or existing statutes. And these costs have been rising compared to the private sector. *USA Today* journalist Dennis Cauchon reports that, from 2002 to 2009, for every $1-an-hour pay increase, public employees have gotten $1.17 in new benefits; private sector workers, meanwhile, have received just 58 cents in added benefits.

Pension costs are rising in many places.[25] Depending on the accounting methods used, estimates of states' pension liabilities range from $600 million at the low end to $3 trillion at the high end. For example, in 2009, New Jersey's unfunded liability was $130 billion, which was more than four times the state's 2008 fiscal year budget. California, which faced a $25.4 billion budget gap in 2011, paid $100,000-plus pensions to more than 12,000 state and municipal retirees that year. Pensions will soon begin to consume a bigger share of state and local budgets. Today they account, on average, for 4.6 percent of state and local revenues. But if they only earn a 4 percent return on their investments over the next decade, pension contributions will have to rise to 14.5 percent of revenue, becoming the third-largest slice of many state budgets, after schools and healthcare. The increased cost of meeting the annual required pension contribution means that states must either raise new revenues, cut services, issue more debt, or some probably unappetizing combination of all three. Furthermore, part of what is driving up the liabilities is the attractiveness of early retirement for many public workers. In the first decade of the twenty-first century, the number of people receiving government-sponsored pensions shot up by 38 percent to 8.25 million, while the number of workers on the job contributing to public pension funds only increased 5 percent. As the ratio of workers to beneficiaries fell, costs exploded, doubling from $100 billion to $200 billion.

Turning to healthcare benefits, across the nation, 86 percent of state and local government workers have access to employer-provided health insurance, while only 45 percent of private sector workers do. In many cases, these plans involve meager contributions from employees, or none at all—in New Jersey, for instance, 88 percent of public school teachers pay nothing toward their insurance premiums. Estimates of the states' healthcare liability vary widely. Looking at 75 plans, Alicia Munnell estimated the total liability to be $588 billion in 2012. The Pew Center on the States estimates the total state unfunded liability to be $627 billion. Total liabilities are, however, likely to be much higher because many health plans are locally administered and not on the states' books. But insofar as localities are legal creations of the states, the states could become liable if local units of government require a bailout. Other studies have found the total liability to be as much as $1.6 trillion.[26] And these liabilities have been increasing, as healthcare costs rise.[27]

There are a number of different types of retiree healthcare plans offered by states and municipalities. In some cases, these are plans that cover workers who retire before they are eligible for Medicare at age 65.[28] In other places, plans supplement Medicare coverage for the rest of a worker's life. Some government plan sponsors contribute almost nothing to these plans, while in other cases the employer makes fairly generous contributions.

Most health plans in the public sector operate on a pay-as-you-go basis, meaning that the government sponsor uses funds from its general operating budget. Fewer than 10 states have undertaken any sort of prefunding, and even in those cases the amount of assets they have accumulated varies. Most states have not yet adopted a long-term strategy for funding these liabilities. Nor have America's big cities. As of 2009, the 61 cities with a population greater than 500,000 had a $118 billion liability and had only set aside enough money to cover 6 percent of it.[29]

School Districts

School districts form some 37,000 individual government units in the United States and are integral parts of local government. Like states and cities, they too are under enormous budgetary pressure from pension and healthcare commitments, in their case, to teachers. Analysts estimate the total unfunded liability of US teacher pensions to be somewhere between $390 billion, on the low end, and nearly $1 trillion dollars, on the high end, which is almost double the total annual budget of all American public education.[30] Analysts at the Thomas B. Fordham Institute examined the Milwaukee, Cleveland, and Philadelphia school districts to estimate the impact of their pension and retiree healthcare obligations on everything else these districts might want to do.[31] By 2020, the Philadelphia school system—the worst off of the three districts studied—could be spending as much $2,361 per pupil on retiree costs alone, an increase of $1,923 from today.[32] That will mean less money for teacher salaries, new instructional tools, and more specialized classroom activities.

Change will be difficult for school districts. Districts cannot generally change pension rules and financing mechanisms, which are set by states. They can, however, try to reduce teacher health benefits. But even this is a heavy lift politically. Many teachers' health benefits are set by collective bargaining agreements and unions will fight tooth and nail to prevent the reduction of these benefits. And given the influence teachers' unions can exercise on school boards, pushing back on benefits becomes very difficult, since negotiators for the district have little support in the face of union demands. Even if some districts are able to save money through reducing health expenditures, it is not likely to be enough to cover the pension obligations. Consequently, barring new revenues from property tax increases, school districts will be forced to make cuts to such things as extracurricular activities, student counseling, or administrative staff. In some cases, the districts may need to cut teacher salaries or increase class sizes.

THE CONSEQUENCES FOR GOVERNMENT
SPENDING AND SERVICES

Employee pensions and healthcare are putting increased pressure on state and local officials to manage their balance sheets. Indeed, even as state and local government payrolls have declined during and after the Great Recession, state and local government spending has not. Since 2009, state government payrolls have declined by 161,000 and local payrolls by 560,000, but state and local spending have increased in many places. From 2008 through 2010, state spending actually rose by $200 billion to $1.9 trillion. Even pushing government workers into early retirement does not provide much fiscal relief. The city of Chicago reduced the size of its workforce by 20 percent over the last decade, but costs still went up 15 percent. State and local government is now spending more but doing less.

As these costs rise, they may cause the redirection of state and local spending away from more traditional priorities like road maintenance, libraries, parks, and public transport. With taxes hard to raise, revenue scarce, and spending commitments locked in on pensions and healthcare, money must be taken from other programs. For example, in Massachusetts, hundreds of millions of dollars in school funding have never reached a classroom because they were used to pay for the healthcare of education workers. This sort of situation helps explain why the major increases in spending on education over the last 30 years have had so little effect on student performance. In the Bay State's cities and towns, employee healthcare costs jumped about 85 percent from 2001 to 2006, according to the *Boston Globe*. Consequently, the town of Stoneham, for example, was forced to cut a dozen jobs in the police and fire departments and reduce other services by reducing the hours of town employees.[33] Other cities have had to take even more dramatic action: Scranton, Pennsylvania, temporarily cut the pay of all city workers to the minimum wage.

Last year, the National Conference on State Legislatures forecast that for 10 states, employee retirement and benefit costs will be their fastest-growing budget area.[34] Illinois Governor Pat Quinn's budget director, David Vaught, has remarked that "our revenue growth is not enough to keep up with pensions and Medicaid. It creates a squeeze for everything else." Or as he put it in his State of the State Address, pension costs are "squeezing out education, public safety and other vital services to the tune of $17 million a day."[35]

These facts have made change urgent. Since 2009, some 40 states have undertaken some sort of "reform." But many of the changes have largely been cosmetic and have not really addressed the underfunding problem.[36] One strategy is to offer less generous pensions or increase the retirement age for newly hired workers. But the savings from such moves won't show up for years and may reduce the attraction of government work for talented people.

Yet, the biggest problem for state and local finances may be the cost of healthcare, which has been rising rapidly. While the Affordable Care and Patient Protection Act takes some small steps toward reigning in costs, how much it will be able to do so remains highly uncertain. In addition, many state workforces are older and many baby boomers are approaching retirement. It's a one-two punch of rising costs and a growing number of retirees. And because these plans are mostly funded on a pay-as-you-go basis, they will increasingly pinch state budgets. On the upside for states, as they increase their retirement ages for public employees, the cost of the most expensive form of health insurance—coverage for those under 65— may decrease. Supplementary benefits to Medicare are comparatively less expensive, which cover some prescription drugs, eye and dental care, and other procedures.

Overall, however, instead of paying for these health benefits, states have tried to reduce costs by instituting wellness programs, restricting coverage, and requiring workers to pay more for their plans. The latter is the main strategy by increasing the percentage of the premium paid by the employee and increasing copayments and deductibles. Yet such steps are unlikely to be enough.

Where all this rubber really meets the road, however, is at the local level. As Mayor of Syracuse, New York, Stephanie Miner wrote in the *New York Times*, "Our labor costs are too high—less because of salaries, more because of the rising costs of pensions and health care."[37] The cities facing the toughest choices produced by crowding out are ones that experienced big declines in property values or in states like California that limit munic- ipalities' power to raise revenues. In addition, nearly a third of the Golden State's cities require collective bargaining and prohibit outsourcing public services to private contractors.[38]

The Pew Research Center reports that the most populous cities across America have a gap of more than $217 billion between what they had promised their workers in pensions and retiree healthcare and what they had saved to make good on that promise.[39] Pittsburgh, for example, has one of the worst-funded city pensions in the country. In 2011, actuaries estimated that it had set aside only 30 percent of the funds needed to cover future promises to city workers. (A plan with a funding ration of 75 per- cent is usually considered well funded.) The city has now sued to remove the tax-exempt nonprofit status of the University of Pittsburgh Medical Center, one of the city's largest employers.[40] More generally, unfunded urban pension liabilities grew 15 percent in just one year from 2009 to 2010. Such figures indicate that other things city government wants to do must be put on the back burner or forced off the table entirely—unless, of course, they take on more debt, raise new revenue through taxes and fees, or paper things over with accounting gimmicks.

Consider New York City. Between 2005 and 2012, city spending on pen- sions increased from $3.2 billion to $7.8 billion. This increase meant that pensions went from consuming 6.1 percent of the city's budget to 11.7 per- cent. If one adds fringe and other benefit payments to city workers in 2012, they consumed nearly a fifth of the budget (17 percent).[41] Former Mayor Michael Bloomberg describes the problem: "We now spend more on pen- sions than we do on the operating budget of the NYPD, the Fire Department and the Sanitation Department—combined." Almost all city revenue gen- erated by income taxes goes to cover pensions. Again, Bloomberg: "Next year, every penny in personal income tax we collect will go to cover our pension bill." According to Bloomberg, pension costs prevent the city from spending on social programs: "Because as pensions consume an ever larger portion of our annual budget, that leaves less and less for everything else. The $6.5 billion more that we are spending on pensions is money that we're not using to fund child care, housing for the homeless, libraries, summer jobs for teens, senior centers and parks and environmental protection."[42]

Such talk has become a common refrain from other mayors. In Los Angeles, pension costs have risen over the past decade from 3 percent to 18 percent of the city's budget, and the Little Hoover Commission predicts they could rise to 37 percent of the budget by 2015, which is why some now warn that the city verges on insolvency.[43] Today, 91 percent of Los Angeles's general fund revenues are dedicated to employee salaries and benefits.[44] Over the past two years in Des Moines, Iowa, police and fire pension costs have increased by 20 percent at a time when its property tax revenue has been shrinking. In response, the city has raised property taxes and cut services by closing the library one day a week, picking up trash collection in parks less often, and reducing street cleaning.[45]

Finally, in Chicago, Mayor Rahm Emanuel is moving to close 11 percent of the city's elementary schools, possibly the largest number of schools closed at one time, to reduce a yawning $1 billion budget deficit—further straining his relationship with the city's teachers' union.[46] This move comes in light of the fact that a new state law mandates that, starting in 2015, the city must contribute more to its $19 billion pension liability. That will likely mean an increase of $550 million in its annual required contribution in the first year the law takes effect (Figure 8.4). And, on top of the increased pension cost, the city comptroller reports that the Windy City's subsides for retiree healthcare are projected to increase from $109 million today to $500 million over the next decade—this is largely thanks to an increasing number of retirees and healthcare costs.[47] These budget woes formed the backdrop of the strike called in the fall of 2012 by the Chicago

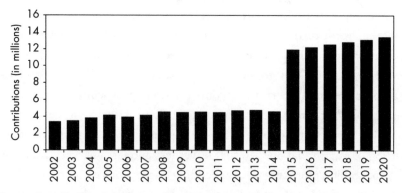

Figure 8.4 Chicago Pension Contribution (Historical and Projected).

Source: City of Chicago, Annual Financial Analysis, 2012.

Teachers Union. All told, these costs create a steep fiscal cliff for the city, forcing it to take dramatic action, including school closings, in response.

As these examples and others attest, states and cities are likely going to have to take more dramatic steps to get their fiscal affairs on a sustainable path. Otherwise, citizens will be receiving fewer and shoddier services at the same or even greater cost.

PUBLIC SECTOR UNIONS AND CROWDING OUT

How do public sector unions affect this situation? In three ways: One is by increasing the generosity of the benefit plans. Another is that in some jurisdictions, government unions have pushed to increase the total number of workers on the public payroll, which costs government more. And lastly, by fighting against any effort to reduce pensions (usually for future workers) or heath benefits (sometimes for those currently employed), they raise the political costs of taking action and limit reform options. In some places these three effects are combined.

It is a basic fact that public employee unions have a powerful incentive to push for larger budgets insofar as parts of that budget are allocated to improving working conditions for their members (salaries, benefits, and costly work rules). As we have seen, this is one reason that states with strong government unions tend to have higher debt.[48] Yet, there is a trade-off unions must make between hiring more workers and compensating them as much as possible. That is, for any state or local budget, when there are fewer public workers, that means that those on the job can be paid more. This gives unions an incentive to limit the labor supply and rein in hiring. Yet, employing more workers means more union members and more workers paying union dues, which translates into more power for the union. Under such conditions a union can argue that it needs more members and money to push for higher wages.

How this trade-off is managed in practice has not been intensively studied, and one can imagine a variety of union strategies for dealing with it. It seems likely that in most cases the union leadership will face the greatest and most immediate pressure from existing members to raise compensation and the organizational imperatives of the union itself will take a back seat. However, union leaders are frequently re-elected by large margins of a modest percentage of members in a bargaining unit, which gives them substantial autonomy in crafting strategy. So even though the benefits to existing members of hiring more workers are not immediately and tangibly apparent to workers the way that salary increases are, the leadership may have the opportunity and motive to prioritize them.

Partly due to the fact that we just don't know that much about how this trade-off is managed in practice, the existing studies of public sector unions' effect on government employment levels have not yielded a consensus. Some find that unions increase government employment. Others, however, show that they have no impact and total government employment as a percentage of the population has remained stable. So even if unions manage to expand segments of the public workforce, they simultaneously cause a contraction in employment in nonunionized sectors. And still others find that they reduce the number of government jobs.[49] Most recently, Sarah Anzia and Terry Moe found that unionization of municipal fire and police departments in the 1970s and 1980s led to increases in both firefighter and police compensation and per capita fire (7.6 percent) and police (2.3 percent) protection. Both staffing levels and payroll went up when these groups unionized.

When it comes to the politics of public employee benefit reforms, however, the picture is clear. Public sector unions are the leading forces of opposition to any change that might reduce the generosity of existing plans. As political alignments form over these issues, the unions' stand has been remarkably consistent and predictable: make every effort to block reform. Of course, that doesn't always mean the unions win. In Wisconsin, Governor Scott Walker forced public employees to make greater contributions to their pension and healthcare plans. The unions agreed with this part of his "budget repair bill," insofar as they were even more concerned about staving off restrictions to collective bargaining. In New York, Governor Andrew Cuomo forced the Empire State's unions to accept a new pension scheme for new employees, which is less generous to new hires. And over the intense opposition of the New Jersey Education Association, Governor Chris Christie got the legislature to pass a measure increasing teachers' contributions to their healthcare plans. However, in states like Illinois and California, the unions have been surprisingly effective at either blocking benefit reforms entirely or watering them down significantly.

THE CONSEQUENCES FOR GOVERNING AND PUBLIC TRUST

A great deal is known about the behavior of policymakers when the size of the budget pie is growing. Indeed, we have had much time to observe them, as it has taken decades of sustained effort to build activist government. However, less is known about what they will do when the pie isn't getting any bigger—or when big slices of it have already been served. As political scientist Paul Pierson observed, we shouldn't expect the politics of retrenchment to mirror the politics of government expansion.[50] Trying to reduce expenditures, especially on programs funded by formulas, is particularly difficult, and the reordering of government priorities is painful. Sacrificing a huge swath of state and local government spending on education, health, and poor relief to pay for the benefits of a vastly smaller slice of people that worked for government is hardly a wise allocation of scarce resources. Yet, in many cases these programs are on autopilot and the hands of politicians are tied, and if they do start to tinker they risk raising the ire of public sector unions.

Historically, budgeting at all levels of American government received little attention from the press. It was a low-key horse-trading affair that occurred in the relative obscurity of legislative committees. Yet the growth of pension and health liabilities has made budget battles front-page news. The paradox is that media attention has increased at the moment when policymakers' margin of maneuver has shrunk. Activist government has narrowed the scope of budget decision making. Consequently, the tenor of the public debate about budgets has also changed. Referring to the national budget, political scientist Eric Patashnik has spoken of the "fiscalization of the policy debate," wherein "programs are no longer debated on their merits but rather on their impact on the budget."[51] When one is debating the details of policy, as was the case in the past, many things hinge on details that can be negotiated pragmatically among experts. On the other hand, a fiscalized debate expands the boundaries of discussion and raises the stakes to a debate over the appropriate size and role of government. Hence, budget battles are now more intense and may well abet partisan polarization.

For politicians, managing crowding out is likely to be an exercise in what Kent Weaver has called "blame avoidance" rather than credit claiming.[52] Hitherto, politicians touted how they "brought home the bacon":

securing new programs and benefits for their constituents. Now they try not to be seen as taking anything away—just look at how much recent business in the US Senate is conducted after midnight. Politicians are reluctant, to say the least, to be seen as cutting popular benefits, especially from deserving groups. Under conditions of austerity budgeting, then, politicians are inclined to obscure causal chains in their behavior that lead to unpopular actions. This can involve using obscure parliamentary procedures and abstract rhetoric—especially when politicians are trying to raise income and sales taxes. Finally, some states and cities will resort to the sort of fiscal gimmickry that has plagued Illinois and New Jersey. Unable to raise revenue, politicians will be tempted to borrow more by doing things like issuing pension bonds. Indeed, states and cities over the last 25 years have racked up a bill of $60 billion bonding pensions.

All of these tactics are meant to cover policymakers' tracks and make it more difficult for average citizens to divine what is going on. This is hardly a recipe for encouraging a healthy public debate about the alternatives facing various levels of American government. Nor is it a means for winning citizens' trust to undertake the tough decisions that the country faces, decisions that will affect all of us in small ways and some of us in acutely painful ones. For instance, state and local pension plans cover 15 million government workers (11 percent of the national workforce) and provide benefits to 8 million retirees. Changing these plans will have significant economic effects on every state, city, and town in the nation. And because many state pension commitments are constitutionally protected, there is no easy way out of this financial sinkhole. Yet, a recent court decision in Detroit indicates that pension obligations may not have to be fulfilled if city governments declare bankruptcy.

The new politics of retirement benefits are also driven by significant political asymmetries in mobilization and attention to the issues. Public employee unions are engaged and vigilant about protecting state and local workers' salaries, pensions, and healthcare benefits, while the consumers of public services are largely disorganized. This is because pension and health benefits provide concentrated and direct benefits to public workers, which in fact are their livelihood, while imposing diffuse and mostly indirect costs on taxpayers. Thus, trying to reduce the share of the pie these compensation costs are consuming is an uphill battle. In sum, particular characteristics of these programs provide powerful incentives for the mobilization of retrenchment opponents.

However, all is not lost. We have some examples of politicians defying many of the incentives and expectations of the current fiscal and political landscape. The most prominent example is Rhode Island State Treasurer Gina Raimondo, who engineered a major reform of her state's failing pension system, which was only 48 percent funded in 2010 (75 percent funded is seen as the minimum threshold for a healthy fund). (What sparked her interest in the state's pension problem was the crowding-out effect, whereby pension costs were forcing cuts in Providence's library hours and bus services.)[53] After launching a "Truth in Numbers" campaign, where she focused on the math rather than the politics to raise public awareness of the problem, she brokered a deal with Democrats in the legislature who were allied with the state's public employee unions. The Rhode Island Retirement Security Act (RIRSA) was enacted by the state legislature in the fall of 2012, with bipartisan support in both chambers. Raimondo's example provides hope that it is possible to achieve significant reform by being frank with key stakeholders and the American public.

While clearly not undertaken in the conciliatory mode of Raimondo, Wisconsin Governor Scott Walker's signature piece of legislation, Act 10 of 2011, has averted, at least in the near term, the huge escalation of pension and healthcare costs for the Milwaukee Public School System. Act 10 removed healthcare as a subject of collective bargaining, forced public employees to contribute more toward their pensions, and encouraged the teachers' union to offer more affordable health insurance plans than the one controlled by the union itself. It sparked massive resistance in the form of huge protests, lawsuits that reached the state supreme court, and recall elections of the governor and a host of state legislators. Yet, without Act 10, teacher retirement costs per student in Milwaukee would have reached $3,500 by 2020. With Act 10 in place, those costs will be held constant at about $2,000 per student from now until 2020. Walker's actions demonstrate that determined politicians, who are willing to spend lots of political capital, can bring these costs under control.

Ultimately, the state and local budget crunch is likely to impinge significantly on the extent and quality of the important services government provides. We'll be spending more and receiving less: the paradox of big government that does few tangible things. And public sector unions make it even harder to get out of the straitjacket government has gotten itself into.

SHELTER FROM THE STORM

I think that the teachers' productivity can be measured very easily. It is—what we do is affect the productivity of everybody else in society, the computer people and the lawyers and the doctors and the engineers. I think teachers in our society have been very productive. The fact that we are the wealthiest nation on earth, the fact that we have moved so quickly, I think if teachers hadn't done their job, the rest of that productivity wouldn't be there. I don't know how else one would measure a teacher's productivity.

—Albert Shanker, UFT President[1]

I need some of my management rights back.

—James Tilton, California Department of Corrections[2]

Ever since Thomas Jefferson and Alexander Hamilton squared off in President George Washington's cabinet, the size of government has been a central ideological debate in American politics. Since the New Deal, American liberals have preferred a larger and more active government, while conservatives have called for a smaller government that does less. Often lost in the fray is appreciation of government flexibility. A big but flexible government could experiment with many policies until it found ones that worked. A small flexible government could rely on private organizations and still get a lot done. However, government becomes less flexible as public sector unions negotiate work rules and lobby for laws, ordinances, and regulations that protect workers at the expense of innovation. Government becomes more rigid and ossified. Experiments that might yield improvements are squelched. Inefficiencies persist. Bureaucratic routines triumph.

Anyone who has ever visited government offices knows that they are often shabby places lacking the spit and polish of corporate America. In many, the lighting is bad, the furniture dated, and the equipment antiquated. Public employees often complain that they are treated like automatons rather than professionals. The prevailing spirit of heavy regulation in government employment can sap workers' energy, undermine pride in a job well done, and reduce initiative.[3] Yet, whatever the condition of the physical plant and the rules under which public employees toil, government employment is a safe harbor compared to the private sector, where cutthroat competition, regular performance evaluations, and managerial discretion predominate. In some ways, public employees trade plusher offices, autonomy, and flexibility for security, regularity, and predictability. Add unionization, and this security, regularity, and predictability is a given. This chapter explores how public employee unions affect government efficiency, responsiveness, and the services the public receives.

The security and consistency of government employment can be seen in the aggregate in a few statistics. Take unemployment rates. In the private sector they swing significantly based on economic conditions. When the economy is doing well, unemployment rates fall; during recessions, they rise quickly. Unemployment tends to be rarer in the public sector and layoffs less frequent, especially during downturns.[4] And what are often described as public sector "layoffs" are really failures to hire people for positions vacated through attrition or early retirement.[5] Furthermore, the rates at which people voluntarily leave their jobs in the private sector (called "quit rates") are far higher than in the public sector. Finally, if one inspects the rules constraining managers in the public sector, they will find that it is much harder for managers to treat their employees capriciously. The steps required to hire, fire, promote, demote, transfer, or discipline workers are far more numerous in government than in business. In short, company managers wield a lot more discretion. While the security and consistency of public employment may have some advantages for government workers, the efficiency and quality of the services received by the public suffer as a result.

Optimists imagine that amicable negotiations between public employees and agency mangers will produce favorable outcomes all around: effective and efficient governmental organization, well-served citizens, and pleased taxpayers. However, the likelihood of scoring such a trifecta is, in reality, very low.

Collective bargaining in government is actually structured to produce less-than-optimal organizational outcomes. This is not because union leaders or administrators proceed in bad faith or are bad people (notwithstanding the "antiworker" label unions attach to critics of the collective bargaining process). Rather, it's due to the structure of incentives created by the adversarial nature of collective bargaining. Union leaders must put their members' interests first. If they don't do that, they will face an electoral challenge within the union. And contrary to the polemics of some conservatives who label the workers "good" but their union bosses "bad," many union leaders share the preferences of the rank and file, especially when it comes to bread-and-butter issues.

Therefore, even if elected officials and agency managers were to push back against the unions, any deal reached will favor public workers over sound governmental organization. In the real world, public officials are unlikely to push very far. In part, this is because they struggle to envision alternatives to the status quo, especially when the policies at issue are detailed and complex. Also, some elected officials are beholden to the unions for their election. Others may have been union members at one time—and therefore sympathetic to the union's position. With at least a few elected officials allied with the union, the government as a whole cannot be counted on to push back against the unions' demands with all its force. This is a key difference from private sector collective bargaining, where management has many incentives to present a united front. Consequently, collective bargaining in government skews outcomes in favor of public employees over those of nonunion citizens. One side of the bargaining table is allied with some members on the other, which tends to undermine the delivery of public services.

Government becomes like Gulliver in Lilliput: tied down by thousands of rules lobbied for and negotiated by public sector unions. Ultimately, the public's interest in an efficient, adaptable, and affordable government is ignored. The progressive hope of using government as a problem-solving tool is dashed.

TWO WORLDS OF WORK

The activities of public sector unions over the past 30 years have helped create what policy scholar John Donahue calls the "two worlds of work": the one that exists in the private sector and the other that endures in the public sector. In the former, competition is intense. In the latter, stability and regularity predominate. As Donahue puts it, "A gap [has] opened between the worlds of work in government and the rest of the U.S. economy."[6] The government's world is much less responsive, flexible, and efficient than it might otherwise be. This is the consequence of many factors; some are accidental, others not. One contributing factor is public employee unions' negotiation of work rules that greatly restrict managerial discretion and innovation.

However, it must be said at the outset that public sector unions do not cause many of the differences between the public and private sector work. Indeed, the locus of most of the changes separating the two sectors is the private economy. And many of the reasons government work is slow to change have to do with the peculiar nature of government as an employer. Many of the restrictions imposed on government derive, ultimately, from citizens' demands: demands channeled through elections, legislatures, interest groups, and courts. Nonetheless, public sector unions are not off the hook. Since the 1970s, they have consistently composed the camp resisting organizational enhancements embraced by the private sector, blocking efforts to privatize and streamline services, and seeking to make government more rule bound and risk averse.

In large measure, public employment is distinct because of the radical changes that have occurred in the private sector. The economy has become more global, more competitive, more diverse, and more technologically sophisticated since the 1970s. Today, people with talent and ambition—to say nothing of good luck—can make out fantastically well. People without those traits are often just trying to keep their heads above water. Risk is high. New opportunities abound. Private sector unions have largely disappeared. Economic inequality has increased. A winner-take-all ethos predominates.[7]

Little of this portrait applies to the public sector. If the capitalist economy is as Joseph Schumpeter described it, a "perennial gale of creative destruction," government remains an island of routinized stability.[8] Government work continues to resemble the economy of the post–World War II period. Salary disparities between the top and bottom of the workforce are smaller. Workers retain significant job protections. Unions are powerful. Layoffs are rare. Retirements come early. Governments never go out of business. The fact that government work has changed so little in its productive capacity isolates it from the storms ravaging the private sector.[9] When consumers can perform so many transactions in seconds, they struggle to understand why public services often take so long. Questions abound: Why does government still rely on paper rather than digital records? Why are government forms and websites so poorly designed and hard to use? Why are there so many rigid rules?

One of the major differences between public and private employment is the degree of managerial discretion. In the private sector, most workers are "at will" employees, meaning that they can be legally dismissed without cause. Managers have nearly full authority to hire, promote, fire, transfer, discipline, and reassign workers. Such flexibility is necessary to adjust to shifts in demand for companies' products and services, as well as the talents and abilities of their workers. In government, however, managers lack such flexibility. As former Indianapolis mayor Stephen Goldsmith has remarked, government's mentality is "the only way to prevent abuse of discretion is to prevent discretion."[10] The thrust of work rules is to replace a large share of management's functions by specifying detailed procedures in advance. Whether they are prison wardens, fire chiefs, or school principals, many of their staffing decisions are shaped by civil service laws and work rules that are negotiated in collective bargaining. Promotions and salary increases take place on rigid schedules that are not determined by performance but by time on the job (seniority) and levels of education (degrees). The pace of advancement for all workers—high and low performers alike—is roughly the same. And that pace, especially for high performers, is slow.

With poor prospects in the rough-and-tumble competition of the private sector, government work is increasingly desirable for those with limited skills. Conversely, the wage compression imposed by unions and civil service rules make government employment less attractive to those whose abilities are in high demand. Consequently, some analysts point to a "brain drain" at the top end of the government workforce, as many of the country's most talented people opt for jobs in the private sector where they can be richly rewarded for their skills and bypass the intricate work rules and glacial advancement through big bureaucracies inherent in government work. Private firms, on the other hand, obsess over cultivating and nurturing top talent.[11] Public policy scholar Paul Light also argues that government employment "caters more to the security-craver than the risk-taker."[12] And because government employs more of the former and fewer of the latter, it is less flexible, less responsive, and less innovative. And, as we have seen, it is also more expensive.

Insofar as government collective bargaining agreements touch on a wide range of decisions, public sector unions have extraordinary influence over the way government work gets done. In one case over what is negotiable, the Maryland Court of Appeals described the situation as follows: "virtually every managerial decision in some way relates to 'salaries, wages, hours, and other working conditions,' and is therefore negotiable."[13] Even collective bargaining over something as basic as wages touches on public policy broadly speaking, insofar as it has implications for the allocation of scarce public resources. When management pushes back on the scope of bargainable matters, the result is often litigation over the definition of that scope. The adversarial conversation over what labor and management will even include in their discussion reduces the possibility of collaboration and, in turn, productivity.[14] Such a legalized environment paralyzes public agencies and renders them unable to act decisively.[15]

Over the long term, negotiated work rules can drive public policy in directions that neither elected officials nor voters desire. In an investigative series on the Long Island Railroad, the *New York Times* discovered that "union contracts inflate operating costs through arcane work rules … which pad employee paychecks, boosting pension and disability payments in turn."[16] Once enacted, these policies can prove very hard to reverse, even through elections. A new mayor or governor—no matter how hard-charging a reformer—will often find his or her hands tied by the agreements unions managed to extract from his or her predecessors. For example, when then New York governor George Pataki and Albany lawmakers appointed a special authority to handle the distressed finances of Nassau County, Long Island, even that authority couldn't alter union

contracts. In a decade under its watch, generous new contracts were negotiated with six-figure salaries for police officers and "strange perks" such as
"paid time off for giving blood."[17]

PRODUCTIVITY AND GOVERNMENT

Productivity is all about inputs and outputs. It includes efficiency (produc-
ing the most possible outputs using the least resources) and effectiveness
(the output's quantity and quality). Yet, measuring the "productivity" of
government is no easy task.[18] Entire academic journals are devoted to the
subject.[19] Many government functions do not lend themselves to precise
measurements. There is no standard unit of measurement. For business
firms in a competitive marketplace, a fungible unit that all actors seek to
maximize measures the "bottom line": money. Hence, economists have
a common metric by which to measure private sector performance and
efficiency.

In government, public agencies are trying to realize many different
goals. We want sanitation workers to pick up the trash, but we also want
government to hire workers that reflect the population demographically, to shield them from risk of injury, and many other things. Some
agencies have ambiguous goals, such as "educate children," "prevent
crime," or "punish criminals." Are corrections officers doing a good
job? It's hard to say. It depends on what you think they are supposed
to be doing. Should they be punishing criminals, rehabilitating them,
or some amalgam? And still others have goals that are in dispute. For
instance, what does it mean to say that schools should educate children
if we can't agree on what constitutes a good education? Should things
like "emotional intelligence" count as much or nearly as much as read-
ing, writing, and arithmetic? It's hard to keep score when one isn't sure
what counts as a point.

Furthermore, government managers are powerfully limited by what
they can do to improve the efficacy of the larger organization. There is a
huge list of environmental, organizational, and personal factors that can
make realizing efficiency gains in the public sector much harder than in
the private sector—among which worker unionization is only one.[20] Such
things include a lack of market pressures, the influence of politics, a focus
on outputs more than outcomes, "spend it or lose it" budgets, and excessive

layers of middle management.[21] As political scientist James Q. Wilson noted, government managers lack "control over revenues, productive factors, and agency goals," all of which are "vested to an important degree in entities external to the organization—legislatures, courts, politicians, and interest groups."[22] Consequently, agency managers must pay constant heed to those outside entities rather than to the tasks of their organization. The effect of unionization is only to exacerbate these contextual constraints, adding one more outside entity managers must worry about: unions and their leaders.

Three major problems afflicting government work are accountability, equity, and fiscal integrity.[23] Regarding the first, it is difficult to get government bureaucracies to serve singular goals, as they contain many competing interests. Government cares about more than time spent and money collected. It values many outputs, including securing the support of various interest groups. Responsibility is more diffuse in the public sector. So cost overruns and unexpected problems don't usually cost civil servants their jobs. The poor performance of bureaucracies has rarely cost smart politicians their offices. Indeed, they can often spin such performance to their electoral advantage. Cutting red tape and improving how government works are perennial campaign themes because they are perennial problems. So while agency managers are constrained by groups, neither they nor anyone else is likely to be held accountable with authority so diffusely allocated.

The second problem is that government needs to treat all citizens fairly when delivering goods and services. This requires government to spell out clear rules in advance. These rules are designed to reduce the discretion that government service providers might exercise to the detriment of some citizens. The aim is to prevent favoritism and discrimination. For rules to be universally applied, they must be detailed enough to eliminate the need for individual judgment in particular cases. Red tape ensues.

It is the democratic desire for equity that very often compromises efficiency. Political scientist Herbert Kaufman once asked where red tape came from. His answer: us.[24] Consequently, the desire for fairness, when inscribed in law, forces government agencies to centralize decision making, to ignore cost–benefit calculations, to constrain human energy and judgment, and to shy away from straightforward procedures. Process trumps productivity.

The third issue is that to prevent government corruption, agencies require detailed proposals from contractors with whom they do business so that everything is recorded, and jobs must be given to the lowest bidder irrespective of that bidder's reputation. In the private sector, companies can contract with firms with whom they have good experience. They can begin work without complete plans and adjust matters with their suppliers as the project proceeds. Of course, if things go wrong in the private sector, companies suffer a financial loss and managers can be fired. In government, misuse of the public's money undermines trust in government—yet rarely is anyone fired for cost overruns.

So when thinking about productivity and efficiency in government, we need to take a more capacious view of the valued inputs and outputs, as they go well beyond the time and money it takes to deliver a good or service. If those two inputs were the only considerations, the private sector would almost always be more efficient. Yet, even if projects take longer and cost more to complete, a bureaucracy that is responsive, deliberate, and equitable might be considered reasonably efficient relative to people's expectations of the public sector.

Bearing all that in mind, however, not every constraint on public agencies makes sense, and not every agency responds to the reasonable demands of worthy external constituencies. Excessively rigid rules may be a response to the unreasonable demands of unworthy groups. This is, in part, why eliminating red tape is a constant campaign theme. It is why President Bill Clinton campaigned on a platform to "reinvent" government by streamlining the federal bureaucracy. President Barack Obama has promised similar things through "regulatory review." Governors across the country say they will do the same. The trouble is that one man's parasitical interest group is another's noble cause. Some people view public employee unions as salutary forces protecting government workers from capricious managers. Others see them as feathering their members' nests and wasting the public's time and money. The reality is both—and more.

Government Unions and Productivity

Public employee unions place constraints on public agencies through collective bargaining and their lobbying activities. To protect workers, they must constrain management.[25] To constrain management, they must get more rules on the books. More rules increase the routinization of work and make public agencies less nimble. Rules can come in the form of laws and ordinances passed by state legislatures and city councils or they can be negotiated into collective bargaining agreements. Nonetheless, it is theoretically possible that while unions increase government's costs per worker (see chapter 7), that cost is offset by an increase in productivity. Indeed, some studies of the private sector show that unions increase the productivity of workers on the job.[26]

The number of academic studies on the relationship between unionization and productivity in government is, however, small. And there is not a scholarly consensus on many of the issues involved. Yet, basic economic theory says that when there is little competition and vague performance metrics in the provision of a good or service, worker productivity will decline. One can also look at the effect of union work rules on industries that, like government, face little competition. The data on such industries suggest that union work rules can substantially reduce efficiency. Economist James A. Schmitz estimated that when there was limited competition in the iron ore industry, output per worker fell by roughly 50 percent.[27] After analyzing studies of both the public and private sector, economist Barry Hirsch concluded that positive effects of unionization on productivity "are largely restricted to the private, for-profit sectors. Notably absent are positive productivity effects for school construction, public libraries, government bureaus, schools, and law enforcement."[28] In sum, there appears to be a difference between the productivity gains unions can achieve in the private sector, which can offset the costs they impose on employers, and their inability to do so in the public sector.[29]

That unionization decreases productivity in the public sector could be the fault of individual unions. However, that is unlikely. It is more probable that the nature of public work is different, and unions only exacerbate the things that make government less productive. Given that public employment is already more rule bound, and the objectives of public agencies are multiple and complex, there are more opportunities for shirking in government work. Once again we see that unions in the public and private sectors have different effects.

Private sector firms usually have a clearly defined "chain of command." In public sector agencies, however, there are many breaks in that chain.

For instance, workers are allowed to go outside the chain of command and report actions of their supervisors to union stewards, who can then complain to the supervisor's boss or file a formal grievance. A worker who had been politely asked to adjust his nameplate reported his New York City Parks Department supervisor to the union grievance officer. The worker alleged harassment (even though the supervisor reportedly asked nicely) and further complained that the supervisor's appearance at the jobsite constituted an "inappropriate unannounced visit" under the contract's work rules.[30] The ensuing "grievance" procedure took up a good deal of the supervisor's time.

Finally, in California's prison system, the prison guards' 1999–2001 contract, agreed to by then governor Gray Davis, stipulated that 70 percent of prison positions would be doled out on the basis of seniority—irrespective of whether officers' skills matched particular jobs.[31] Prison managers simply cannot assign the most effective guards where they are most needed. In short, contracts and civil service laws make workers more autonomous from management.

Not only is management constricted by union contracts from assigning work consonant with workers' skills, but also they face the prospect of difficult personnel matters. If managers try to change working conditions without following procedures spelled out in contracts in even minor ways, the unions can and probably will file grievances. This creates more work for administrators and freezes even minor policy changes in their tracks. It also means management cannot make changes without full worker support, which may sound like a good thing but renders the notion of management virtually meaningless. Many managers complain that they do not undertake many worthwhile initiatives because they fear they will be drowned in a tsunami of grievance procedures.

Furthermore, contract stipulations make it difficult for managers to monitor and sanction workers who are protected by an array of contractual rights. Many union leaders complain about the aggressiveness of managers. However, such claims may also overlook high levels of misconduct or disobedience among workers. These processes can become very adversarial, as the union provides workers free legal counsel. Many unions have negotiated contract stipulations that allow or require a union representative to be present when an employee is being hired, investigated, disciplined, or fired. During investigations of misconduct, such procedures can reduce how forthcoming witnesses are likely to be. It is these kinds of provisions that protected the California corrections officers at Corcoran prison who allegedly organized "gladiator days"—orchestrated fights among rival inmate gangs for officers to watch and bet on.[32] At every turn, investigators claimed that union officials stymied their inquiry into instances of misconduct. Before and during the trials of a few officers, the union ran television and radio ads saying that the officers' jobs were extremely dangerous and the inmates were violent predators. None of the eight officers tried was convicted of wrongdoing.[33]

Ultimately, many public agencies, which lack extensive bureaucratic capacity, simply cannot compete with the unions and their extensive resources. The unions have lawyers and staff at the ready to assist members in cases of misconduct. On the other side, the government often has weak investigative abilities. The legal staff is overextended. Managers must deal with grievance procedures and still carry out their regular duties.

Productivity and Strikes

The most serious constraint on productivity an organization can face is when workers won't work at all or won't work to their full capacity. Unions are instrumental in organizing such collective actions. Like their private sector counterparts, many public employee unions have sought to induce change through a series of semilegal "job actions." These are often referred to as "slow downs" and coordinated "sick outs" and "working to code," which means following the rule book to the letter, causing major delays in the delivery of public services. The most spectacular of these tactics is the strike, when workers walk off the job. Strikes can have a huge negative effect on productivity, as a number of workdays are lost. Such stoppages not only hold the public hostage but also create big backlogs of work.

Take the 2012 Chicago teachers' strike. The Chicago Teachers Union (CTU) represents some 26,000 teachers. The teachers opposed efforts by Mayor Rahm Emanuel to lengthen the school day, enhance teacher evaluations, and hold the line on salary increases. Unable to come to a deal in the fall of 2012, 90 percent of CTU members voted to strike. (Illinois is one of the few states where public sector strikes are legal.) The two-week-long strike affected the third-largest school district in the country with some 350,000 students. Parents were forced to juggle schedules and pay for substitute childcare. Yet, whatever the costs to students and parents for lost days, the union got much of what it wanted. It won 17.6 percent pay raises over four years, the elimination of merit pay provisions, and a revised teacher evaluation formula that reduced the weight of student test scores.[34] In sum, the teachers got more money and job protections, and the students got a two-week vacation at the beginning of the school year. But at what cost to taxpayers and parents?

Even allies of organized labor have seen strikes in government as suspect, which explains why they are illegal in all but a few states. Viewing the state as the "supreme, absolute, and uncontrollable" sovereign as an employer, President Franklin Roosevelt argued that "a strike of public employees manifests nothing less than an intent on their part to obstruct the operations of government until their demands are satisfied. Such action looking toward the paralysis of government by those who have sworn to support it is unthinkable and intolerable."[35]

Many early opponents of public employee unionism rested their understanding on the *essentiality* of government services. As a matter of public duty, they argued, public services must not stop. And a conceptual matter, the people (i.e., the government) cannot strike against *the people*.[36] As long-time *New York Times* labor reporter A. H. Raskin put it: "The community cannot tolerate the notion that it is defenseless at the hands of organized workers to whom it has entrusted responsibility for essential services."[37] Such stoppages were not simply inefficient but morally suspect as well.

However, the Chicago strike is today something of an outlier. Public sector strikes were far more common in the 1960s and 1970s. Some strikes were used to pressure policymakers to grant workers collective bargaining rights, or they were employed to make sharp and steep early gains in pay, benefits, and working conditions—the purpose of the original organizing drives. Since the initial wave of strikes crested, however, there have been far fewer public sector strikes. Partly this is because they are illegal in most places. Yet, there have been a few big strikes that have made headlines. The 2005 pre-Christmas illegal strike by the Transportation Workers Union Local 100, which operates the subways and buses in New York City, nearly bankrupted the union with fines and legal fees.[38] (Of course, it also cost the city millions in lost economic activity.)

Some analysts trace the decline of strikes in both the public and private sectors to the most famous public sector strike in American history: the federal air traffic controllers' standoff with President Ronald Reagan.[39] After failing to make much headway on issues important to the union by the end of the 1970s, the Professional Air Traffic Controllers Organization (PATCO) was extremely militant. Salaries had not kept pace with inflation, since the Carter administration had held down federal salaries to fight stagflation. As the sole representative of workers providing a vital service over which the government held a monopoly, PATCO believed it had the leverage to get a better deal—irrespective of economic conditions. This conviction led to disaster. Even after winning a better contract from the Carter administration than other federal workers received, PATCO militants staged a palace coup that dethroned the union's moderate president in favor of a less experienced but more assertive leader.

The problem was that PATCO's demands—which included wage increases and a shorter workweek—went well into "nonnegotiable" territory under federal law. Yet the union clung to the idea that a serious strike threat would cow the Reagan administration. Although strikes by federal workers were illegal, PATCO leaders regularly reminded Federal Aviation Administration (FAA) officials in early 1981 that "the only illegal strike is an unsuccessful strike." Surprisingly, the Reagan administration went a long way toward meeting the union's demands, in part because it feared that a strike would cost the economy $150 million per day. "Never before had the government offered so much in a negotiation with a federal employees' union," historian Joseph McCartin claims. But PATCO ignored several warning signs—including pleas to desist from the American Federation of Labor–Congress of Industrial Organizations (AFL-CIO) and Democratic Speaker of the House Tip O'Neill—ultimately rejecting the administration's offer and calling a strike anyway.

Reagan reacted adamantly. In a White House meeting, he said, "Dammit, the law is the law and the law says they cannot strike." He then issued an ultimatum that all controllers who did not return to work within 48 hours would be fired and replaced. The FAA swung into action, putting supervisors, most of whom had once been controllers, back to work and calling in controllers from the military. The nation's airline system struggled for the next few years as new controllers were trained and hired. In a departure from past labor conflicts in the federal government, however,

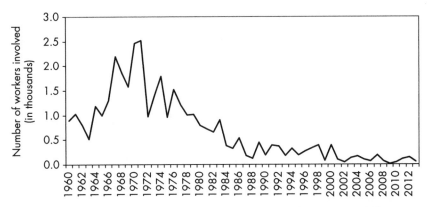

Figure 9.1 Work Stoppages Involving 1,000 or More Workers, 1960–2013.

Source: Bureau of Labor Statistics.

the FAA never rehired most of the fired PATCO strikers. Breaking the PATCO strike forged a lasting image of Reagan's toughness as a leader—an image that Governor Scott Walker invoked in his pursuit of collective bargaining changes in Wisconsin law.

Reagan's legitimization of employers' "fire and replace" response to strikes blunted unions' most powerful weapon in industrial relations. Because the entire nation witnessed Reagan's decision, McCartin argues, it encouraged business managers to see the tactic as justifiable. And once "remember PATCO" became a widespread warning, it became more difficult for unions to mobilize their members for strikes. Indeed, since the 1980s, strikes in the public and private sectors have declined dramatically (Figure 9.1). In 2009, there were only five major work stoppages, involving a mere 13,000 workers, according to the Bureau of Labor Statistics. While once a serious problem for government efficiency, the strike is no longer a major threat to public service. The ultimate symbol of organized labor's strength has been voided, for which unions in the private sector can reasonably blame PATCO and President Reagan.

Collective Bargaining and Schools

Popular press accounts of negotiations between teachers' unions and school districts often focus on salaries and benefits. These are, indeed, central elements of the negotiations. However, to a greater degree than other unionized public servants, teachers are inclined to believe that they can run schools as well as or better than school districts and principals.[40] Therefore, another big negotiation point is securing rules insulating their jobs from managerial discretion. Individual teachers often complain that they are kept busy filling out reports and preparing students for high-stakes tests. Many claim they are treated like interchangeable parts rather than professionals. However, in their collective action through unions, teachers consistently oppose any steps—such as vouchers, merit pay, open enroll-ment, charter schools, or stronger principals—that would give them more autonomy on the job. In short, teachers' unions regularly trade autonomy for security in contract negotiations.[41]

This helps explain why teachers' contracts run into the hundreds of pages. If the contract were all about wages and benefits, contracts would be about 10 pages long. The work rules that require such detail include such things as transfer prerogatives, requirements that principals give advance notice before observing classes, demands that student test scores not count in teachers' evaluations, extensive grievance procedures that must be followed before disciplining or firing a teacher, limits on the number of minutes teachers must spend each day with students, limits on the number and length of parent–teacher conferences, stipulations about accumulat-ing unused sick leave for cash payouts, limits on class size, and on and on.[42] By the end of a teacher contract, principals, the main managers in schools, have seen their authority greatly limited—yet they are still paid respect-able salaries and sometimes held accountable for school performance.[43] This is how collective bargaining has a big effect on how schools are orga-nized and run.

The rules negotiated tell the school district how to allocate its resources. This means that the district is not free to decide how to provide children the best possible education. If it wants to do that, its schools will need to be orga-nized accordingly—even if there is considerable dispute about what exactly the best possible education is. However, there is a big contradiction between optimal organizational arrangements and what actually exists today. The reason is that many features of school organization are designed to pro-tect teachers rather than to deliver the best possible education for students. Prioritizing the former over the latter greatly undercuts productivity.[44]

Policy analysts Katherine Strunk and Jason Grissom found that the more powerful teachers' unions are, especially in large cities, the more restrictive the work rules negotiated into contracts. These work rules reduced school boards' flexibility in amending policies. They found that "districts with stronger unions, measured by both board members' evaluations of union power and union support of board members in recent elections, allow school district administrators less flexibility than do contracts in districts with weaker, less active unions."[45] For many things teachers' unions strongly support—such as requiring state teaching licenses, extra pay for master's degrees, and teacher tenure—little evidence has been forthcoming that they increase teacher effectiveness in the classroom.[46]

Take salaries. However crass it is to say it, money is a motivator. Yet, given their duty to equally represent all teachers, unions have imposed rigid salary schedules. Only two things impact most teachers' salaries: length of service and additional education obtained. Salary schedules are a grid with "steps" representing seniority and "lanes" indicating degrees earned and additional educational credits.[47] A contract rule specifies where teachers start and how they advance on that grid to determine their salary. Teachers in the same school district are, then, compensated at the same level regardless of whether they are effective in the classroom and kids are learning anything. No amount of extra effort or outstanding classroom performance on the part of an individual teacher can change his or her salary.

The problem is that if a workplace does not reward talent, the talented will go elsewhere.[48] And the salary schedule makes it nearly impossible for principals to use financial incentives to punish or reward performance as nearly every private sector enterprise does. And while "merit pay" has been much discussed and implemented in a few places, the amounts offerable ($1,000 to $2,000) are usually too paltry to change behavior. Finally, considering what would most help students—having highly motivated teachers in the classroom with incentives to help them learn more—the teachers' salary schedule arrangement makes little sense.

And it's not just the work rules in union contracts that have a big impact on the organization and productivity of America's schools; so, too, does the number and quality of teachers. For the last half century, teachers' unions have pushed to increase the number of teachers and thereby reduce the student–teacher ratio. With help from many quarters, they have succeeded. In 2012, there were 3.27 million teachers, or 1 for every 15 students—down from a 22-to-1 ratio in 1970. On its face this change appears to be a good thing. It implies greater personal attention for each student. It would also seem to be an instance where teachers' interests in more manageable classrooms (to say nothing of less work grading student papers) and the interests of students converge.

Not so fast. This change has downsides too. First of all, to hire more teachers, school districts must hold down salaries. If fewer teachers had been hired, each teacher could have been paid more, or merit pay could have been offered to outstanding teachers. Hiring more teachers also meant fishing deeper in the teacher labor pool, where weaker performers are found. As education scholar Jay P. Greene has argued, as the number of teachers increased, quality quite possibly decreased. And insofar as hiring more teachers slowed the rise in salaries, talented people were unlikely to be drawn to teaching. It is possible, then, that students would have been better off with less personal attention, higher student–teacher ratios, and more talented teachers attracted by higher pay. Fewer teachers would have also placed less stress on budgets, given the long-term costs more teachers impose on pension and health benefits.[49]

Other things that teachers' unions negotiate into contracts are the number of sick and paid personal days a teacher can take each year. In many districts, teachers receive 10 sick days, two to three personal days, and three days for professional development (all with pay). Recall that teachers only work nine months a year. On average, teachers are absent 5 to 6 percent of all school days, which is nearly three times the rate of professional or managerial workers in the economy as a whole.[50] It is highly unlikely that such absenteeism is good for students, as substitutes are more likely to assign "busy work."

Then there are the contested issues of teacher evaluation, discipline, and dismissal. Many contracts contain detailed procedures that must be followed to the letter if a principal makes the tough decision to discipline or fire a poorly performing teacher. And the teachers' unions do not just rely on provisions in contracts for such procedural protections from management: they have also pushed in many states for detailed statutes that have the same effect. (Therefore, in some parts of the country these things are absent from contracts because they are already enshrined in state law.)

Furthermore, because many attempts to discipline or dismiss a teacher will be based on evaluations, the teachers' unions have consistently pushed for weakening evaluation standards. Indeed, until very recently, they have fought tooth and nail against efforts to craft more rigorous methods and use student test scores as part of teacher evaluations.[51] In

New York City, until 2013, teachers could only be rated on a binary scale (satisfactory or unsatisfactory) and over 95 percent were rated satisfactory.[52] In order to participate in President Obama's Race-to-the-Top program, however, New York State had to improve its evaluation system. After a bruising battle, New York City Mayor Bloomberg and his school's Chancellor Dennis Walcott failed to reach an agreement with the United Federation of Teachers (UFT) on a teacher evaluation system. The city's schools then had to stomach a $450 million midyear budget cut, which clearly wasn't good for students.[53] The issue is that UFT has every incentive to push for the maximum job protections for its members (i.e., to shield them from any negative consequences of more meaningful evaluations, which would include student test scores).[54] In the end, the state education commissioner had to step in and impose a new evaluation system—one very much along the lines of what the mayor proposed—to end the stalemate. And even then the degree to which student test scores will be used in teacher evaluations is very limited and not scheduled to begin until 2017.

Given how difficult it is in practice to evaluate, discipline, or fire a poorly performing teacher, most principals don't even try. They know that if they don't follow every procedural stipulation to the letter, the union-appointed lawyer defending the teacher will win on technicalities. These cases are almost never decided on the basis of whether or not the teacher is good or bad. In addition, the costs can be enormous. In California, 0.002 percent (which is to say effectively zero) of teachers are dismissed for performance-based reasons in a given year, compared to 1 percent of all public workers and 8 percent of private sector workers.[55] It cost the Los Angeles school district $3.5 million in legal fees and nearly a decade trying to dismiss seven teachers—four were ultimately dismissed but two of them received large payouts.[56] In Illinois, it costs an average of $219,000 to dismiss one teacher. According to the movie Waiting for "Superman," 1 out of every 57 doctors loses his or her license to practice medicine and 1 out of every 97 lawyers loses his or her license to practice law. But in America's big cities, only 1 out of 1,000 teachers is fired for performance-related reasons.[57]

Clearly, having poorly performing teachers in the classroom, even if they are only a small percentage of all teachers, is not good for children. Yet given the unions' duty to protect all members equally, they must protect poor performers as well. Here is another case where collective bargaining and unionization serve public employees' interests over the interests of students, parents, and the public, who all have an interest in better-educated young people.

This conclusion, while contestable, is borne out by solid social science research on the subject.[58] Two top-of-the-line studies, one by Caroline Hoxby and another by Terry Moe, find that collective bargaining has a negative impact on student performance—after controlling for a host of other factors. Hoxby's study looks at all school districts over time to see what difference it makes when districts start engaging in collective bargaining and teachers become unionized. She shows that these factors lead districts to increase total spending on schools, increase teacher salaries, and reduce student–teacher ratios. To put it bluntly, the unions get more of what they care about most, which is money and jobs. However, while unions increase inputs they care about, they decrease productivity, as outputs such as the student dropout rate get worse.[59]

Moe's study focuses on California and codes teacher union contracts based on the level of restrictiveness of their contracts. After controlling for a large number of factors, he finds that as teacher contracts become denser with rules, student achievement falls, especially for minority students.[60] Given the persistent gap in test scores between white and Asian students on one side and black and Latinos on the other, the effect of restrictive work rules further disadvantages some of America's most disadvantaged children. It appears that not only does collective bargaining and unionization affect productivity but it also tends to affect the least fortunate students. The taxpaying public is providing too many resources—or those resources are being directed to the wrong things—to achieve more efficient education production.[61]

There are many other studies of the effect of teacher collective bargaining on student performance. However, unlike those cited previously, which employ the most rigorous statistical methodology and have been published in top peer-reviewed journals, the other studies vary enormously in methodology, approach, and quality. Some reach opposing conclusions. Because we are dealing with an empirical social science question, the matter is unlikely to ever be fully settled. However, the fact that the best studies by the top scholars point in the same direction as common-sense analysis of the structure of the incentives inherent in collective bargaining is a powerful indication that unionization and collective bargaining negatively affect school productivity. This, in turn, has huge spillover effects, as the consequent loss of human capital depresses economic growth and society as a whole.

PRODUCTIVITY, DISCIPLINE,
AND THE PROTECTIVE SERVICES

Examining the effects of productivity on other areas of public service is difficult because fewer in-depth studies exist. However, whether one considers firefighters, police officers, or corrections officers, collective bargaining incentives remain similarly structured to those of teachers and school districts. Union representatives must prioritize the day-to-day occupational interests of their members at the bargaining table. They are prioritized over whether fires are put out or criminals caught. Of course, when public safety is at stake, government negotiators will push hard for a deal that will benefit the electorate. Yet the same potential for political influence across the bargaining table still exists for the unions. To illustrate this, it is useful to look at a few cases exposed by the press.

Over the past 35 years, the number of fires in the United States has fallen by more than 40 percent, while the number of career firefighters has increased by more than 40 percent.[62] When most people call the Los Angeles Fire Department, it is not to report a fire, but to request transportation of a sick person. In fact, only 2 percent of calls were for actual fires—and most were small ones confined to dumpsters, cars, and garbage cans. However, the department retains the workforce, fire trucks, ladders, hoses, and other equipment for fighting big fires—at a significant cost to the city.[63] Similarly, according to Nightline, it costs $3,500 every time a fire truck pulls out of a fire station in Washington, DC. And 25 calls in a 24-hour shift is not uncommon, so the cost to taxpayers is quite significant.[64]

Many of the calls to the fire department are false alarms. Twenty-five years ago false alarms were equal to just half the number of actual fires; today, false alarms significantly exceed the number of fires.[65] But union power and other factors have increased the amount of fire protection, and risk-averse citizens now believe there are fires or emergencies that require the attention of the fire department far more often.

If protecting citizens from actual fires were the only goal, then current arrangements would be a vast waste of money and manpower. Government could design ways to weed out the false alarms, transfer medical emergencies to hospitals, and reduce the need for fully staffed fire trucks to respond to certain situations. However, firefighters' unions have negotiated contract rules that require their constant presence, so these expensive and bloated arrangements are actually rational, in a sense. The inefficient allocation of resources occurs because fire departments respond to a powerful outside constituency that is demanding more work for its members, and more of them. Similar things happen in other agencies.

In New York State, Governor Andrew Cuomo sought to save $50 million by closing a juvenile detention center that was not being used. Although empty, the facility was staffed by a few dozen corrections officers. Therefore, the governor was stymied by a law that prevents closing a state facility with union employees without one year of advance notice. So the state just spent the $50 million to keep the facility open for another year.[66] While this was a drop in the bucket in the Empire State's $133 billion annual budget, it was money that only benefited unionized corrections officers at everyone else's expense. And such waste can pile up fast.

Or consider Florida's Police Benevolent Association (PBA) and Fraternal Order of Police. Until the mid-1990s, the two unions had supported Democrats. But a disagreement with Democratic Governor Lawton Chiles over a pension sweetener favored by the union led them to consider political alternatives. In 1994, the PBA backed Republican Jeb Bush in an unsuccessful bid to unseat Chiles. When Bush ran successfully for governor four years later, the PBA supported him again. The first bill that Governor Bush signed was the pension sweetener that Chiles had opposed.

The PBA had other objectives as well. One was protecting members from disciplinary action. The body responsible for policing the police was the Criminal Justice Standards and Training Commission, which the Florida legislature created in 1977. With their ally in office, the PBA sought to weaken the commission. Bush proved compliant and appointed Ernie George, the head of the PBA, to chair the commission's disciplinary panel. With George at the helm, more union representatives sat on the disciplinary panel, giving union officials more say over who else could sit on the panel. The panel limited the amount of negative evidence the commission could see, and even eliminated its ability to punish officers who lied under investigation. In a note to his membership in 2006, George summed up his accomplishments: "We were able to lobby the Legislature and pass major pieces of legislation other unions only dream about." According to data analyzed by the *Miami Herald-Tribune*, there has been a 20 percent decline in the number of officers who have lost their certification since 2000, compared with the 15 years prior.[67] Again, the interests of Florida's police union and the public interest conflicted. The union sought to protect it members. Yet protecting its members meant that more police officers who had been charged with serious misconduct could remain on the job without facing any penalties.[68]

The California Correctional Peace Officers Union (CCPOA) also shows how a union can capture a hugely important policy area with negative consequences for the common good. The union supported an explosion of prison construction in the 1980s and 1990s and then backed the state's notorious 1994 three-strikes law, which greatly inflated the state's prison population. Between 1980 and 2000, the population jumped from 25,000 inmates to 160,000. In 2008, there were 172,000 inmates plus another 30,000 in county jails. The Department of Corrections expanded its staff to deal with the system, becoming the largest in the state with 162,000 employees. The CCPOA also grew from 15,000 to 30,000 dues-paying members. Yet, by the beginning of the twenty-first century, California's prisons were badly overcrowded and unmanageable. Due to these conditions, a panel of judges concluded that one inmate a week was unnecessarily dying.[69]

In the midst of all this, the CCPOA won huge benefits for its members. Prison guards in California now earn twice as much in total compensation as prison guards in other states. Many critics have pointed out this pernicious cycle: the union supports tougher sentences for criminals and the construction of more prisons, the prison population grows, more guards are needed, the ranks of the union increase, its coffers swell, and those monies can in turn be used to pressure politicians for more tough sentences and prison construction. Such a massive investment in punitive incarceration is hardly efficient. And the CCPOA has made it nearly impossible to change the current state of affairs.

The work rules negotiated by the union have also hamstrung management, which cannot discipline guards without the union's approval. The CCPOA also reportedly uses its political influence to block the appointment of wardens who they deem anathema to their interests. In towns with prisons, district attorneys are reportedly afraid to prosecute corrections officers accused of violations for fear of their union—this even includes officers accused of staging "gladiator fights" among inmates. According to sociologist Joshua Page, "As [the CCPOA] grew and became a formidable political force, the union influenced the nature, purpose, and scope of imprisonment and associated functions in California.... [It] promoted particularly moralistic conceptions of law-breaking and tough penal policies, helped redefine penal expertise, and empowered actors that supported its interests and views on criminal punishment."[70] The CCPOA thus influences the design and implementation of state policies with harsh consequences for lawbreakers, public budgets, and even the rule of law.

Similar dynamics were at work in a sordid scandal at the Baltimore City Detention Center. By all accounts the inmates were running the jail. One gang leader sired four children with different female corrections officers. Drugs were trafficked in the center and a bustling money-laundering operation took place.[71] While all this was going on, the corrections officers union (an affiliate of the 30,000-member-strong American Federation of State, County and Municipal Employees [AFSCME]) lobbied the Maryland legislature for legislation that made it nearly impossible for prison managers to transfer, fire, or discipline officers.[72] Because the corrections officers make up nearly a quarter of all AFSCME members in Maryland, they are a potent political force. Bill sponsor Sen. Donald Munson (R-Hagerstown) said that he "looked at it, read it, and thought it was fair" but admitted that "much of the work was done by lobbyists for the corrections officers," since he "simply didn't have the time to put into it."[73] The Democratic legislature also complied with the union and Governor Martin O'Malley signed a bill that basically emasculated jail managers and prison wardens. The Corrections Officers Bill of Rights (COBR) effectively gave corruption in Maryland's correctional facilities legal protection.[74] Legal red tape produced a situation in which, according to the language of the federal indictment against the officers, "the prospect of actual punishment [is] very remote. Often suspected corrections officers were merely transferred to another facility in the immediate vicinity."[75] The union, of course, downplayed this point.[76]

This is an extreme case to be sure. The larger point is that the protections afforded to many public safety officers make it very hard to discipline or remove police officers, firefighters, and correction officers from duty. Summarizing the Baltimore jail case, *Washington Post* columnist Charles Lane notes that "Maryland's COBR ... give[s] corrections officers' unions extra influence over employee discipline, a process in which the unions have a special interest." And the law does this, he concludes, "in deference to union political power—and despite the public's interest in [a disciplinary] process that is as impartial as possible."[77] These are the sort of job protections from management that the vast majority of "at will" employees in the private sector can only dream of. Arguably, the effect of such protections is to attract a certain type of people to government in both management and rank-and-file roles. Few hard-charging executives want to head organizations where their freedom to innovate and improve matters is constrained by extensive red tape. On the other hand, many people looking for job security and orderly routines are drawn to public employment.

EFFICIENCY AND THE PUBLIC INTEREST

I've focused here on teachers, firefighters, and police officers because these occupations have long-established traditions of unionization and are well organized in almost all cities.

For instance, the Fraternal Order of Police, founded in 1915, has over 325,000 members organized in 2,100 local chapters. The International Association of Firefighters, founded in 1918, has 298,000 members in more than 3,200 locals. The American Federation of Teachers, founded in 1916, has 1.1 million members in around 600 locals. The National Education Association, the larger of the two main teachers' unions, has 2.3 million members and nearly 1,000 locals. The services provided by cops, firefighters, and teachers are also very hard to evaluate in terms of efficiency. Few agree on what a proper education looks like. Police officers and firefighters are only deemed "effective" once the criminal is caught, prosecuted, and imprisoned or the fire is put out and the children saved from smoke and flames. This is why it is so easy for unions to layer on rules that protect their members.

James Q. Wilson once remarked that "to evaluate the efficiency of a government agency one must first judge the value of the constraints under which it operates; to improve its efficiency one must decide which constraints one is willing to sacrifice."[78] Many have tried to do this by comparing whether a private firm delivers the good or service better than a public agency. In the many cases that scholars have studied, the private firms did the jobs more cheaply and more quickly.[79] These included trash collection, street cleaning, school bus operation, vehicle maintenance, and road repair. David Osborne and Ted Gaebler reviewed a series of studies and found that "on average public service delivery is 35 to 95 percent more expensive than contracting, even when the cost of administering the contracts in included."[80] Public agencies have also been made more efficient when they have had to compete with private providers for government work—an arrangement called managed competition.

Not all services can or should be privatized. Yet many can be. Public policy scholar John Donahue argues that "tasks that are well-defined, easy to monitor and available from competitive suppliers—call them 'commodity tasks'—are prime candidates for privatization. Tasks that are complex and mutable, lack clear benchmarks or are immune from competition—'custom tasks'—should be kept in-house."[81] Yet, such a rational allocation is less common than it should be. In Chicago, refuse collectors work on average five-and-a-half hours a day and make $70,000 a year. The garbage truck routes, worked out through union contracts and ward politics, are an amazing maze that wears down the trucks and wastes fuel and employees' time. Trash disposal in the Windy City costs $231 per ton compared to $129 in Los Angeles and $74 in Dallas.[82]

Many factors are at work, of course, but public employee unions are usually dead set against privatization of public services.[83] The staunchest opponent of privatization of prisons in California has been the CCPOA. Private prison management companies do not use union labor, they threaten the job security of prison guards, and they have the potential to undercut the political power of the union itself. The CCPOA is single-handedly responsible for the absence of private prisons in the Golden State.[84] Privatization of prisons has only gained traction in right-to-work states such as Florida, Tennessee, and Texas, which lack strong prison guard unions to oppose the private prison lobby. Of course, one's opinion of privatized penal institutions must factor in the reality of government directly empowering workers to use violence against people.

Union opposition to privatization means that government still does many "commodity tasks." Werner Z. Hirsch found that the lower a state's public unionization rate is, the more likely it is to contract out services.[85] Timothy Chandler and Peter Feuille examined 740 cities and found that when sanitation workers were unionized, cities were less likely to consider contracting out the service.[86] More recently, unions representing employees of liquor stores in Pennsylvania (which are state-run enterprises in the Keystone State) have opposed privatization of alcohol sales.[87] Again, we find public employee unions blocking change that favors more efficient and effective government.

Only in rare instances—such as during Stephen Goldsmith's celebrated mayorship of Indianapolis—have elected officials been able to persuade rather than force government workers' unions to accept managed competition or privatization schemes.[88] To make such arrangements work, the unions require protections for their workers so they will be transferred rather than fired, allotted sufficient time to prepare for competition with private providers, and treated with respect. In Indianapolis, the AFSCME eventually came to support managed competition and bid on jobs just like private firms. It came to see managed competition as an opportunity to challenge the argument that government is less efficient than the private sector and to possibly win back some government work that had already been privatized.[89] Yet, embracing managed competition required a big gamble on the part of the union leadership, which had to work hard to win member support. And the union only undertook this arduous task because Mayor Goldsmith promised to wage an even broader privatization campaign.

Ideally, innovative, flexible government would experiment through trial and error, but that process is blocked by the work rules imposed by unions through collective bargaining and sometimes through law. So government can't try things, discover that they don't work, and discard them. On the contrary, once something is tried and found to be congenial to workers and their union representatives, it is very difficult to change. Once public sector employees find a particular work rule, practice, or program beneficial to them, they use their power of union organization to defend it. Given the status quo bias of American political institutions, the lobbying power of public sector unions means that many programs, once begun, are nearly impossible to change or eliminate. And because old rules never seem to die, agency managers can't try out new things. "Today," Jonathan Rauch notes, "we expect that anything the government tries this year will still be with us fifty years from now."[90]

Furthermore, the political costs for legislators reduce their incentive to challenge the unions. Instead, it's popular to offer ever more employment conditions that government workers like, even if they reduce productivity even further. Trying to change unproductive work rules leads to trench warfare with the unions—politicians know they are unlikely to emerge unscathed. Inefficient government might be unsatisfying for politicians, but, rationally, they don't pursue a more flexible approach because the political costs of opposing the unions outweigh the credit earned from the voting public. Similarly, agency managers lack the political support to initiate change that will probably likely produce only modest efficiency gains, which the public will never notice. In short, the incentives for political leaders to push for greater productivity are low. This is a classic political problem: concentrated benefits for a particular group, with diffused costs.[91] Unlike the trial-and-error model that prevails in the private sector, in state and local government, many initiatives are extraordinarily durable.

What we have, then, is a situation where change is very hard to achieve. Politicians and agency managers might want change, but the entrenched forces of public sector unions block them from taking action. Something has to give. New policies just get layered on top of old ones, sometimes increasing dysfunction. The bureaucracy thickens. Government becomes less flexible and less rational.

Marginal Gains

People should not expect government to be as "efficient" as private enterprise, especially if efficiency is defined simply in terms of time and money. Time and money are not the only things government and the public value—even if some taxpayers are not so quick to admit it. Nonetheless, that does not mean that government couldn't be more effective at delivering services to citizens at lower prices with fewer conflicts of interest between government workers and the citizens they serve. Unionization and collective bargaining distort the purposes of public agencies such that optimal outcomes for taxpayers rarely materialize.

Getting government to be responsible, accountable, and reasonably effective is hard. Adding unionization and mandating collective bargaining raise the hurdles to achieving those goals. And the beneficiaries of the rigid work rules and salary schedules introduced and maintained by collective bargaining are often the poorest performers: reckless cops, inept teachers, and lazy firefighters. The many police officers, firefighters, and teachers who love their jobs and work above and beyond the call of duty are, if anything, penalized by such organizational imperatives.

Finally, one could reasonably argue that eliminating collective bargaining from the public sector would only produce marginal gains in productivity. Yet marginal gains are the only kind that can be made in government performance. And they are often worth far more than their price tag suggests. Just think if schools were optimally organized to educate students—rather than to also accommodate adults' work preferences. Such schools might not cost much less to operate (and may even cost slightly more), but they would deliver a superior product to students that would produce myriad spillover benefits to the economy and society.

A DAY OF RECKONING?

My central claim in this book is that unionization and collective bargaining in state and local government impose significant costs on society while providing few broadly shared benefits. The costs are primarily borne by taxpayers who fund government services and citizens who rely on them, while the benefits accrue overwhelmingly to those who are public employees. Since the former greatly outnumber the latter, the case against government unions deserves a hearing. As this book has documented, the interests of public employees run afoul of the interests of the broader public in multiple instances.

Still, it's worth reviewing the case *for* public sector unionism outlined in chapter 1 to see how well it holds up. The core claims of the pro-union position are that unionization:

1. ensures "labor peace,"
2. enables "industrial democracy,"
3. provides public employees representation in the political arena and offers a counterweight to business,
4. reduces the power inequalities between employers and workers,
5. improves government workers' lives by increasing salaries and benefits,

6. protects the fundamental right of collective bargaining, and

7. ensures investment in public goods.

Before considering each claim, it should be noted that only two of the eight claims (1 and 7) imply that unionization and collective bargaining benefit society as a whole rather than public workers alone. Claims 2 through 6 relate to the benefits unionization gives to government employees. While there may be some beneficial side effects—for example, better-paid public servants will have more disposable income and boost consumer spending during economic downturns—those effects are likely to be relatively weak, not least because public employment would perform this function without unionization. In short, defenders of public employee unions have yet to make a convincing case that these organizations in fact benefit the broader society.

Businesses, too, are undoubtedly self-interested, but the market helps ensure that their pursuit of their private interests yields public benefits in the form of innovative products, new jobs, and economic growth. Government workers' unions offer few if any such generalized benefits. (At best, defenders of the unions argue that they provide a counterweight to conservatives and big business and have made government more productive in some areas—primarily by reducing turnover among workers. These are arguments derived from the market economy, wherein private sector unions would make firms more efficient.[1]) Yet, in the public sector where there are few market pressures, these arguments are weak reeds on which to hang the defense of unionization and collective bargaining. This is especially true if we recall that turnover in government employment tends to be lower than in the private sector even when employees are not unionized. Moreover, some unions may even encourage turnover among younger employees if they are more protective of senior employees and push for better pay and benefits for them at the expense of more generous salaries for newly hired workers.

In recent public debates, defenders of government unions have largely confined themselves to arguing that public employees are not overpaid, have not contributed to recent state budget deficits, are not responsible for the underfunding of public pension systems, and that such unions have smaller effects on compensation than those in the private sector.[2] Yet, these points amount to little more than denials that unions do harm and therefore shouldn't be challenged. None demonstrates that government unions provide concrete benefits to society at large. (By extension, in the eyes of these authors, it would seem that the status quo of public sector labor relations, where bargaining and unions exist, cannot be improved to the benefit of the public—with the possible exception of introducing collective bargaining in states with weak legal provisions.) Missing is a well-developed *positive* argument for public sector unions' broad social, economic, and political benefits. That case would require proving more than that public employees have a right to form associations on their own and engage in the political process. Defenders of unions must go further and justify the coercive aspects of public unionism, including the agency shop, dues check-off, and mandatory collective bargaining. These practices reduce the liberty and discretion of individual workers and government employers.

In this respect, again, public sector unions are different from private sector ones. Defenders of private sector unions can and do argue—with considerable justice and some evidence on their side—that they benefit not only their members but also other similarly situated workers by inducing other companies to raise wages to avert unionization. Four-fifths of workers are employed in the private sector, where there is greater means and motive to exploit workers, which bolsters the case for unionism. There is some evidence that unions have made companies more productive; that's an effect that benefits consumers and, more broadly, the economy. Strong private sector labor unions have also helped reduce economic inequality. Yet public sector unions fail to provide such wider gains (i.e., ones that benefit society as a whole). As sociologist Jake Rosenfeld points out, "Threat effects ... are less likely to operate in the public sector, where the government is the employer."[3] Therefore, unionizing one group, say, police officers or firefighters, does not raise the wages of nonunion government employees or similarly situated employees in the private sector.

Now let's turn to the individual arguments. It is clear that unionization and binding arbitration (imposed to prevent strikes) have dramatically reduced the frequency and duration of public sector strikes since the 1960s and 1970s, when government workers first began to unionize. This is one of the more powerful claims on behalf of unionization in government. Yet in hindsight, the militancy of the 1960s and 1970s was really an outlier driven by other factors, among them rapid population and economic growth. Before then, public sector labor peace didn't require collective bargaining and unionization. In addition, many of the strikes of the militant period occurred *after* collective bargaining rights had been granted.[4] As we have seen, it is hardly true that public sector employees are an oppressed or exploited lot. Few leave public employment voluntarily, and those who spend their careers in the public sector tend to have better lives in retirement than similarly situated private sector workers. Finally, one must ask at what cost to the public finances and the productivity of service delivery the supposed labor peace was achieved.

Unionization in government does offer public employees a means to express discontent about their working conditions without fear of reprisals from management. This is the case even though union leadership elections are often very low-turnout affairs and most workers hardly participate in union activities.[5] Through collective bargaining, public employees win salary and benefit increases, as well as work rules that protect them from management. However, with limited government resources, there are always trade-offs. Giving more to one set of government workers may reduce resources for others; providing public workers better compensation may squeeze the tax dollars available for other priorities. Furthermore, giving workers greater protections from management could also protect poor performers, reducing productivity and discouraging talented employees.

Unionization has given government workers a powerful voice in their workplace and in American politics. They are among the largest donors to candidates and parties during elections at all levels of government. They take to the airwaves and produce their own ads during campaigns. Their members attend local, state, and national party conventions. They organize protests and support the protests of other groups. They are pivotal players in initiatives and referenda. They run sophisticated lobbying machines. Of course, the effects of these activities are the subject of debate. Liberals champion them; conservatives deplore them.

Unionization has tended to reduce inequalities in the governmental workplace. The salary scale in government is far more compressed than in the private sector. Collectively bargained work rules significantly limit management's prerogatives and protect workers from capricious supervisors. However, reducing these inequalities comes at the price of making government work less attractive to the talented and ambitious, reducing productivity, and driving up the costs of government services. Government salary scales would still be compressed without unions. The government as an employer simply cannot afford—fiscally or politically—to match top private sector salaries. Furthermore, unlike private sector unions, unions may reduce income inequality among public servants, but they do nothing to address income inequality in the private sector, where the vast majority of Americans work and which has grown over the last three decades. In fact, the rise of public sector unionism has correlated with the rise in income inequality over the last 30 years. And the states and cities where government unions are the strongest are also the ones where income inequality is highest.

Collective bargaining is undoubtedly a legal right where it exists. Yet, legal rights can be modified or rescinded.[6] Whether it is a universal social and economic right, which all governments are duty-bound to enforce, is another matter. (Were it such a right, the American states and the federal government that do not permit collective bargaining in the public sector would be in violation of it.) Given the highly uneven extension of this right in the United States—to say nothing of the world at large—the universalization of collective bargaining in public sector labor relations appears to be more an aspiration than a right.

Collective bargaining in the public sector may also violate other rights, particularly freedom of speech and association. Bargaining collectively with government, even over such a basic issue as wages, is inherently political insofar as it requires the union to advocate for a particular allocation of scarce public resources. In two recent Supreme Court cases, *Knox v. SEIU Local 100* (2012) and *Harris* v. *Quinn* (2014), the Supreme Court has considered whether requiring public-employee agency fees for collective bargaining violate the First Amendment.[7] Both cases questioned the constitutional grounding of *Abood v. Detroit Board of Education* (1977), the precedent that permitted agency fees for nonunion members in the public sector. As Justice Anthony Kennedy noted in oral argument in *Harris*, the activities of public-employee unions in collective bargaining unavoidably affect the size of government, which, he remarked, involves a "fundamental issue of political belief."[8] In that way, workers who do not join the union are compelled to financially support political positions in collective bargaining that they do not believe in. In his majority opinion in *Knox*, Justice Samuel Alito argued that the idea that free-rider problems require fair-share fees does not sit well with the First Amendment rights of workers who choose not to join the union. As he noted: "Such free-rider arguments … are generally insufficient to overcome First Amendment objections." In *Harris* Alito also noted *"Abood's* questionable foundations." While the court came very close to saying that agency fees violate the Constitution when granted in the public sector, it decided both cases on narrower grounds. Overturning *Abood* would in effect create a national right-to-work law for the public sector. However the court ultimately decides this issue, one can at least say that there is significant tension between a right to collective bargain and other fundamental constitutional rights.

Public sector unions do increase government spending on public goods such as personal security, education, criminal justice, and fire protection. However, the way that spending is directed and channeled by unions does not necessarily rebound to the benefit of the public. As we have seen, the costs of public employee pensions, healthcare, and "fringe" benefits have increasingly caused many government functions to be whittled down. The result—a government that spends more but does less—is hardly the sort of broad public provision that liberals champion. And it's a less attractive version of the "big government," which conservatives already oppose.

If collective bargaining were the most effective way to organize public sector labor relations, it is surprising that more than half the states have not seen fit to grant collective bargaining rights to all public workers. The Pew Charitable Trusts regularly ranks the states where public sector collective bargaining is prohibited or strictly limited among the best in public management performance.[9] Thirty-seven states provide collective bargaining rights for at least one of the following categories of workers: state workers, police officers, firefighters, teachers, or local workers. A few other states, such as Arizona, Colorado, and Texas, allow for procedures comparable to collective bargaining in their big cities. The states that don't are all in the South or the border states.

And even if it is an efficient way to deal with wages, benefits, and working conditions, those positive effects can still negate the benefits. In our system of competitive federalism, if a state government's practice establishes itself as superior, then other states and the federal government are likely to evolve in that direction. That has not happened with public sector collective bargaining. If anything, there has been a move away from it, which is telling.

LOOKING AHEAD

There are short-term and long-term sources of today's troubles in public finance.[10] National, state, and local budgets are struggling to provide high quality services to citizens—and ideally launch new, innovative programs. The short-term cause is the disruption created by the financial crisis of 2008 and the subsequent Great Recession. (When state and local government faced decreased tax revenue during the recession, some of the perks won by public sector unions were scrutinized.) The longer-term cause stems from the welfare state model created by the New Deal, extended in the Great Society, and capped by the passage of the Patient Protection and Affordable Care Act (aka Obamacare). This model was predicated on macroeconomic regulation of the economy through Keynesian interventions, government-provided retirement pensions for the aged, a mix of public and private universal health care, a growing population, and expanded consumerism. The dollar would remain the world's reserve currency and liberal international trade would ensure increasing prosperity. A nice formula—if it were sustainable.

However, to finance such an extensive state apparatus in the face of constitutional barriers and citizen opposition to high taxes, government plunged into debt financing. Politicians are often afflicted with myopia when they dispense benefits. This has been the case in state and local government, where politicians often heedlessly agreed to generous pensions and expansive retiree health benefits with little thought about the bills coming due. They benefited politically from such promises but stuck the public with the tab. America's states may have constitutional balanced-budget requirements, but many engage in gimmicks to run up debt, including the issue of bonds designed to circumvent legal limits on borrowing.[11] These liabilities, coupled with pension and healthcare commitments to public workers, are now crowding out spending on core functions that citizens expect government to perform.

The resulting conflict over competing government priorities in the face of tight budgets has divided both political parties and is one of the sources of polarization between them at every level of government. These pressures have also produced intraparty divisions. On the Democratic side, tension exists between centrists and populists who want to tax Wall Street and the wealthy to sustain the status quo—and possibly secure increases in the size of government. Moderate and centrist Democrats worry that overtaxing the wealthy and excessively regulating Wall Street will threaten the progressive tax bases of blue states and cities by causing firms and wealthy individuals to restructure their pretax income.[12] On the Republican side, Tea Party activists have battled tax increases and demanded budget cuts, while moderate Republicans have grappled with the tough trade-offs.

Interparty divisions are also at a high point. From the New Deal to Obamacare, the Democratic Party has built a series of kaleidoscopic coalitions, promising public spending and recruiting new groups with the enticement of more government programs. One of the mainstays of the Democratic Party since at least the 1930s has been organized labor. However, as private sector unions began a long, slow decline in the 1960s, Democrats turned to organizing and mobilizing public sector unions as a serviceable replacement. As we have seen, these new types of unions now form the bedrock foundation of the party in many states.[13] The Democrats have evolved, as analyst James Pierson puts it, into a party "that finds its votes and organizational strength in public sector unions, government employees and contractors, and beneficiaries of government programs."[14] The consequence is increased conflict with the Republican Party, which has developed much differently. The organizational backbone of the GOP is business, especially small business owners concerned about the costs of commerce: taxes, regulations, and government intrusiveness that cut into their bottom line. One party champions government; the other bewails it.

It should come as no surprise, then, that the red versus blue political maps that began with the 2000 presidential election tend to correspond with the nationwide distribution of public sector union membership. In states where public sector unions are strong and the costs of government high, Democrats tend to dominate. Where such unions are weak, the GOP tends to be in charge. This became even more apparent after the 2010 and 2012 elections. Heading into the 2014 elections, the GOP controls 30 governorships (representing 58 percent of the US population) and the governorship and the state legislature in 25 states (representing 52 percent of the population). The Democrats maintain unified control of only 14 states, representing just 33 percent of the country. However, the Democratic party continues to rule the roost in some of the largest and wealthiest states with strong government unions: New York, California, Illinois, Connecticut, and Massachusetts. It is not surprising that swing states like Wisconsin,

Ohio, Michigan, and Pennsylvania have been ground zero for the battle over collective bargaining, union security measures, and public worker retiree benefits. In sum, the two parties' agendas are incompatible, not just in Washington, but in states and localities as well.

Party polarization in state government has set up a natural experiment to test each party's governing philosophy. Both sides have admirable qualities, but the GOP deserves credit: most Republican states have lower unemployment rates as the nation emerges from the recession (7.2 percent in the 25 Republican states compared to 8.4 percent in the 14 Democratic states). According to the Bureau of Economic Analysis, the reason is that the economies of those states are growing faster. And right-to-work states have created more jobs in recent years than heavily unionized states. Not surprisingly, these states have better credit ratings as well.[15] Nonetheless, many of the blue states remain among the wealthiest and most desirable places in the country to live. The test of governance has yet to be determined.

America's big cities are another proving ground, as most of them are dominated by Democrats with strong ties to public sector unions. Detroit's bankruptcy highlighted the fiscal maladies of many big cities at a time when cities are becoming more important to the nation's role in the global economy. The percentage of Americans living in them is growing. Many cities are one-party strongholds. With Washington mired in gridlock, mayors and city councils must try to get things done. In particular, they must woo businesses.[16] Various analysts have noted that the denser the city, the more economically innovative it is.[17] Under current budget conditions, mayors will no longer be able to expand public payrolls and inflate pay to win over unions. Making cities more business friendly but also crafting policies that increase upward mobility and protect citizens from risk are today's central challenges.[18]

Sources of Change

Political scientists differ on when and how policy change occurs. One useful framework is called "punctuated equilibrium"—and its cousin is called "path dependence."[19] In this view, policies and supporting political arrangements become entrenched over time. The communities with a stake in a policy become the preserve of experienced practitioners to the exclusion of the broad public. In such cases, policies achieve a sort of equilibrium, where some tinkering and refinement of the policy may occur but its general direction persists over time. Occasionally, however, that static bubble bursts, creating opportunities for change. This is caused by various crises, a buildup of technological and societal changes, or major electoral shifts. Once the equilibrium is destabilized, a burst of effort addressing big problems quickly is common, rather than small-ball reform.

Over the last 30 years, collective bargaining, agency shops, and other union security measures enjoyed policy equilibrium in the states and cities that adopted these measures. The same was true for public pension plans, which continued to expand and offer more generous benefits to government workers. The media paid little attention to the looming problems in pension finance. Contract negotiations received little if any press coverage—unless, of course, there was an occasional strike. Collective bargaining was (and still is) largely conducted by experienced lawyers—often far out of view from average citizens. Those involved in public sector labor relations—on both sides of the bargaining table—got to know each other. In the political realm, public sector unions—teachers' unions aside—received little attention in the popular press and even less from academics. Most stories about organized labor focused on the travails of unions in the private sector.

Under these conditions, only small incremental reforms could have been expected, and in fact, that's what happened. They rarely captured the attention of the news media or the public. An iron triangle of public sector unions, elected officials, and public agencies developed and became immune to outside pressure or media scrutiny. Democrats maintained their political alliances with public employee unions and favored the expansion of benefits. Republicans tended to go along largely because there was little pressure on them to oppose expansion. The issues were technical, the public was uninformed and probably uninterested, and the problems did not appear to be pressing. The unions had the political playing field to themselves. There was little effort to make big changes to pensions, especially with the economy growing well in the 1990s.

However, the Great Recession and the Tea Party–fueled Republican electoral sweep of the 2010 elections upset the apple cart. Before the recession, Republican state legislators could look the other way when it came to overly generous contracts and pension sweeteners, as there was very little pressure from citizens or interest groups to scrutinize them. The press didn't cover such things. In short, for many Republicans, acquiescence on those issues made other issues easier to handle. All that changed in 2010. Public sector unions and the government pension problem were and are likely to remain in the news. Citizens are aware of some of the problems. New interest groups have emerged. Older ones have taken an interest in these subjects. Republicans will be pressured to oppose public sector unions and reduce the generosity of pensions. Furthermore, the politics of collective bargaining and public pensions are likely to be more partisan and polarized than ever.

As for the Democrats, they are increasingly divided over public sector unions and pension politics. Many Democratic mayors and governors are concerned about benefits squeezing their budgets. They are open to reform, and sometimes they're leading it. Other Democrats—especially those who hold legislative seats—retain close ties to the unions and remain opposed to reducing the generosity of government pension and health benefits.

Longer-term pressures, especially state and local government commitments to provide healthcare and pensions to their employees, may force states to act. As former governor Richard Lamm of Colorado, a Democrat, has remarked: "We have to take this on, if there is any way of bringing fiscal sanity to our children .... The New Deal is demographically obsolete. You can't fund the dream of the 1960s on the economy of 2010."[20] With public sector unions standing in the way of taking any action to address those obligations, politicians may be moved to remove or at least reduce the obstacles to reform.

A slow decline of public sector unionism may begin to occur at the municipal level. This is because municipal government budgets devote so much to employee compensation. States will be receiving less federal aid, as the federal budget is squeezed by entitlements. In turn, states will be forced to send less aid to localities. Changing interest rates could pressure the municipal bond market. Cities, therefore, will likely initiate the momentum to change. This movement is likely to start with a slowly unfolding crisis over pension and healthcare costs for public employees.

Ultimately, the political cooperation of government workers' unions is essential to remedying the pension funding crisis. And that will depend, at least in many places, on the talent and skill of individual state and local governments. Political leadership will determine how to distribute the painful impact of this crisis across unionized and nonunionized voters and citizens.

WHAT MIGHT BE DONE?

The wide variance of legal and political arrangements in states and cities makes reform a challenge. There is no uniform solution. Improving government productivity is hard. Politically, especially in largely one-party cities, matters are even more complicated, as change often requires Democratic politicians to betray their erstwhile allies. Yet there are a number of reform opportunities states and cities might consider. Only the urgent need to cancel or renegotiate major public debts and the structure of public finance will allow for real change. All of the reform options aim to prevent public sector unions from having two bites of the apple: either restrict their collective bargaining activities or limit their political operations.

One recommendation is to limit the deal points in collective bargaining. In most places pensions are not bargained over, but they should be omitted from negotiations in places where they are. Another is to remove health benefits from collective bargaining agreements and return the matter to elected officials, because these benefits are one of government's biggest spending commitments. Finally, government should index for inflation the upper limit of union wage demands.

Reformers might also experiment with eliminating agency shops in the public sector. Reformers need not immediately implement a right-to-work law, as Indiana and Michigan did recently. They might indeed leave the private sector labor movement alone, especially since the case for agency fees is stronger in the private than in the public sector. This would force public sector unions to use the same techniques as other interest groups to attract members and their dues, rather than have government coerce membership.

Or reformers might consider allowing money from dues check-off to be used only for collective bargaining—not politics. If government unions wish to engage in politics they should do it on their own dime, without government facilitating it. The object is to extract the state from determining which funds are in effect donations to an interest group.[21] Unions would have to surmount this new obstacle by devoting their own administrative resources to collecting political contributions—just like any other interest group.

In some states, such as New York, the rules regarding the arbitration process that must be followed when contracts expire could be modified. The 1982 Triborough Amendment to New York's Taylor Law has particularly pernicious consequences for taxpayers insofar as it discourages unions from making concessions in collective bargaining.[22] Under this provision, all elements of a collectively bargained contract remain in place—including inefficient work rules, salary schedules, and sick and vacation pay—after a contract expires until a new contract has been negotiated. The law encourages unions to fight significant changes to their contracts because if negotiations break down, the worst possible outcome for the union is the preservation of the status quo. Even with a base salary freeze during the Great Recession, the law cost the Empire State $140 million and automatic step salary increases for teachers cost school districts some $300 million.[23] This helps explain why every municipal workers' union in New York City allowed their contract to expire in the final years of Mayor Michael Bloomberg's administration: they hoped that they could negotiate a better deal with a new mayor elected with their support in the fall of 2013. The contract negotiated in the spring of 2014 by Bloomberg's successor, Bill de Blasio, included expensive 4 percent retroactive raises, at a cost of $3.6 billion, and 1 percent to 3 percent raises for the next five years in exchange for unspecified savings in public employees' healthcare plans. Teachers' base pay will increase 19.5 percent over the life of the contract. The teachers union's strategy looks wise in retrospect.

Finally, reformers could alter state–city relations to empower cities to take greater action in how they deal with public employee unions on their own. States could provide cities with relief from a variety of mandates that constrain their freedom. Governments could then consider changing the way they deliver services. Governments are often bad at designing and organizing the ways they interact with citizens and businesses. Agency managers are concerned with the outside organizations that constrain them—namely, courts, legislatures, and interest groups—and they therefore have a hard time thinking about things from the consumer's point of view. Bruce Katz and Jennifer Bradley of the Brookings Institution argue that cities are capable of doing much more than they currently do.[24] To do more, cities must reform public sector labor relations and get their fiscal houses in order.

Beyond government's direct relations to their unions, local and state government must regain control of their budgets. Primarily, this means abandoning the accounting tricks and gimmicks they have used to calculate their pension and health liabilities. The Institute for Truth and Accounting notes that states and localities are using "antiquated budgeting rules and accounting standards" and that many debts they have accumulated don't appear on their balance sheets.[25] Only when the fiscal problems of governments are presented in stark relief can politicians ask the public to make sacrifices.

Next, governments should pursue more increases in the retirement age for public employees—especially new workers. That would reduce long-term pension liabilities and those related to healthcare. Governments' most expensive health plans offer to cover their workers if they retire before 65, when they are eligible for Medicare. If governments owe workers just several fewer years of these expensive plans, this will significantly reduce health liabilities.

Two other changes worth pursuing have been championed by California Governor Jerry Brown. One is to expand the number of years from which an employee's final peak salary is calculated for pension purposes. This reduced pension-"spiking" schemes, such as workers cashing in sick days during their last year to inflate their salary, working excessive overtime, and using other means to drive up their salaries artificially. By averaging a worker's pension salary over three to five years instead of just one, states can reduce their long-term pension liabilities. A second proposal is for states to cap the size of the pension a worker can receive. California has limited pensions for new recruits to $110,000.

Finally, states should move quickly to introduce defined contribution or 401(k)-style retirement plans. Under these plans, workers' retirement income depends much more on what they set aside during their employment years. The liability therefore falls on the individual worker rather than on the government and taxpayers. To ease the transition, some governments might consider offering new workers the option either to join the old-style defined benefit plan or to join a defined contribution plan. Especially for younger workers, the portability of the latter might be very attractive.[26] My own employer, the City University of New York (CUNY), has offered this option since the 1950s. Those who plan to spend their entire careers in public service can stick with the defined benefit plan. But those planning to work for government for a short time should not be penalized for doing so.

There are some signs that voters support pension reform. A few states have adopted defined contribution plans, including Alaska, Utah, and Michigan. (Nebraska also has a defined contribution plan but it was adopted in 1967.) Reformers also have drawn motivation from the experiences of San Diego and San Jose, California. In 2012 referenda, voters in the Golden State's second- and third-largest cities approved significant changes to their municipal pension schemes (neither participate in CalPERS). San Jose voters passed an initiative that raises employee contribution rates to the pension system or alternatively permits them to select a less generous plan. San Diego fully embraced defined contribution plans. Perhaps not surprisingly, public sector unions have sued in both cities, hoping to overturn the will of voters and block the implementation of the new measures.

The Bailout Society

The deepest question posed to American democracy is not how to address the fiscal imbalances induced by unionizing government work. It is about the character of American democracy itself. One need not go as far as Alexis de Tocqueville, who claimed that "mores are more important than laws," to believe that democracy cannot flourish unless its citizens cherish certain values, maintain certain habits, and share certain traditions.[27] A bedrock American principle is that people have the ability and responsibility to govern their own lives—"individualism rightly understood," Tocqueville called it. The old-fashioned view was that individuals acting collectively to govern themselves—popular sovereignty—were responsible for the public weal. The challenge is that that view is now considered outmoded and even retrograde in many quarters.

Now that our cities, states, and the federal government are suffering fiscally, some argue that no individuals need be held responsible. Popular sovereignty and the responsibility it entails are just fictions that lead to financial pain. Rather than reform bad governance and mismanagement, some argue that it's better to bail out the decision makers.

Such reasoning implies that there is no going back to responsible government. The size and scope of government—or, essentially, the benefits it delivers—are sacrosanct. Goods and services provided by the government are now considered legal rights, so if they become unaffordable, new monies must be found—either from more revenues, especially from the rich, or from borrowing. It's simple fairness—or "social justice."[28] Why should pensioners in Detroit living on $1,800 a month accept a cut in benefits—even if the city is bankrupt? It takes a hard person to say they should. So many say they shouldn't.

Rather, if the tax base isn't robust enough to produce more revenue, the solution to insolvency is to issue more debt. If public sector pensions and healthcare are devouring state and local budgets, borrow more. Federal entitlements are squeezing other priorities: borrow more. General Motors overextended itself: bail it out. Detroit and Illinois overextended themselves: bail them out. People bought homes they couldn't afford: bail them out.

Holding in abeyance the question of economic sustainability (nobody really knows if such an approach is sustainable, as Japan's experience attests), the bigger problem with the bailout society is that it corrodes the foundation of democratic governance, which is built on the principle that the people rule. Impersonal economic, social, and demographic forces render it a chimera. To combat these forces under the banner of fairness and social justice, only one power will do: government. The consequence is the increasing collectivization of the wealth of society to pay the mutual debts of an interdependent society. During her campaign for a US Senate seat, former Harvard professor and head of the Consumer Financial Protection Bureau Elizabeth Warren championed this collectivist mentality:

> You built a factory out there? Good for you. But I want to be clear: you moved your goods to market on the roads the rest of us paid for; you hired workers the rest of us paid to educate; you were safe in your factory because of police forces and fire forces that the rest of us paid for. You didn't have to worry that marauding bands would come and seize everything at your factory, and hire someone to protect against this, because of the work the rest of us did.[29]

Because we all pay for public goods—roads, education, environmental protection, and public safety—all property should be considered public, not private. This implies government will manage things; in cooperation, of course, with its unionized workers. Individuals and smaller collectives such as cities, counties, towns, business firms, and maybe even irresponsible states will not be held liable. They can always be bailed out by Washington.

This sort of distributional politics threatens America with a case of what was called the "British disease" in the 1970s—today it might be called the "French disease."[30] That disease is economic sclerosis resulting from the demands of public sector unions, social service providers, and other interest groups. The French government today spends the equivalent of 56 percent of its gross domestic product, the highest in the Eurozone, and has been unable to undertake meaningful structural reforms to reduce public spending. Democracies are vulnerable to this disease because politicians continually offer small concessions, which ratchet-up the size of the constituencies that benefit from government spending.[31] Those constituencies then defend tooth and nail their newly acquired benefits, making rollback difficult. The disease can be fatal: elected officials concede to wage and benefit increases for the unions, expand social provision, tax the most profitable local industry until it becomes uncompetitive, borrow money to make up any differences, and set the jurisdiction on the road to fiscal crisis.[32]

Yet, the deepest danger of distributional politics is that it actually works and is fairly sustainable. As Tocqueville pointed out, the creation of a vast tutelary power can undermine a people's belief that they can govern themselves. Such a government saps individual energy and initiative. As he put it:

> The sovereign extends its arms over society as a whole; it covers its surface with a network of small, complicated, painstaking, uniform rules through which the most original minds and the most vigorous souls cannot clear a way to surpass the crowd; it does not break wills, but it softens them, bends them, and directs them; it does not destroy, it prevents things from being born; it does not tyrannize, it hinders, compromises, enervates, extinguishes, dazes, and finally

reduces [the] nation to being nothing more than a herd of timid and industrious animals of which the government is the shepherd.[33]

The restoration of political and economic vitality in America's states and cities requires, among many other things, a recalibration of its public sector labor relations. America's 40-year experiment with unionized government has been, on balance, misguided. While there are clearly benefits to this mode of organizing public sector labor relations—especially to public workers themselves—they do not outweigh the significant costs to the public. Unionized government overburdens taxpayers, makes services on which the poor and middle class rely less effective, and distorts the democratic process.

There is hope. American politicians are endlessly creative. There are a range of reforms with which to experiment. Liberals, who since Franklin Roosevelt have championed government experimentation, should seize the day. Such experimentation would stem from nobler, more selfless motives than sometimes animate conservatives. Yet, whether liberals or conservatives drive reform matters little, given the looming fiscal challenges states and localities face. Crises in Los Angeles, New York, Chicago, and elsewhere will likely spur action. Of course, we can all hope that sharp and steep economic growth just on the horizon will ease the pain and offer space for creative action. By properly reforming government labor relations, we can behold a remedy for one of the diseases most incident to contemporary American democracy.

NOTES

CHAPTER 1

1. "Six-Figure Pensions More Common for Police and Firefighters," Empire Center of New York Policy, Press Release, June 12, 2013.
2. Andrew Biggs, *Not so Modest: Pension Benefits for Full-Career State Government Employees* (Economic Perspectives, American Enterprise Institute, Washington, DC, March 2014); Biggs, "How to Become a (Public Pension) Millionaire," *Wall Street Journal*, March 14, 2014.
3. Stephane Fitch, "Gilt-Edged Pensions," *Forbes*, February 16, 2009; Rich Karlgaard, "The Millionaire Cop Next-Door," *Forbes*, June, 10, 2010.
4. Diane Rado, "Chicago-Area Teachers Top State in Earning Six-Figure Salaries," *Chicago Tribune*, July 14, 2010.
5. Catherine Saillant and Mike Reicher, "Lifeguards Special Status Pension under Scrutiny in California," *Los Angeles Times*, June 16, 2011.
6. US Census Bureau, "Median Household Income, 2007–2011," http://quickfacts. census.gov/qfd/states/00000.html; E. J. McMahon and Josh Barro, "Public vs. Private Retirements," *New York Post*, December 19, 2010.
7. Alan Crawford, "Having It All: The Rise of Government Unions and the Decline of the Work Ethic," *Washington Monthly* (January 1983): 33–39.
8. Bureau of Labor Statistics, "The Employment Situation," Press Release, May 2, 2014.
9. D. Roderick Kiewiet and Matthew D. McCubbins, "State and Local Government Finance: The New Fiscal Ice Age," *Annual Review of Political Science* 13, no. 49 (December 2013): 105–122.
10. Joshua Rauh, "Are State Public Pensions Sustainable? Why the Federal Government Should Worry About State Pension Liabilities," *National Tax Journal* 63, no. 3 (2010): 585–602; Byron Lutz and Louise Sheiner, "The Fiscal Stress Arising from State and Local Retiree Health Obligations" (Working Paper 19779, National Bureau of Economic Research, January 2014); Douglas J. Elliot, "State and Local Pension Funding Deficits: A Primer" (Report, Brookings Institution, Washington, D.C., December 2010).
11. Andrew Biggs, *The Multiplying Risk of Public Employee Pensions to State and Local Government Budgets* (Economic Perspectives, American Enterprise Institute, Washington, DC, December 2013).

12. Nicholas Johnson, "State and Local Job Cuts Continue, Especially in Education," Center for Budget and Policy Priorities, September 2, 2011, http://www.off-thechartsblog.org/state-and-local-job-cuts-continue-especially-in-education/; William Selway "States Cut Taxes, Increase Spending as Economy Improves," *Bloomberg News*, December 10, 2013, http://www.bloomberg.com/news/2013-12-10/states-cut-taxes-increase-spending-as-economy-improves.html; Kiewiet and McCubbins, "State and Local Government Finance," *Annual Review of Political Science* 13, no. 49 (December 2013).

13. Don Bellante, David Denholm, and Ivan Osorio, *Vallejo Con Dios: Why Public Sector Unionism Is a Bad Deal for Taxpayers and Representative Government* (Policy Analysis, No. 645, Cato Institute, Washington, DC, 2009).

14. Samuel L. Gompers, "What Does the Working Man Want?" International May Day address, Louisville, Kentucky (1890).

15. James Madison, "The Vices of the Political System of the United States," chap. 5, doc. 16 in *The Papers of James Madison*, vol. 1, ed. William T. Hutchinson et al. (Chicago and London: University of Chicago Press, 1962–77).

16. It should be noted that Meany later changed his position when it became clear that public employment was the last avenue for the expansion of the labor movement in the 1960s.

17. Martha Derthick helped me frame matters in this way.

18. Martin H. Malin, "The Legislative Upheaval in Public-Sector Labor Law: A Search for Common Elements," 27 *ABA Journal of Labor and Employment Law* 149 (2012): 149-64; Steven G. Greenhouse, "Ohio's Anti-Union Law Is Tougher Than Wisconsin's," *New York Times*, March 31, 2011; Angela Delli Santi, "New Jersey Anti-Union Bill Approved, Governor Christie Signs into Law," *Huffington Post*, June 28, 2011; Monica Davey, "Michigan Governor Signs Laws Limiting Unions," *New York Times*, December 11, 2012; Richard Locker, "Tennessee Legislature OK's Ban of Teacher Bargaining," *The Commercial Appeal*, May 20, 2011; Joy Resmovitz, "Education Ballot Initiative Results Show Mixed Returns on School Reform," *Huffington Post*, November 11, 2012.

19. Scott Walker, "Why I'm Fighting in Wisconsin," *Wall Street Journal*, March 10, 2011; Monica Davey, "Organizers Say 1 Million Signed Petition to Recall Wisconsin Governor," *New York Times*, January 18, 2012; Shushannah Walshe, "30 Million Pouring in to Influence Wisconsin's Recall Elections," ABC News, August 4, 2011.

20. Quoted in Vicki Needham, "McConnell Blames Public Workers Unions for Tea Party Targeting," *The Hill*, June 21, 2013.

21. Quoted in Brady Dennis and Peter Wallsten, "Obama Joins Wisconsin's Budget Battle, Opposing Republican Anti-Union Bill," *Washington Post*, February 11, 2011.

22. André Blais, Donald E. Blake, and Stéphane Dion, *Governments, Parties, and Public Sector Employees* (Pittsburgh: University of Pittsburgh Press, 1997).

23. See, for example, the reaction of a former Democratic city councilwoman in California to the role of public employee unions in her city. Marti Brown, "Vallejo Poised to Make to Make Same Financial Decisions That Led to Bankruptcy,"

Sacramento Bee, November 2, 2013. Pete Peterson and Kevin Klowden, "Democrats versus Unions?" *City Journal Online*, April 25, 2014, http://www. city-journal.org/2014/cjc0425ppkk.html.

24. Matthew Yglesias, "The Populist Democrat's Dilemma," *Slate*, November 11, 2013. For example, in New York State, the top 1 percent of taxpayers contributed 43 percent of tax revenues in 2007—the highest percentage on record. Such a skewed distribution of taxes is highly unstable given the dependence of high earners on financial markets. See *New York State Assembly Revenue Report* (Ways and Means Committee, February 2009), 40; *New York State 2010–11 Executive Budget, Economic and Revenue Outlook*, 193; E. J. McMahon, *Testimony: New York State Budget* (Joint Legislative Fiscal Committees, February 14, 2011).

25. Monica Davey, "As Teachers Strike Goes On, Mayor Digs In," *New York Times*, September 17, 2012.

26. Patrick McGuinn, "Presidential Policymaking: Race to the Top, Executive Power, and the Obama Education Agenda," *The Forum* 12, no. 1 (2014).

27. Paul E. Peterson, Michael Henderson, and Martin R. West, *Teachers versus the Public: What Americans Think about Schools and How to Fix Them* (Washington, DC: Brookings Institution Press, 2014), 42–44, 120–24.

28. Quoted in Patrick J. McDonnell and David Zahniser, "Villaraigosa Takes on Teachers Union," *Los Angeles Times*, December 10, 2010. See also, Antonio Villaraigosa, "Why are Teachers Unions So Opposed to Change?" *Wall Street Journal*, July 20, 2014.

29. The NAACP has loudly opposed school choice measures in general and vouchers in particular. Yet it has also received substantial funding support from the teachers' unions. So perhaps its opposition to those items is less surprising given the distribution of African American opinion on education policy.

30. Quoted in Steven Greenhut, "San Jose Shows the Way Out of Pension Sinkhole," *Bloomberg View*, May 30, 2012.

31. *Why Public Sector Union Reform Is Bipartisan* (Union Watch, California Public Policy Institute, January 22, 2012), http://unionwatch.org/why-public-sector-union-reform-is-nonpartisan-2/; Allysia Finley, "Gloria Romero: The Trials of a Democratic Reformer," *Wall Street Journal*, August 31, 2012; Richard Kahlenberg, "Bipartisan, but Unfounded: The Assault on Teachers' Unions," *American Educator* 35, no. 4 (Winter 2011–12).

32. Most of the books written by journalists and others outside the academy tend to be critical of government unions and situated on the political Right. See Myron Lieberman, *The Teachers Unions: How Now the NEA and AFT Sabotage Reform and Hold Students, Parents, Teachers, and Taxpayers Hostage to Bureaucracy* (New York: Free Press, 1997); Peter Brimelow, *The Worm in the Apple: How Teachers Unions Are Destroying American Education* (New York: HarperCollins, 2003); Steve Brill, *Class Warfare: Inside the Fight to Fix America's Schools* (New York: Simon and Schuster, 2011); Steven Greenhut, *Plunder: How Public Employees Are Raiding Our Treasuries, Controlling Our Lives, and Bankrupting the Nation* (Santa Ana, CA: The Forum Press, 2009); Roger Lowenstein, *While America Aged: How Pension Debts Ruined General Motors, Stopped the NYC Subways, Bankrupted San Diego, and Loom as the Next Financial Crisis*

(New York: Penguin Press, 2008); Steven Malanga, *The New New Left: How American Politics Works Today* (New York: Ivan R. Dee, 2005); Malanga, *Shakedown: The Continuing Conspiracy against the American Taxpayer* (New York: Ivan R. Dee, 2010); Mallory Factor with Elizabeth Factor, *Shadowbosses: Government Unions Control America and Rob Taxpayers Blind* (New York: Center Street Press, 2012).

33. Harold Meyerson, "Wisconsin Is Only Party of the GOP War against Unions," *Washington Post*, February 23, 2011. Another variant on this argument is that the unions protect government services from politicians who might be inclined to cut them during tight fiscal times. See Larry Bartels, "Public Sector Unions Promote Government, Not Government Jobs," The Monkey Cage Blog, *Washington Post*, October 24, 2013, http://www.washingtonpost.com/blogs/monkey-cage/wp/2013/10/24/public-sector-unions-promote-government-not-government-jobs/.

34. Jonathan Chait, "Learning Curve," *New Republic*, April 7, 2011. This view harkens back to John Kenneth Galbraith, who carried on the progressive argument that a powerful state was necessary to counterbalance the power of corporations. See Galbraith, *The New Industrial State* (Boston: Houghton-Mifflin, 1967).

35. Elbert Ventura, "At Our Service," *Democracy: A Journal of Ideas* 29 (Summer 2013).

36. For a variant of the political balance argument, see E. J. Dionne, "Wisconsin Reaches for the Last Resort," *Washington Post*, May 30, 2012.

37. Robert Reich, "Public Employees Are GOPs Scapegoats," *San Francisco Chronicle*, January 16, 2011; see also Stanley Aronowitz, "One, Two, Many Madisons: The War on Public Sector Workers," *New Labor Forum* 20, no. 2 (Spring 2011): 5.

38. Walter Russell Mead, "The Madison Blues," Via Media Blog, *The American Interest*, February 18, 2011, http://blogs.the-american-interest.com/wrm/2011/02/18/the-madison-blues/.

39. For a debate about this issue as it relates to education, see Richard D. Kahlenberg and Jay P. Greene, "Unions and the Public Interest: Is Collective Bargaining for Teachers Good for Students," *Education Next* 12, no. 1 (Winter 2012).

40. Benjamin I. Page and Walter Y. Shapiro, *The Rational Public: Fifty Years of Trends in Americans' Policy Preferences* (Chicago: University of Chicago Press, 1992).

41. For a version of this argument, see Charles Lane, "Who's Progressive in Wisconsin," *Washington Post*, February 6, 2012; Lane, "The Democrats Dubious Alliance with Public Sector Unions," Post-Partisan blog, *Washington Post*, October 18, 2010, http://voices.washingtonpost.com/postpartisan/2010/10/the_democrats_dubious_alliance.html.

42. The rise to prominence of public sector unions, which gave organized labor a more affluent and educated profile, may help explain why the Democratic Party began in the 1970s to emphasize the postmaterial lifestyle issues that prioritized aesthetics, morality, and rights over the basic material concerns of lunch-pail economics and personal security. Regarding postmaterialism, see Ronald Inglehart, *The Silent Revolution* (Princeton, NJ: Princeton University Press, 1977). For an analysis of how public sector unions' concerns differ from private sector unions',

see Jake Rosenfeld, *What Unions No Longer Do* (Cambridge, MA: Harvard University Press, 2014), 64–67.

43. David Osborne and Ted Gaebler, *Reinventing Government: How the Entrepreneurial Spirit Is Transforming the Public Sector* (New York: Plume, 1993).

44. David Madland and Karla Walter, *Why Is the Public Suddenly Down on Unions?* (American Worker Project, Center for American Progress Action Fund, July 2010).

45. Seymour Martin Lipset, "Labor Unions in the Public Mind," in *Unions in Transition,* ed. Seymour Martin Lipset (San Francisco: ICS Press, 1986).

46. Lydia Saad, "Labor Unions See Sharp Slide in U.S. Public Support," Gallup, September 3, 2009.

47. Paul E. Peterson, William Howell, and Martin West, "Teachers Unions Have a Popularity Problem," *Wall Street Journal,* June 4, 2012. For further analysis of the gap between the public's education policy preferences and those of teachers, see Peterson, Henderson, and West, *Teachers versus the Public.*

48. California Research Corporation, "The Field Poll," Release #2458, December 13, 2013. See also George Skelton, "Unions Need to Give the Public a Break," *Los Angeles Times,* December 18, 2013.

49. Michael Cooper and Megan Thee-Brenan, "Majority in Poll Back Public Sector Unions," *New York Times,* February 28, 2011.

50. Ben Smith, "Poll: Public Unions a Hard Sell," *Politico,* February 18, 2011.

51. Lydia Saad, "New York and Tri-State Region Gripes Most about State Taxes," Gallup, April 9, 2014, http://www.gallup.com/poll/168419/new-york-tri-st ate-region-gripes-state-taxes.aspx#2.

52. For a review of the recent studies by economists, see Eileen Norcross, "Public Sector Unionism: A Review" (Working Paper, No. 11–26, Mercatus Center at George Mason University, May 2011).

53. Norma M. Ruccucci, "Public Sector Labor Relations Scholarship: Is There a 'There'?" *Public Administration Review* 71, no. 2 (March/April 2011): 203–9.

54. Robert Shaffer, "Where Are the Organized Public Employees? The Absence of Public Employee Unionism from U.S. History Textbooks and Why It Matters," *Labor History* 43, no. 3 (2002): 315, 331.

55. Joseph A. McCartin, "Bringing the State's Workers In: Time to Rectify an Imbalanced US Labor Historiography," *Labor History* 47, no. 1 (February 2006): 74. For a few exceptions, see Marjorie Murphy, *Blackboard Unions: The AFT and NEA 1900-1980* (Ithaca, NY: Cornell University Press, 1992); Paul Johnston, *Success While Others Fail* (Ithaca, NY: Cornell University ILR Press, 1994).

56. Richard Kahlenberg, *Tough Liberal: Albert Shanker and the Battles Over Schools, Unions, Race, and Democracy* (New York: Columbia University Press, 2009).

57. Wallace Sayre and Herbert Kaufman, *Governing New York City: Politics in the Metropolis* (New York: Russell Sage Foundation, 1960); Paul Peterson, *School Politics, Chicago Style* (Chicago: University of Chicago Press, 1976); William T. Grinshaw, *Union Rule in the Schools: Big City Politics in Transition* (Lexington, KY: Lexington Books, 1979); Margaret Levi, *Bureaucratic Insurgency: The Case*

of Police Unions (Lexington, KY: Lexington Books, 1977); Maurice Berube, *Teacher Politics* (New York: Greenwood Press, 1988).

58. J. David Greenstone, *Labor in American Politics* (New York: Knopf, 1969).

59. Levi, "Organizing Power"; Taylor Dark, *The Unions and the Democrats* (Ithaca, NY: Cornell University ILR Press, 1999); Herbert B. Asher, Eric S. Heberling, Randal B. Ripley, and Karen Synder, *American Labor Unions in the Electoral Arena* (Lanham, MD: Rowman & Littlefield Publishers, 2001).

60. Tracy Roof, *American Labor, Congress, and the Welfare State, 1935-2010* (Baltimore: Johns Hopkins University Press, 2011); Dorian Warren, "The American Labor Movement in the Age of Obama: The Challenges and Opportunities of a Racialized Political Economy," *Perspectives on Politics* 8 (2010): 847–60; Benjamin Radcliff and Martin Saiz, "Labor Organization and Public Policy in the American States," *Journal of Politics* 60 (1998): 11–32; Benjamin Radcliffe and Patricia Davis, "Labor Organization and Electoral Participation in Industrial Democracies," *American Journal of Political Science* 44 (2000): 132–41.

61. Terry Moe, *Special Interest: Teachers Unions and America's Public Schools* (Washington, DC: Brookings Institution, 2011); Moe, "Political Control and the Power of the Agent," *Journal of Law, Economics, and Organization* 22 (2006): 1–22; Moe, "The Union Label on the Ballot Box," *Education Next* 6, no. 3 (Summer 2006).

62. Sarah F. Anzia, *Timing and Turnout: How Off-Cycle Elections Favor Organized groups* (Chicago: University of Chicago Press, 2013); Anzia, "Election Timing and the Electoral Influence of Interest Groups," *Journal of Politics* 73, no. 2 (2011): 412–27.

63. Terry Moe and Sarah F. Anzia, "Public Sector Unions and the Costs of Government," *Journal of Politics* (Forthcoming, 2015); Anzia and Moe, "The Politics of Pensions," paper presented at the American Political Science Association Annual Meeting, Chicago, IL, August 29–September 1, 2013.

64. Paul Johnston, *Success While Others Fail* (Ithaca, NY: Cornell University ILR Press, 1994).

65. Joshua Page, *The Toughest Beat: Politics, Punishment, and the Prison Officers Union in California* (New York: Oxford University Press, 2011).

66. Rosenfeld, *What Unions No Longer Do.*

67. Johnston, *Success While Others Fail.*

68. Leo Troy, *The New Unionism in the New Society: Public Sector Unions in the Redistributive State* (Fairfax, VA: George Mason University Press, 1994).

69. For a full discussion of how profoundly important it is that public sector unions can exercise influence on the very officials who are supposed to be managing them by campaigning on their behalf, see Moe, "Political Control and the Power of the Agent," *Journal of Law, Economics, and Organization* 22 (2006); and Moe, *Special Interest.*

70. Charles Tiebout, "A Pure Theory of Local Expenditures," *Journal of Political Economy* 64, no. 5 (1956): 416-24; Michael S. Greve, *Real Federalism: Why It Matters, and How It Could Happen* (Washington, DC: AEI Press, 1999).

71. John Ostrower, "Boeing Union Approves New Eight-Year Contract," *Wall Street Journal,* January 4, 2014.

72. "Bold Action Big Change: About AFSCME's New Plan," *AFSCME Public Employee*, Special Edition (September 2006): 7.

73. Clyde W. Summers, "Public Employee Bargaining: A Political Perspective," *Yale Law Journal* 83 (1974): 1156-1200.

74. "After Detroit, Who's Next?" *Wall Street Journal*, July 21, 2013; Richard Riordan and Tim Rutten, "A Plan to Avert the Pension Crisis," *New York Times*, August 4, 2013.

75. Summers, "Public Employee Bargaining."

76. Eugene G. Eisner, "First Amendment Right of Association for Public Employee Union Members," *Labor Law Journal* 20 (1969).

77. Moe, *Special Interest*, chap. 9 and 10.

78. Michael Hartney and Patrick Flavin, "From the Schoolhouse to the Statehouse: Teacher Union Political Activism and U.S. Education Reform Policy," *State Politics &Policy Quarterly* 11, no. 3(September 2011): 251-68.

79. Peter H. Schuck, *Why Government Fails So Often* (Princeton, NJ: Princeton University Press), 321.

80. I once raised the issue of first principles at a public debate. My principal interlocutor and most of the audience took it as a joke and responded in kind. However, having probably considered the matter settled for so long, none of them were able to offer much of an answer when they realized I was serious.

81. Clyde W. Summers, "From Industrial Democracy to Union Democracy," *Journal of Labor Research* 21, no. 2 (2000): 3-14.

82. Walter Lippman, *Drift and Mastery* (Madison: University of Wisconsin Press, 1985), 59.

83. Bowen cited in David Sims, "CUNY Professor: Just Being Truthful about Public Payroll's Drain," *The Chief-Leader*, April 16, 2010.

84. Richard Steier, "A Neocon Skeptic Grows at City College," *The Chief-Leader*, May 6, 2011.

CHAPTER 2

1. Harry H. Wellington and Ralph K. Winter, "The Limits of Collective Bargaining in Public Employment," *Yale Law Journal* 77, no. 7 (1969): 1107–27.

2. Richard Epstein, "The Public Mischief of Public Unions," *Forbes*, March 3, 2009.

3. Henry Wellington and Ralph Winter, *The Unions and the Cities* (Washington, DC: Brookings Institution, 1971); Robert S. Summers, *Collective Bargaining and Public Benefit Conferral: A Jurisprudential Critique* (Ithaca, NY: Institute of Public Employment, New York State School of Industrial and Labor Relations, 1976). For a critique of this view, see Sanford Cohen, "Does Public Employee Unionism Diminish Democracy?" *Industrial and Labor Relations Review* 32, no. 2 (1979): 189–95.

4. Lawrence M. Spizman, "Public Employee Unions: A Study in the Economics of Power," *Journal of Labor Research* 1, no. 2 (Fall 1980): 265–73.

5. *Abood v. Detroit Board of Education* 341 U.S. 209 (1977). In *Abood*, the Supreme Court held that non-members may be assessed dues for "collective bargaining, contract administration, and grievance adjustment purposes" but not for political or ideological causes.

6. Thomas L. Gais, Mark A. Peterson, and Jack L. Walker, "Interest Groups, Iron Triangles and Representative Institutions in American National Government," *British Journal of Political Science* 14, no. 2 (April 1984): 161–85.

7. Theodore Lowi, *The End of Liberalism* (New York: Norton, 1969). For an example using teachers' unions, school boards, and departments of education, see Martin R. West, Michael Henderson, and Paul E. Peterson, "The Education Iron Triangle," *The Forum* 10, no. 1 (Spring 2012).

8. Mary Williams Walsh, "Padded Pensions Add to New York's Fiscal Woes," *New York Times*, May 20, 2010; Nicole Gelinas, "Pension Tension and the Crime Spike," *New York Post*, July 15, 2012.

9. Alicia Munnell, *State and Local Pensions: What Now?* (Washington, D.C.: Brookings Institution Press, 2012); Josh Barro, "Dodging the Pension Disaster," *National Affairs* 7 (Spring 2011): 3–20.

10. Cited in Benjamin Wallace-Wells, "What Is Chris Christie Doing Right?" *New York Magazine*, August 4, 2013.

11. Tyler Cowen, *Average Is Over: Powering America beyond the Great Stagnation* (New York: Penguin, 2013); Lane Kenworthy, *Social Democratic America* (New York: Oxford University Press, 2014).

12. Josh McGeee and Marcus A. Winters, *Better Pay, Fairer Pensions* (Civic Report No. 79, Manhattan Institute for Policy Research, September 2013).

13. "A Tale of Two Counties," *Washington Post*, May 30, 2010.

14. Jan Leighley and Jonathan Nagler, "Unions, Voter Turnout, and Class Bias in the U.S. Electorate, 1964–2004," *Journal of Politics* 69 (2007): 430.

15. David Blachflower, "International Patterns of Union Membership," *British Journal of Industrial Relations* 45 (2006): 1–28.

16. Jake Rosenfeld, *What Unions No Longer Do* (Cambridge, MA: Harvard University Press, 2014), 66, 164–73.

17. "Why Public Sector Union Compensation Matters," E21 blog, January 12, 2011, http://economics21.org/commentary/why-public-sector-union-compensation-matters.

18. Barry Bluestone, "A New 'Grand Bargain' for Public Sector Workers," presentation to the John LaWare Forum, Federal Reserve Bank of Boston, March 24, 2009.

19. Richard B. Freeman and Eunice S. Han, "The War on Public Sector Collective Bargaining in the U.S.," *Journal of Industrial Relations* 54, no. 386 (Spring 2012): 386–408.

20. Thomas DiNapoli, *Debt Impact Study: An Analysis of New York State's Debt Burden* (Office of the New York State Comptroller, January 2013).

21. Ryan Murphy and Patrick Bachman, *The Public 'Union' Effect: Pushing Up Unfunded Liabilities and State Debt* (Report, Beacon Hill Institute at Suffolk University, May 2013).

22. Charles V. Bagli, "Cuomo Gains Ally in Looming Fight with Public-Employee Unions," *New York Times*, December 9, 2010.

23. Raymond Hernandez, "New York Business Leaders Plan Push in Council Races," *New York Times*, May 30, 2013.

24. Matt Friedman, "Showing Off Union Support, Christie Rallies with Laborers," *Newark Star-Ledger*, September 30, 2013; Steven Malanga, "How Chris Christie

Split the Labor Movement in New Jersey," *Wall Street Journal*, September 28, 2013.

25. Eric A. Hanushek, "Teacher Deselection," in *Creating a New Teaching Profession*, ed. Dan Goldhaber and Jane Hannaway (Washington, DC: Urban Institute Press, 2009), 165–80; Hanushek and Kati Haycock, "An Effective Teacher in Every Classroom: A Lofty Goal, but How to Do It?" *Education Next* 10, no. 3 (Summer 2010): 46–52.

26. Terry M. Moe, *Special Interest: Teachers Unions and America's Public Schools* (Washington, DC: Brookings Institution, 2011), 174–214.

27. Moe, *Special Interest*, 52, and nn. 42, 420.

28. Brad Shannon, "State Workers Getting a Smaller Share of the Budget," *Seattle Times*, October 14, 2011.

29. Eric Patashnik, "Budgeting More, Deciding Less," *Public Interest* 138 (Winter 2000).

30. Moody's Investor Service, *Adjusted Pension Liabilities for U.S. States* (Median Report, June 27, 2013).

31. Steven Greenhut, "California Cities and Counties Consider Bankruptcy Option," *Union Watch*, March 16, 2012, http://unionwatch.org/californias-br oke-cities-and-counties-consider-bankruptcy-option/.

32. Jon Hurdle, "With Philadelphia Shortfall, Schools Face Renewed Cuts," *New York Times*, April 25, 2014.

33. Take the results of a brief scan of the international news in the summer of 2013, which in many countries covered battles between government and public sector unions. See, for example, Jeffrey Simpson, "When Politicians Campaign against Public Sector Unions," *The Globe and Mail*, June 1, 2013; "Maestros causan destrozos en la Cámara de Diputados de México," *Univision Noticias*, August 20, 2013; Philippe Jacqué, "En grève, les cheminots veulent peser sur l'évolution du système ferroviaire," *Le Monde*, June 12, 2013.

34. Yuval Levin, "Beyond the Welfare State," *National Affairs* 7 (Spring 2011): 21–38.

CHAPTER 3

1. "Union Members—2009," News Release, Bureau of Labor Statistics, January 22, 2010.

2. These changes have also altered the demographic profile of the workers unions represent, as there are now many more women, minorities, and those with college degrees in their ranks.

3. Jefferson Cowie, *Stayin' Alive: The 1970s and the Last Days of the Working Class* (New York: New Press, 2010).

4. Kate Bronfenbrenner et al., "Introduction," in *Organizing to Win: New Research on Union Strategies*, ed. Kate Bronfenbrenner, Sheldon Friedman, Richard W. Hurd, Rudolph A. Oswald, and Ronald L. Seeber (Ithaca, NY: ILR Press, 1998), 2.

5. Albert Shanker, "Where We Stand: The Flagrant One-Sidedness of the Taylor Law," *New York Times*, September 9, 1972.

6. Richard B. Freeman, "Unionism Comes to the Public Sector," *Journal of Economic Literature* 24, no. 1 (March 1986): 41–86.

7. Jeffrey H. Keefe, "A Reconsideration and Empirical Evaluation of Wellington's and Winter's *The Unions and the Cities*," *Comparative Labor Law & Policy Journal* 34, no. 2 (Winter 2013): 262.

8. The Supreme Court proscribed the "closed shop" in *National Labor Relations Board v. General Motors*, 373 U.S. 734 (1963). In that case, the court said that workers cannot be forced to join unions. However, it allowed for unions who act as the "agent" of workers in a collective bargaining to assess workers who refuse to join the union with "agency fees," which are often nearly as much in dollar terms as union dues. So while membership cannot be coerced, contributions to union coffers can be. Workers refusing to join and objecting to the use of their agency fees for noncollective bargaining purposes, usually political activity, can exercise a "claw-back" provision. But few actually do. For the background on these legal distinctions, see Charles W. Baird, "Right to Work before and after 14(b)," *Journal of Labor Research* 19, no. 3 (Summer 1998): 471–93.

9. For data on the occupational variation of collective bargaining rights, see Henry S. Farber, "Union Membership in the United States: The Divergence between the Public and Private Sectors," Working Paper #503 Princeton University Industrial Relations Section (September 2005).

10. Baird, "Right to Work before and after 14(b)."

11. Barry T. Hirsch and David A. Macpherson, BLS data compiled at http://www.unionstats.com. See also Hirsch and Macpherson, "Union Membership and Coverage," *Industrial and Labor Relations Review* 56, no. 2 (January 2003): 349–54. Linda N. Edwards, "The Future of Public Sector Unions: Stagnation or Growth?" *American Economic Review* 79, no. 2 (May 1989): 161–65.

12. Steven Malanga, "The Real Engine of Blue America," *City Journal* 16, no. 1 (Winter 2005).

13. Center for Responsive Politics, "Top All-Time Donors, 1989–2012," http://www.opensecrets.org/orgs/list.php; and National Institute for Money in State Politics, http://www.followthemoney.org/database/IndustryTotals.phtml. See also Troy Senik, "The Worst Union in America," *City Journal* 22, no. 2(Spring 2012).

14. For a good review of all the legal changes, see Joseph E. Slater, "Public Sector Labor in the Age of Obama," *Indiana Law Journal* 87, no. 1 (2012): 189–229.

15. Stephen Skowronek and Karen Orren, *The Search for American Political Development* (New York: Cambridge University Press, 2004), 123.

16. Nick Salvatore, "A Brief Ascendancy: American Labor after 1945," *The Forum* 10, no. 1 (Spring 2012).

17. *Railway Mail Association v. Murphy*, 180 Misc. 868, 875, NYS 2nd 601, 607, (1945). As one judge wrote in this case: "To tolerate or recognize any combination of civil service employees of the government as a labor organization or union is not only incompatible with the spirit of democracy, but inconsistent with every principle upon which our government is founded. Nothing is more dangerous to public welfare than to admit hired servants of the state can dictate to government the hours, the wages and conditions under which they will carry

on essential services vital to the welfare, safety, and security of the citizen .... To admit as true that government employees have power to halt or check the functions of government unless their demands are satisfied, is to transfer to them all legislative, executive and judicial power. Nothing could be more ridiculous."

18. LaGuardia, who pledged to make New York a "one hundred percent [private sector] union" town, had a civic vision of public employees as the people's workers, exemplars of the common good. LaGuardia explained that he did "not want any of the pinochle club atmosphere to take hold" in his city government. "The right to strike against the government," he insisted, "is not and cannot be recognized." Cited in Fred Siegel, *The Prince of the City* (New York: Encounter Books, 2003), 2–6.

19. National Labor Relations Act (NLRA), 29 U.S.C. §§ 151–169, Section 1.

20. Samuel I. Rosenman, ed. *The Public Papers and Addresses of Franklin D. Roosevelt* (New York: Random House 1937), chap 6: 325, as cited by William Gomberg in "The Problem of Arbitration-The Resolution of Public Sector Disputes," *Proceedings of the American Philosophical Society* 118, no. 5 (Oct. 15, 1974), 409–14. Viewing the state as the "supreme, absolute, and uncontrollable" sovereign, Roosevelt argued that "a strike of public employees manifests nothing less than an intent on their part to obstruct the operations of government until their demands are satisfied. Such action looking toward the paralysis of government by those who have sworn to support it is unthinkable and intolerable." Letter from Franklin D. Roosevelt to L. C. Stewart, president, National Federation of Federal Employees, August 16, 1937.

21. The essentiality issue is discussed by Leonard D. White, "Strikes in the Public Service," *Public Personnel Review* 10 (January 1949): 3–10.

22. For findings that support the view that the laws as an endogenous factor spurred union growth in the public sector, see Casey Ichniowski, "Public Sector Union Growth and Bargaining Laws: A Proportional Hazards Approach with Time Varying Treatments," in *When Public Sector Workers Unionize*, ed. Ichniowski and Richard B. Freeman (National Bureau of Economic Research, Chicago: University of Chicago Press, 1988); Jeffrey Zax and Casey Ichniowski, "Bargaining Laws in the Local Public Sector," in *When Public Sector Workers Unionize*; Gregory M. Satlzman, "Bargaining Laws as a Cause and Consequence of the Growth of Teacher Unionism," *Industrial and Labor Relations Review* 38, no. 3(April 1985): 335–51. For evidence that the direction of causation is not from law to unionization, see John F. Burton and Terry Thomason, "The Extent of Collective Bargaining in the Public Sector," in *Public Sector Bargaining*, 2nd ed., ed. Benjamin Aaron, Joyce Najita, and James L. Stern (Madison, WI: IRRA, 1988): 1–51.

23. Melissa Waters and William J. Moore, "The Theory of Economic Regulation and Public Choice and the Determinants of Public Sector Bargaining Legislation," *Public Choice* 66, no. 2 (1990), 161. See also Joseph D. Reid and Michael M. Kurth, "Public Employees in Political Firms: Part B. Civil Service and Militancy," *Public Choice* 60, no. 1 (1989), 41–54.

24. For a different list of possible conditions shaping bargaining laws, see Satlzman, "Bargaining Laws as a Cause and Consequence of the Growth of Teacher

Unionism"; and Waters and Moore, "The Theory of Economic Regulation and Public Choice and the Determinants of Public Sector Bargaining Legislation."

25. Martin West, "Bargaining with Authority: The Political Origins of Public-Sector Collective Bargaining," paper presented at the Policy History Conference, St. Louis, MO, June 3–5, 2008.

26. Mike Royko, *Boss: Richard J. Daley of Chicago* (New York: Dutton, 1971), 61.

27. Gregory Saltzman, "Public Sector Bargaining Laws Really Matter," in *When Public Sector Workers Unionize*, ed. Freeman and Ichniowski, 53.

28. A. James Reichley, *The Life of the Parties* (Lanham, MD: Rowman and Littlefield, 1992), 251–59.

29. Roger Lutchin, "Power and Policy: American City Politics between Two World Wars," in *Ethics, Machines, and the American Urban Future*, ed. Scott Greer (Cambridge, MA: Schenkman, 1963), 26.

30. Even school boards were often under the thumb of party machines. See Paul E. Peterson, *The Politics of School Reform, 1870-1940* (Chicago: University of Chicago Press, 1985).

31. Leo Kramer, *Labor's Paradox: The American Federation of State, County, and Municipal Employees* (New York: Wiley, 1962), 27.

32. Edward C. Banfield and James Q. Wilson, *City Politics* (Cambridge, MA: Harvard University Press, 1963), 206–7.

33. Harvey C. Mansfield Jr., "The Prestige of Public Employment," in *Public Employee Unions: A Study of the Crisis of Public Sector Labor Relations*, ed. A. Lawrence Chickering (San Francisco: Institute for Contemporary Studies, 1976), 35–50.

34. Stephen Ansolabehere, Alan Gerber, and James N. Synder, "Equal Votes, Equal Money: Court-Ordered Redistricting and Public Expenditures in the American States," *American Political Science Review* 96, no. 4 (December 2002): 767–77. For further discussion, see Ansolabehere and Synder, *The End of Inequality: One Person, One Vote, and the Transformation of American Politics* (New York: W.W. Norton, 2008).

35. Saltzman, "Bargaining Laws as a Cause and Consequence of the Growth of Teacher Unionism," 350; Terry M. Moe, *Special Interest: Teachers Unions and America's Public Schools* (Washington, DC: Brookings Institution, 2011), 113–33; Marjorie Murphy, *Blackboard Unions: The AFT and NEA 1900-1980* (Ithaca, NY: Cornell University Press, 1992).

36. James C. Garand, "Explaining Government Growth in the U.S. States," *American Political Science Review* 82, no. 3 (September 1988): 837–49.

37. Thomas R. Dye, "Party and Policy in the States," *Journal of Politics* 46, no. 4 (November 1984): 1097–116; James C. Garand, "Partisan Change and Shifting Expenditure Priorities in the American States, 1945–1978," *American Politics Quarterly* 13 (1985): 335–92.

38. US Counsel of Economic Advisors, *Economic Report to the President* (Washington, DC: USGPO, 1988), Table B-43.

39. US Census Bureau, *Statistical Abstract of the United States, 1970* (1970), 239.

40. US Census Bureau, "Boomers Life," July 1, 2008, http://www.boomerslife.org/baby_boom_population_us_census_bureau_by_state.htm.

41. Bureau of Labor Statistics, *Work Stoppages in Government, 1958–1968* (Report 348, 1970), 9; *Government Work Stoppages, 1960, 1969, 1970, 1971*).
42. Terry O'Neil and E.J. McMahon, "Taylor Made: The Costs and Consequences of New York's Public Sector Labor Law," Special Report S4-07, Empire Center for New York Policy (October 207), 10. For an argument that the PATCO strike effectively ended strikes in both: the public or private sectors, see Joseph A. McCartin, *Collision Course: Ronald Reagan, The Air Traffic Controllers, and the Strike that Changed America* (New York: Oxford University Press, 2011), 340–2, 350–1, 363.
43. John Ahlquist, "Public Sector Workers Need Private Sector Workers or Why the Wisconsin Protests Were Not Labor's Lazarus Moment," *The Forum* 10, no. 1 (2012): 2.
44. McCartin, *Collision Course*, 32.
45. Early institutional and legal developments in public sector unionism, especially in New York City, are discussed in James L. Perry and Charles H. Levine, "An Interorganizational Analysis of Power, Conflict, and Settlements in Public Sector Collective Bargaining," *American Political Science Review* 70, no. 4 (December 1976): 1185–201. See also E. J. McMahon and Fred Siegel, "Gotham's Fiscal Crisis: Lessons Unlearned," *Public Interest* no. 158 (Winter 2005).
46. Joseph E. Slater, *Public Workers: Government Employee Unions, the Law, and the State, 1900–1962* (Ithaca, NY: ILR Press, 2004), 179.
47. For the most thorough account of the development of EO 10988, see McCartin, *Collision Course*, 31–43.
48. The law was named after the head of a commission designated by Governor Nelson Rockefeller to study public sector labor relations in the state.
49. O'Neil and McMahon, "Taylor Made," 9. See also Ronald Donovan, *Administering the Taylor Law: Public Employee Relations in New York* (Ithaca, NY: Cornell University ILR Press, 1990), 67.
50. "New Taylor Law Has Wide Impact," *New York Times*, May 5, 1968.
51. John Kincaid, "Constitutional Federalism: Labor's Role in Displacing Places to Benefit Persons," *PS: Political Science and Politics* 26, no. 2 (June 1993): 173.
52. *Report of the President and Headquarters Departments* (International Convention, American Federation of State, County, and Municipal Employees, AFL-CIO, 1972), 30–32.
53. *Proceedings of the International Convention, American Federation of State, County, and Municipal Employees* (1970), 15; *AFSCME Proceedings* (1964), 179.
54. John Matthews, "Now, a Federal Law on Teacher Bargaining?" *Compact* 9, no. 1 (1975); Transcript, Albert Shanker and James Harris on the TODAY Show with Barbara Walters, February 26, 1975, AFT News, AFT Speeches Collection, Walter P. Ruether Library.
55. Nicol C. Rae, *The Decline and Fall of the Liberal Republicans: 1952 to the Present* (New York: Oxford University Press, 1989). See also Byron E. Shafer, *The Two Majorities and the Puzzle of American Politics* (Lawrence: University of Kansas Press, 2003), 143–56.
56. Joshua B. Freeman, *Working Class New York: Life and Labor since World War II* (New York: New Press, 2000), 211.

57. Michael Goldfield, *The Decline of Organized Labor in American Politics* (Chicago: University of Chicago Press, 1987); Paul Edward Johnson, "Organized Labor in an Era of Blue-Collar Decline," in *Interest Group Politics*, 3rd ed., ed. Allan J. Cigler and Burdett A. Loomis (Washington, DC: CQ Press, 1991); Bruce Western, "A Comparative Study of Working-Class Disorganization: Union Decline in Eighteen Advanced Capitalist Countries," *American Sociological Review* 60, no. 2 (April 1995): 179–201; Harold Meyerson, "Rolling the Union On," *Dissent* (Winter 2000): 47–55.

58. Margaret Levi, "Organizing Power: The Prospects for an American Labor Movement," *Perspectives on Politics* 1, no. 1 (March 2003): 45.

59. Gary M. Fink, "Labor Law Revision and the End of the Postwar Labor Accord," in *Organizing Labor and American Politics, 1894-1994: The Labor-Liberal Alliance*, ed. Kevin Boyle (New York: SUNY-Albany Press, 1998).

60. "Union Members—2012," News Release, Bureau of Labor Statistics, January 22, 2013.

61. Jacob Hacker and Paul Pierson, *Winner-Take-All Politics: How Washington Made the Rich Richer—and Turned Its Back on the Middle Class* (New York: Simon and Schuster, 2010); Benjamin Radcliff and Martin Saiz, "Labor Organization and Public Policy in the American States," *Journal of Politics* 60, no. 1 (February 1998): 113–25; Karen Orren, "Union Politics and Postwar Liberalism in the United States, 1946–1979," *Studies in American Political Development* 1 (1986): 215–52.

62. Andrew E. Busch, *Reagan's Victory: The Presidential Election of 1980 and the Rise of the Right* (Lawrence: University of Kansas Press, 2005); Dan Balz and Ronald Brownstein, *Storming the Gates: Protest Politics and the Republican Revival* (Boston: Little, Brown, 1996); Godfrey Hodgson, *The World Turned Right Side Up: A History of the Conservative Ascendancy in America* (Boston: Houghton-Mifflin, 1996); Sean Wilentz, *The Age of Reagan: A History, 1974–2008* (New York: HarperCollins, 2008); Donald T. Critchlow, *The Conservative Ascendancy: How the GOP Right Made Political History* (Cambridge, MA: Harvard University Press, 2007).

63. For two significantly different perspectives, see Goldfield, *The Decline of Organized Labor in American Politics* and Charles B. Craver, *Can Unions Survive? The Rejuvenation of the American Labor Movement* (New York: New York University Press, 1993).

64. Melvyn Dubofsky, "Does Organized Labor Have A Future?" *Logos: A Journal of Modern Society and Culture* 12, no. 2 (Winter 2013).

65. Rich Yeselson, "Fortress Unionism," *Democracy: A Journal of Ideas* 29 (Summer 2013); Shafer, *Two Majorities and Puzzle of Modern American Politics*, 132–43.

66. Paul Frymer, *Black and Blue: African Americans, the Labor Movement, and the Decline of the Democratic Party* (Princeton, NJ: Princeton University Press, 2008).

67. Kimberly Philips-Fein, *Invisible Hands: The Making of the Conservative Movement from the New Deal to Reagan* (New York: W. W. Norton, 2009), 87–115.

68. Before 1960, public attitudes toward unions were favorable. In 2009, for the first time in the modern era, less than half of Americans told pollsters that

they approved of labor unions. See Benjamin I. Page and Walter Y. Shapiro, *The Rational Public: Fifty Years of Trends in Americans' Policy Preferences* (Chicago: University of Chicago Press, 1992); Seymour Martin Lipset, "Labor Unions in the Public Mind," in *Unions in Transition*, ed. Seymour Martin Lipset (San Francisco: ICS Press, 1986); Lydia Saad, "Labor Unions See Sharp Slide in U.S. Public Support," Gallup, September 3, 2009.

69. Joseph A. McCartin, "Bringing the State's Workers In: Time to Rectify an Imbalanced US Labor Historiography," *Labor History* 47, no. 1 (February 2006): 83–7.

70. For recent attitudes toward public sector unions and collective bargaining, see "A Manhattan Institute Poll Conducted by Doug Schoen," September 25, 2011, http://www.publicsectorinc.org/events/CSLL092011.html.

71. Ben Wattenberg, "Meany 'Perhapses,'" *Daily Gazette*, December 12, 1972.

72. Roger M. Williams, "The Clamor over Municipal Unions," *Saturday Review*, March 5, 1977, 18.

73. Melvyn Dubofsky, "Does Organized Labor Have A Future?" *Logos* 13, no. 1–2 (Spring 2014).

74. Richard B. Freeman, "Spurts in Union Growth: Defining Moments and Social Processes," in *The Defining Moment: The Great Depression and the American Economy in the Twentieth Century*, ed. Michael D. Bordo, Claudia Goldin, and Eugene N. White (Chicago: University of Chicago Press, 1998).

CHAPTER 4

1. David Kocieniewski, "GOP Wants More Details of Corzine Aid," *New York Times*, August 5, 2005. Katz reportedly received $6 million in the break-up settlement from Corzine. See David Kocieniewski and Serve F. Kovaleski, "Romance Over, Union Chief Has Corzine's Number," *New York Times*, May 23, 2007.

2. Paul Mulshine, "Steve Sweeney Might Fight for a Fair Contract," *New Jersey Star-Ledger*, September 20, 2009; Richard D. Jones, "Corzine Gives in on Tax Plan as Trade Off for His Embattled Budget," *New York Times*, June 20, 2006. Corzine also reportedly told union workers at the rally: "I'll stand with you for your pension rights and collective bargaining rights. I want to tell you again, I believe in collective bargaining. It is and has been good for all of New Jersey."

3. Quoted in Steven Brill, "The Teachers Unions Last Stand," *New York Times*, May 17, 2010.

4. Center for Responsive Politics, "Top All-Time Donors, 1989–2012," http://www.opensecrets.org/orgs/list.php; and National Institute for Money in State Politics, "Industry Influence," http://www.followthemoney.org/database/IndustryTotals.phtml. See also Troy Senik, "The Worst Union in America," *City Journal* 22, no. 2 (Spring 2011).

5. Richard Ravitch and Paul Volcker, *Report of the State Budget Crisis Task Force* (New York, NY: State Budget Crisis Task Force, July 2012); Daniel J. Nadler and Sounman Hong, *Institutional Determinants of Tax-Exempt Bond Yields* (Report #11-04, Program on Education and Governance, Harvard Kennedy School, 2012).

6. New Jersey Education Association, "Fact Sheet," http://www.njea.org/about/who-we-are/fact-sheet; Communications Workers of New Jersey, "About Us," http://www.cwanj.org/content/about-us

7. Union dues for full-time teachers in New Jersey in 2012 were $791; for full-time support staff, dues were $395. Multiply those figures by the number of members and you get about $100 million in dues revenue.

8. Kean quoted in Matthew Futterman and James O'Neil, "Despite Setbacks Teachers Union Remains a Force," *Philadelphia Inquirer,* November 14, 1996.

9. The teachers' union members constituted 11 percent of delegates at the Democrats' 1996 National Convention, which was a larger share than the delegation from California, the largest state in the country. See Sol Stern, "How Teachers Unions Handcuff Schools," *City Journal* 7, no. 2 (Spring 2007).

10. Steven Brill, "Teachers Unions' Last Stand," *New York Times,* May 17, 2010. Over the past 25 years, union members (public and private) have been about 25 percent of the delegates at the Democrats' quadrennial national conventions. See Taylor E. Dark, *The Unions and the Democrats: An Enduring Alliance* (Ithaca, NY: ILR/Cornell University Press, 1999), 135.

11. Terry M. Moe, *Special Interest: Teachers Unions and America's Public Schools* (Washington, DC: Brookings Institution, 2011), 291–95.

12. Bill Turgue, "Rhee Dismisses 241 DC Teachers; Union Vows to Contest Firings," *Washington Post,* July 24, 2010.

13. Moe, *Special Interest,* 144–53. See also Moe, "Teachers Unions and School Board Elections," in *Besieged: School Boards and the Future of Education Politics* ed. William G. Howell (Washington, DC: Brookings Institution Press, 2005).

14. Jake Rosenfeld, *What Unions No Longer Do* (Cambridge, MA: Harvard University Press, 2014), 167. Rosenfeld is keen to show that unionizing government workers does not increase voter turnout as much as unionizing blue-collar private sector workers.

15. Rosenfeld, *What Unions No Longer Do,* 170–73.

16. Bob Dole, "Acceptance Speech," Republican National Convention, San Diego, California, August 15, 1996.

17. Mancur Olson, *The Logic of Collective Action: Public Goods and the Theory of Groups* (Cambridge, MA: Harvard University Press, 1965).

18. James Q. Wilson, *Political Organizations,* rev. ed. (Princeton, NJ: Princeton University Press, 1995), 332–6.

19. In *National Labor Relations Board v. General Motors,* 373 U.S. 734 (1963), the Supreme Court determined that workers cannot be forced to join unions and outlawed the "closed shop." However, the court held that it is still constitutional for unions to require contributions to their coffers, even if they cannot require contributing workers to become union members.

20. For example, see New York State Civil Service Law, Chapter 606, Laws of 1992.

21. The US Supreme Court has held that agency fees can be assessed only to cover the expenses of collective bargaining, not political activity. See *Abood v. Detroit Board of Education,* 431 U.S. 209 (1977).

22. *Hudson* rights derive from a Supreme Court case. See *Chicago Teachers Union, Local 1, AFT, AFL-CIO v. Hudson* 475 U.S. 292 (1986). For a state example, see

NYS Law, Chapter 677, Laws of 1977 (as amended by Chapter 678, Laws of 1977 and Chapter 122, Laws of 1978).

23. "Agency Refund Procedure," PSC-CUNY letter to members, 2012.
24. *Knox v. Service Employees International Union, Local 100* 567 U.S. (2012).
25. Moe, *Special Interest*, 52, and nn. 42, 420.
26. Moe, *Special Interest*, 71.
27. Richard B. Freeman and Eunice S. Han, "Public Sector Unionism without Collective Bargaining" (Working Paper, Economics Department, Harvard University, December 2012).
28. Byron Shafer, *The Two Majorities and the Puzzle of Modern American Politics* (Lawrence: Kansas University Press, 2004), 132–69.
29. Sean Farhang and Ira Katznelson, "The Southern Imposition: Congress and Labor in the New and Fair Deals," *Studies in American Political Development* 19 (2005).
30. "Texas Is Prospering while Ohio Lags," *Wall Street Journal*, July 18, 2008; Vincent Vernuccio and Joseph Lehman, "An Inspiration and a Warning from Michigan," *Wall Street Journal*, December 18, 2012.
31. Richard H. Thaler and Cass R. Sunstein, *Nudge: Improving Decisions about Health, Wealth, and Happiness*, rev. and exp. ed. (New York: Penguin, 2009).
32. Christian Schneider, "It's Working in Wisconsin," *City Journal* 22, no. 1 (Winter 2012): 54.
33. George F. Will, "Pension Time Bomb," *Washington Post*, February 11, 2008.
34. George F. Will, "Liberals' Wisconsin Waterloo," *Washington Post*, August 24, 2011.
35. Karen E. Crummy, "Public Unions Invest Heavily in Colorado Elections," *Denver Post*, March 14, 2012.
36. Joe Guillen, "Issue 2 Campaigns Raised More Than $50 Million," *Cleveland Plain Dealer*, December 17, 2011; Jim Siegel and Joe Vardon, "Unions Spend Big on Issue 2," *Columbus Dispatch*, October 28, 2011.
37. Molly Bloom and Ida Lieszkovszky, "Educations Unions Raise Much of $19 Million to Defeat Ohio's Issue 2," State Impact, NPR, October 27, 2011, http://stateimpact.npr.org/ohio/2011/10/27/education-unions-push-campaigns pending-on-ohios-issue-2-sky-high. See also Jason Stein and Patrick Marley, *More Than They Bargained For: Scott Walker, Unions, and the Fight for Wisconsin* (Madison: University of Wisconsin Press, 2012).
38. Campaign Media Analysis Group, http://cmagadfacts.tumblr.com.
39. Brennan Center for Justice, New York University School of Law, "Special Interest TV Spending in Wisconsin Supreme Court Race Tops $3 Million," April 4, 2011, http://www.brennancenter.org/content/resource/special_interest_tv_spending_in_wisconsin_supreme_court_tops_3_million.
40. Shushannah Walshe, "30 Million Pouring in to Influence Wisconsin's Recall Elections," ABC News, August 4, 2011.
41. Monica Davey, "Organizers Say 1 Million Signed Petition to Recall Wisconsin Governor," *New York Times*, January 18, 2012.
42. Joshua Page, *The Toughest Beat: Politics, Punishment, and the Prison Officers Union in California* (New York: Oxford University Press, 2011), 48.

43. Quoted in Steve Lopez, "Donations Create Winners," *Los Angeles Times*, May 22, 2011.

44. "Big Money Talks," California Fair Practices Commission Report (March 2010), 41. See also Page, *The Toughest Beat*, 54–64.

45. See US Department of Labor, http://www.dol.gov/olms/regs/compliance/rrlo/lmrda.htm. See also http://www.unionfacts.com.

46. Editor, "Public Sector Unions and Political Spending," September 23, 2010, http://unionwatch.org/public-sector-unions-political-spending/; Larry Sand, "Teachers' Union Political Funding Inappropriate," *San Jose Mercury*, July 7, 2010.

47. AFSCME's members pay, on average, $390 a year in dues per member. But the dues for teachers are sometimes as much as $1,000 per year. So $500 a year seems fair. See Brody Mullins and John McKinnon, "Campaign's Big Spender," *Wall Street Journal*, October 22, 2010.

48. Kenneth Lovett, "Senate Democrats Have Cozy Office Deal with United Federation of Teachers at Union's Building," *New York Daily News*, January 26, 2012.

49. Moe, *Special Interest*, 282.

50. Amber M. Winkler, Janie Schull, and Dara Zeehandelaar, *How Strong Are U.S. Teacher's Unions? A State-by-State Comparison* (Report, Thomas B. Fordham Institute, October 2012).

51. Moe excluded political donations by party committees, candidate PACs, and wealthy individuals, so that his comparison would be a straight-up comparison of interest groups that give to candidates (mostly for governor or state legislator) and to political parties.

52. Moe, *Special Interest*, 291–94.

53. Fred Siegel, "The Most Powerful Force in the Country," *The Forum* 10, no. 1 (Spring 2012).

54. See "California 2010," National Institute for Money in State Politics, accessed, June 30, 2014. http://www.followthemoney.org/database/state_overview.phtml?y=2010&s=CA.

55. Moe, *Special Interest*, 296–97.

56. See "Heavy Hitters: Top All-Time Donors, 1989–2014," Center for Responsive Politics, accessed June 30, 2014, http://www.opensecrets.org/orgs/list.php?type=A.

57. "Democrats Discovering Campaign Law's Cost," *Washington Post*, June 28, 2003.

58. See "Independent Expenditures and Communications Costs, 1989–2014," Center for Responsive Politics, accessed, June 30, 2014, http://www.opensecrets.org/orgs/indexp.php.

59. Mullins and McKinnon, "Campaign's Big Spender"; and Steven Greenhouse, "Union Spends $91 Million on Midterms," Caucus–*New York Times* Blog, October 22, 2010.

60. James Bennett and William Orzechowski, "The Voting Behavior of Bureaucrats: Some Empirical Evidence," *Public Choice* 41, no. 2 (1983): 271–83.

61. Fernanda Santos and David W. Chen, "Mayoral Hopefuls All Make Time for Teacher Union Leader," *New York Times*, March 20, 2012; Javier Hernandez,

"Energized by Bloomberg's Exit, Labor Chiefs Try to Sway Race," *New York Times*, June 19, 2013.

62. Holger Sieg and Yu Wang, "The Impact of Unions on Elections and Fiscal Policies in U.S. Cities," paper prepared for the Carnegie-NYU-Rochester Conference on "Aggregate Implications of Local Public Finance," November 7, 2012.

63. Pamela MacLean, "The Strong Arm of the Law: A Small Union of California Prison Guards Wields Enormous Power," *California Lawyer* 22, no. 1 (November 2002).

64. "Biography of State Representative Joe Aresimowicz," Connecticut House Democrats, April 30, 2014, http://www.housedems.ct.gov/aresimowicz/bio030.asp

65. Dan Walters, "Democrats Strengthen Unions Noose," *Orange County Register*, July 10, 2009.

66. Editor, "SEIU Spokesperson threatening California lawmakers with union retaliation," *Union Watch*, September, 25, 2010, http://unionwatch.org/seiu-spokesperson-threatening-california-lawmakers-with-union-retaliation/

67. Eric Bailey, "Proposition 98, which Guards Funding for State's Schools, Is Tested Again," *Los Angeles Times*, July 17, 2009.

68. US Census Bureau, Census of Governments, *Preliminary Count of Local Governments by Type and State* (2012); *Summary of Public Employment and Payrolls by Type of Government* (March 2007). This excludes other types of local governments, such as townships (16,519) and counties (3,033).

69. Richard Smolka, quoted in William J. Crotty, *Political Reform and the American Experiment* (New York: Crowell, 1977), 86–87.

70. Zoltan Hajnal, Paul Lewis, and Hugh Louch, *Municipal Elections in California: Turnout, Timing, and Competition* (San Francisco: Public Policy Institute of California, 2002). See also Curtis Wood, "Voter Turnout in City Elections," *Urban Affairs Review* 38, no. 2 (2002): 209–31.

71. "Election 2013: Exit Polls," *New York Times*, http://www.nytimes.com/projects/elections/2013/general/nyc-mayor/exit-polls.html; Ruth Milkman and Stephanie Luce, *State of the Unions 2013: A Profile of Organized Labor in New York City, New York State, and the United States* (Report for the Joseph S. Murphy Institute at the CUNY Graduate Center, September 2013).

72. Sarah F. Anzia, *Timing and Turnout: How Off-Cycle Elections Favor Organized Groups* (Chicago: University of Chicago Press, 2014).

73. Anzia, *Timing and Turnout*, chap. 6.

74. Timothy D. Chandler and Rafael Gely, "Protective Service Unions, Political Activities, and Bargaining Outcomes," *Journal of Public Administration Research and Theory* 5, no. 3 (1995): 295–318; James L. Stern, "A Look Ahead at Public Employee Unionism," *Annals of the American Academy of Political Science* 473 (1984):165-76.

75. By the very nature of their jobs, the police are bound to create some enemies. How and how much they seek to enforce the laws will provoke someone's ire. In addition, police tend to be less well organized because there are a greater variety of job titles.

76. Anzia, *Timing and Turnout*, chap. 5. See also Christopher Berry and Jacob E. Gerson, "Voters, Non-Voters, and the Implications for Election Timing for Public Policy," *Quarterly Journal of Political Science* 6, no. 2 (2011): 103–35.

77. Sarah F. Anzia, "Election Timing and the Electoral Influence of Interest Groups," *Journal of Politics* 73, no. 2: 412–27.

78. Quoted in Anzia, "Election Timing and the Electoral Influence of Interest Groups."

79. Stephen Ansolabehere, John M. de Figueiredo, and James M. Snyder, "Why Is There so Little Money in U.S. Politics?" *Journal of Economic Perspectives* 17 (2003): 105–30.

80. Thomas Stratmann, "Some Talk: Money in Politics," *Public Choice* 124 (2005): 135–56; Stratmann, "Can Special Interests Buy Congressional Votes? Evidence from Financial Services Legislation," *Journal of Law and Economics* 45, no. 2 (2002): 345–74.

81. Richard L. Hall and Frank W. Wayman. "Buying Time: Moneyed Interests and the Mobilization of Bias in Congressional Committees," *American Political Science Review* 84 (1990): 797–820.

82. Lynda W. Powell, "The Influence of Campaign Contributions on Legislative Policy," *The Forum* 11, no. 3 (Fall 2013).

83. Lynda W. Powell, *The Influence of Campaign Contributions on State Legislatures: The Effects of Institutions and Politics* (Ann Arbor: University of Michigan Press, 2012).

84. Stephen Ansolabehere, James M. Snyder, and Michy Tripath, "Are PAC Contributions and Lobbying Linked? New Evidence from the 1995 Lobby Disclosure Act," *Business and Politics* 4, no. 2 (2002): 131–55.

85. David Lowery, Virginia Gray, Jennifer Benz, Mary Deason, Justin Kirkland, and Jennifer Sykes, "Understanding the Relationship between Health PACs and Health Lobbying in the American States," *Publius* 39 (2008): 70–94.

86. Zoltan L. Hajnal and Terry Nichols Clark, "The Local Interest-Group System: Who Governs and Why?" *Social Science Quarterly* 79, no. 1 (1998): 227–41.

87. Cari Lynn Hennessey, "Money and Influence in the Chicago City Council," *The Forum* 11, no. 3 (Fall 2013).

CHAPTER 5

1. For a taste of the political science literature on this subject, see Shaun Bowler and Todd Donovan, *Demanding Choices: Opinion, Voting, and Direct Democracy* (Ann Arbor: University of Michigan Press, 2000); Elisabeth Gerber, *The Populist Paradox: Interest Group Influence and the Promise of Direct Legislation* (Princeton, NJ: Princeton University Press, 1999).

2. For a sample of the divide between the public's preferences and those of teachers and their unions, see Paul E. Peterson, Michael Henderson, and Martin R. West, *Teachers versus the Public: What Americans Think about Schools and How to Fix Them* (Washington, DC: Brookings Institution Press, 2014), 15–73.

3. Alyssia Finely, "Gloria Romero: The Trials of a Democratic Reformer," *Wall Street Journal*, August 31, 2012; Steve Malanga, "The Beholden State," *City Journal* 20, no. 2 (Spring 2010); Joel Kotkin, "The Golden State's War on Itself," *City Journal* 20, no. 3 (Summer 2010).

4. "Jerry Brown's Tax Initiative Officially Qualifies for November Ballot," *Sacramento Bee*, June, 20 2012.

5. James Fallows, "Jerry Brown's Reboot," *Atlantic Monthly*, May 22, 2013.

6. Jon Ortiz, "Move Over Wisconsin—The Union Battle Is Beginning in California," *Sacramento Bee*, June, 10, 2012.

7. Richard Ellis, *Democratic Delusions: The Initiative Process in America* (Lawrence: University of Kansas Press, 2002).

8. Troy Senik, "The Worst Union in America," *City Journal* 22, no. 2 (Spring 2011).

9. Terry Moe, *Special Interest: Teachers Unions and America's Public Schools* (Washington, DC: Brookings Institution, 2010), 291–96.

10. This finding comports with the conventional wisdom in the academic literature that interest groups are better at blocking than advancing their goals through direct democracy procedures. For a good review of this literature and a contrarian's perspective based on data from California, see John M. de Figueiredo, Chang Ho Ji, and Thad Kousser, "Financing Direct Democracy: Revisiting the Research on Campaign Spending and Citizen Initiatives," *Journal of Law, Economics, and Organization* 27, no. 3 (2011): 485–514.

11. John Ortiz, "Union Chips in $2.5 Million to Fight Proposition 32," *Sacramento Bee*, August 14, 2012, http://blogs.sacbee.com/the_state_worker/2012/08/union-chips-in-25-million-to-fight-proposition-32.html.

12. "Not Quite Greek, But Still Weak," *The Economist*, June 16, 2012; William Voegeli, "Failed State," *Claremont Review of Books*, December 17, 2009.

13. Howard Bornstein et al., *Going for Broke: Reforming California's Public Employee Pension Systems* (Stanford Institute for Public Policy Research, April 2010).

14. Edward Luce, "From the California Dream to a Cautionary Tale," *Financial Times*, June 10, 2012.

15. According to the State Budget Crisis Task Force, "California, the most populous state in the country, has the largest number of Medicaid enrollees, 7.5 million. Among the six study states, it also has the highest percentage of its population enrolled in Medicaid, 29 percent. California has been able to roll a number of its state-funded health care programs into Medicaid, thereby gaining federal participation in funding of these programs. Even with the addition of federal funds, however, the state's annual spending per enrollee, $3,364, is the lowest among the six study states and well below the national average of $5,337; its Medicaid spending as a percent of state General Fund spending, 11.8 percent, is also well below the national average of 15.8 percent."

16. Wyatt Buchanan, "CA Legislators Taking on Pension Reform," *San Francisco Chronicle*, August 6, 2012; Jim Christie, "California Lawmakers Set to Approve Pension Reform," *Reuters*, August 31, 2012.

17. The number of signatures to get a measure on the ballot must be equal to at least 8 percent of the total votes cast for the governor at the last gubernatorial election.

18. Brown cited in George Skelton, "Gov. Brown's Proposed Tax Increase? Yes, It's about Pensions Too," *Los Angeles Times*, August 29, 2012.

19. Munger's proposition would have raised taxes on a sliding scale starting at $7,316 in taxable income for single filers and $14,632 for joint filers.

20. Some have argued that the school equity lawsuits that resulted in the *Serrano v. Priest* (1976) decision were a major factor in creating the conditions for the

tax revolt and Proposition 13. As the source of school funding moved from local to state governments, California's per-student spending on education fell to among the lowest in the nation. Proposition 98 was then partly a response to the new source of funds and sought to lock in a commitment from the state government. See William A. Fischel, "Did *Serrano* Cause Proposition 13?" *National Tax Journal* 42, no. 4 (December 1989): 465–74; and Fischel, "How *Serrano* Caused Proposition 13," *Journal of Law and Politics* 12, no. 4 (Fall 1996): 607–36. Also, Martin R. West and Paul E. Peterson, "The Equity Lawsuit: A Critical Appraisal," in *School Money Trials,* ed. West and Peterson (Washington, DC: Brookings Institution, 2007).

21. "The People's Will," *The Economist*, April 2011.
22. Much of the data was generously provided by John G. Matsusaka of the Initiative and Referendum Institute at the University of Southern California, http://www.iandrinstitute.org/.
23. The coding method conducted here follows a study by Daniel J. B. Mitchell, who used the University of California Hastings College of the Law dataset. See Mitchell, "Unions and Direct Democracy in California: A New Pattern Emerging?" *California Policy Options 2008,* ed. Mitchell (Los Angeles: School of Public Affairs, 2008), 197–221. My research assistant, Andrew Marcum, did the first cut of coding. I then coded the measures. We agreed on over 90 percent of the coding decisions. When there was disagreement, it was usually over whether a measure deserved a partisan code or should be placed in the "other" category, not whether it was liberal or conservative.
24. It should be noted that by attempting to concentrate solely on public sector unions, some cases where public and private sector labor were at odds were overlooked. In addition, some nominally private sector unions have local affiliates composed of public sector workers. Therefore, the reader should be advised that there is some static in the data.
25. In addition, the arguments themselves may cite other groups that are either for or against the proposition.
26. Of course, another analyst might choose a few different propositions to be included in the list of most important but there is likely to be broad agreement on most of those included here.
27. Richard Lee Colvin, "Wilson Is Lampooned at Teachers Union 'Boot Camp,'" *Los Angeles Times*, August 26, 1998.
28. Senik, "The Worst Union in America."
29. Moe, *Special Interest,* 298.
30. Senik, "The Worst Union in America." The state attorney general's authority over ballot titles stems from a 1974 measure, Proposition 9, which mandated the creation of a Fair Political Practices Commission.
31. Myron Lieberman, *The Teachers Unions: How the NEA and AFT Sabotage Reform and Hold Students, Parents, and Teachers Hostage to Bureaucracy* (New York: Free Press, 1997), 99.
32. Tom McGinty and Brody Mullins, "Political Spending by Unions Far Exceeds Direct Donations," *Wall Street Journal,* July 10, 2012.

33. Proposition 167 in 1992, which sought to raise income tax rates (and repeal a prior sales tax increase), was rejected by voters 59 percent opposed to 41 percent in favor. Proposition 217 in 1996, which sought to reinstate higher rates on top earners, fared better, losing by the narrow margin of 51 percent opposed to 49 percent in favor. In 1990, an initiative to increase sales taxes to fund drug enforcement and prevention was summarily dismissed, 68 percent against to 32 percent in favor. Over the last 30 years, voters have only enacted 6 out of 21 tax-related initiatives. All but one of these either reduced the tax burden or made it more difficult to raise taxes. Two of the measures were nearly identical repeals of gift and inheritances tax. Another indexed taxes to inflation, thus reducing "bracket creep." Yet another repealed sales taxes on certain foodstuffs. And Proposition 62 in 1986 made it more difficult for local government to raise taxes, requiring a two-thirds majority of the governing body. Only Proposition 99 in 1988 raised taxes on cigarettes and tobacco. The voting behavior of the California electorate chimes with extensive national polling, which suggests that the American public wants the impossible combination of extensive government services and low taxes.

34. David Siders, "Gov. Jerry Brown's Holds Uneasy Lead in the Latest Poll," *Sacramento Bee*, June 9, 2012, A1.

CHAPTER 6

1. Henry Brady, Kay Scholzman, and Sidney Verba, *The Unheavenly Chorus: Unequal Political Voice and the Broken Promise of American Democracy* (Princeton, NJ: Princeton University Press, 2012); Brady, Scholzman, and Verba, *Voice and Equality: Civic Voluntarism and American Politics* (Cambridge, MA: Harvard University Press, 1995); G. William Domhoff, *State Autonomy or Class Dominance: Case Studies on Policy Making in America* (Hawthorne, NY: Aldine de Gruyter, 1996) and C. Wright Mills, *The Power Elite* (New York: Oxford University Press, 1956).

2. For a thorough review of the political science literature, see Frank R. Baumgartner and Beth L. Leech, *Basic Interests: The Importance of Groups in Politics and Political Science* (Princeton, NJ: Princeton University Press, 1998).

3. Gloria Romero, "Fixing California: The Union Chokehold," *San Diego Union Tribune*, August 10, 2013.

4. Zoltan L. Hanjal and Terry Nichols Clark, "The Local Interest Group System: Who Governs and Why?" *Social Science Quarterly* 79, no. 1 (March 1998): 227-41.

5. Kay Scholzman and John Tierney, *Organized Interests and American Democracy* (New York: HarperCollins, 1986); Jack Walker, *Mobilizing Interest Groups in America: Patrons, Professions, and Social Movements* (Ann Arbor: University of Michigan Press, 1991).

6. Frank R. Baumgartner, Jeffrey M. Berry, Marie Hojnacki, David C. Campbell, and Beth L. Leech, *Lobbying and Policy Change: Who Wins, Who Loses, and Why* (Chicago: University of Chicago Press, 2009); Jeffrey Berry, *New Liberalism: The*

Rising Power of Citizen Groups (Washington, DC: Brookings Institution Press, 1999).

7. David M. Hart, "Business Is Not an Interest Group (and, by the Way, There's No Such Thing as 'Business'): On Companies in American National Politics," *Annual Review of Political Science* 7 (2004): 47–67. See also Richard A. Harris, "Politicized Management: The Changing Face of Business in American Politics," in *Remaking American Politics,* ed. Harris and Sidney M. Milkis (Boulder, CO: Westview Press, 1989), 262–96.

8. Jennifer Anderson et al., "Mayflies and Old Bulls: Organizational Persistence in State Interest Communities," *State Politics and Policy Quarterly* 4 (2004): 160–90.

9. Sarah Laskow, *State Lobbying Becomes a Billion Dollar Business* (Report for the Center for Public Integrity, December 2006).

10. "A Closer Look at 2011's Record-Breaking $220M Lobbying Total," New York Public Interest Research Group, Press Release, April 5, 2012.

11. *Hired Guns* (Report for the Center for Public Integrity, March 2007).

12. Gary Andres, "Campaign Style Advocacy: A Broader View of Lobbying," *The Forum* 13, no. 1 (Spring 2013).

13. Robert Dahl, "A Critique of the Ruling Elite Model," *American Political Science Review* 52 (1958): 465.

14. Joshua Page, *The Toughest Beat: Politics, Punishment, and the Prison Officers Union in California* (New York: Oxford University Press, 2011), 82.

15. *Big Money Talks* (Report, California Fair Practices Commission, March 2010), 41.

16. Timothy D. Chandler and Rafael Gely, "Toward Identifying the Determinants of Public Employee Unions' Involvement in Political Activities," *American Review of Public Administration* 26 (1996): 41738.

17. Quoted in Kevin W. Hula, *Lobbying Together: Interest Group Coalitions in Legislative Politics* (Washington, DC: Georgetown University Press, 1999), 47.

18. Jason Stein and Patrick Marley, *More Than They Bargained For: Scott Walker, Unions, and the Fight for Wisconsin* (Madison: University of Wisconsin Press, 2013), 140.

19. Chuck Bennett, "The UFT's Clout Shapes City," *New York Post,* April 13, 2009.

20. Murray Edelman, *The Politics of Symbolic Action* (Chicago: Markham, 1971).

21. Public sector unions traffic in the "valence issues" of public good provision, which are things on which nearly everyone agrees about the goals of public policy. Donald E. Stokes, "Spatial Models of Party Competition," *American Political Science Review* 57, no. 2 (1963): 368–77.

22. John Mark Hansen, "The Political Economy of Group Membership," *American Political Science Review* 79, no. 1 (1985): 79–96.

23. Terry M. Moe, *Special Interest: Teachers Unions and America's Public School* (Washington, DC: Brookings Institution Press, 2011), 68–79.

24. Jerry Wurf Papers, Walter P. Reuther Library, Wayne State University, Series II, Boxes 3–5.

25. Jonathan Rauch, *Demosclerosis: The Silent Killers of American Government* (New York: Times Books, 1994), 68–72; Mancur Olson, *The Rise and Decline of Nations: Economic Growth, Stagflation, and Social Rigidities* (New Haven, CT: Yale University Press, 1984).

26. A cap on the number of charter schools was set at 100 in 1998, expanded to 200 in 2007 after a bruising battle with the state's teachers' union, and then raised again to 460 in 2010. See Jennifer Medina, "New York State Votes to Expand Charter Schools," *New York Times*, May 28, 2010.

27. Sarah Butrymowicz and Geoff Decker, "Union lobby power remains unmatched," The Hechinger Report, March 6, 2013, http://hechingerreport.org/content/unions-lobby-power-remains-unmatched_11399/

28. Rauch, *Demosclerosis*, 100.

29. Paul C. Light, *Thickening Government* (Washington, DC: Brookings Institution, 1995).

30. Gareth Davies, *See Government Grow: Education Politics from Johnson to Reagan* (Lawrence: University of Kansas Press, 2007), 222.

31. For a detailed account of the lobbying process that led to the creation of the Department of Education, see Davies, *See Government Grow*, 233–45.

32. Byron E. Shafer, *Bifurcated Politics: Evolution and Reform in the National Party Convention* (Cambridge, MA: Harvard University Press, 1988), 120–21.

33. Matthew Futterman and James O'Neil, "Despite Setbacks Teachers Union Remains a Force," *Philadelphia Inquirer*, November 14, 1996.

34. Raymond Bauer, Ithiel de Sola Pool, and Lewis Anthony Dexter, *American Business, Public Policy, and the Politics of Foreign Trade*, 2nd ed. (Chicago: Aldine-Atherton, 1972).

35. For a fourfold typology of interest groups' activity based on societal costs and benefits, see James Q. Wilson, *Political Organizations*, rev. ed. (Princeton, NJ: Princeton University Press, 1995), 332–37.

36. Baumgartner, Berry, Hojnacki, Kimball, and Leech, *Lobbying and Policy Change*. For a study of public employee unions on this point, see Terry Moe, "Teachers Unions and the Politics of Blocking," *The Forum* 10, no. 3 (Spring 2012).

37. For a classic statement of the incrementalist view, see Charles E. Lindblom, "The Science of Muddling Through," *Public Administration Review* 19 (Spring 1959): 79–88. For a nuanced theory that tries to account better for significant policy change, see Frank Baumgartner and Bryan D. Jones, *Agendas and Instability in American Politics*, 2nd ed. (Chicago: University of Chicago Press, 2009).

38. John W. Kingdon, *Agendas, Alternatives, and Public Policy*, 2nd ed. (New York: Longman, 2002).

39. Larry M. Bartels, *Unequal Democracy: The Political Economy of the New Gilded Age* (Princeton, NJ: Princeton University Press, 2008); Martin Gilens, *Affluence and Influence: Economic Inequality and Political Power in America* (Princeton, NJ: Princeton University Press, 2012); Daron Acemoglu and James A. Robinson, *Why Nations Fail: The Origins of Power, Prosperity, and Poverty* (New York: Crown Business, 2013).

40. Kay Lehman Scholzman, "Voluntary Organizations in Politics: Who Gets Involved?" in *Representing Interests and Interest Group Representation*, ed. William Crotty, Mildred Schwartz, and John C. Green (Lanham, MD: University of America Press, 1994), 76.

41. Task Force on Inequality and American Democracy, *American Democracy in an Age of Rising Inequality* (American Political Science Association, 2004).

42. Scott Winship, "Overstating the Costs of Inequality," *National Affairs* 15 (Spring 2013).

43. Peter Enns and Christopher Wlezien, *Who Gets Represented?* (New York: Russell Sage Foundation, 2011).

44. Hart, "Business Is Not an Interest Group," *Annual Review of Political Science* 7.

45. Michael Useem, *The Inner Circle* (New York: Oxford University Press, 1984), 6.

46. Dan Clawson, Allan Neustadtl, and Mark Weller, *Dollars and Votes: How Business Campaign Contributions Subvert Democracy* (Philadelphia: Temple University Press, 1998), 168. Other analysts have sought to specify the conditions when firms will forge alliances. See Mark Mizruchi, *The Structure of Corporate Political Action: Interfirm Relations and their Consequences* (Cambridge, MA: Harvard University Press, 1992); Patrick J. Akard, "Corporate Mobilization and Political Power: The Transformation of U.S. Economic Policy in the 1970s," *American Sociological Review* 57 (1992): 597–615.

47. R. Kenneth Godwin and Barry J. Seldon, "What Corporations Really Want from Government: The Public Provision of Private Goods," in *Interest Group Politics*, ed. Allen J. Cigler and Burdett A. Loomis (Washington, DC: CQ Press, 2002).

48. Mark A. Smith, *American Business and Political Power: Public Opinion, Elections, and Democracy* (Chicago: University of Chicago, 2000).

49. The year was 1995. Berry, *New Liberalism*, 127–29.

50. Kevin W. Hula, *Lobbying Together: Interest Group Coalitions in Legislative Politics* (Washington, DC: Georgetown University Press, 1999); Marie Hojnacki, "Interest Groups' Decisions to Join Alliances or Work Alone," *American Journal of Political Science* 41 (1997): 61–87.

51. David Vogel, *Fluctuating Fortunes: The Power of Business in American Politics* (New York: Beard Books, 2003, repr.).

52. Cited in Carol J. Williams, "Justice Kennedy Laments the State of Prisons in California, U.S.," *Los Angeles Times*, February 4, 2010.

53. Page, *The Toughest Beat*; Alexander Volokh, "Privatization and the Law and Economics of Political Advocacy," *Stanford Law Review* 66 (2008): 1197-1253.

54. Terry M. Moe, "Teachers Unions and School Board Elections," in *Besieged: School Boards and the Future of Education Politics*, ed. William G. Howell (Washington, DC: Brookings Institution Press, 2005).

55. Joseph Mozingo, "An L.A. Labor Leader with a Stronger Work Ethic," *Los Angeles Times*, June 22, 2013.

56. Terry Moe and Sarah Anzia, "The Politics of Pensions," paper presented to the American Political Science Annual Convention, Chicago, IL (September 2012). Regarding the power of strikes to pressure politicians, see Harry H. Wellington and Ralph K. Winter, *The Unions and the Cities* (Washington, D.C.: Brookings Institution, 1971).

57. Ruth Milkman and Laura Braslow, *State of the Unions 2012* (Report, Joseph S. Murphy Institute and the Center for Urban Research, City University of New York, September 2012), 14.

58. "NYC 2013: Exit Polls," *New York Times*, http://www.nytimes.com/projects/elections/2013/nyc-primary/mayor/exit-polls.html.

59. David Crane, "Wall Street is No Enemy of Public Pensions," *Bloomberg View*, October 23, 2013; Caleb O. Brown, "The Real Reasons We Have a Public Pension Crisis," *The American*, October 23, 2013.

60. Steven Greenhouse, "Hospital Agreement Provides State-Financed Raises," *New York Times*, January 12, 2002.

61. Leon Fink and Brian Greenberg, *Upheaval in the Quiet Zone: 1199 SEIU and the Politics of Healthcare Unionism*, 2nd ed. (Urbana: University of Illinois Press, 2009), 266.

62. Cunningham, cited in Fink and Greenberg, *Upheaval in the Quiet Zone*, 267.

63. Steven Greenhouse, "1199 SEIU Stands Out in Getting Out the Vote," *New York Times*, October 10, 2001.

64. Bill Hammond, "Cuomo's Special Interest Helper," *New York Daily News*, May 3, 2010.

65. Steve Malanga, "How Political Malpractice Crippled New York's Healthcare," *City Journal* 11, no. 3 (Summer 2001); "On the Air to Battle Pataki's Plan," *New York Times*, March 14, 1995; Ian Fischer, "Pressure on All Sides in Battle of the Budget," *New York Times*, March 14, 1995.

66. Fink and Greenberg, *Upheaval in the Quiet Zone*, 267.

67. Annie Karni, "The Most Powerful Woman in Albany," *New York Post*, December 19, 2010.

68. Adam Nagourney, "Union Crosses Party Lines for Pataki," *New York Times*, March 20, 2002.

69. Quoted in Steven Greenhouse, "Long Climb for New President of Health Care Workers Union," *New York Times*, January 28, 2007.

70. Danny Hakim, "Advisor to Cuomo Is Also Top Lobbyist," *New York Times*, April 29, 2010.

71. Nicholas Confessore, "Amid Cuomo's Medicaid Cuts, Health Care Workers' Union Shapes a Victory," *New York Times*, February 25, 2011; Brendan Scott and Fredric Dicker, "Gov and Health Bigs Forge Medicaid Deal," *New York Post*, February 25, 2011.

72. Anzia and Moe, "The Politics of Pensions."

73. Steve Malanga, "The Pension Fund That Ate California," *City Journal* 23, no. 1 (Winter 2013).

74. Mary Williams Walsh, "Calpers Wears Party, or Union, Label," *New York Times*, October 13, 2002.

75. David Crane, "Taxpayers Covering Legislature's Bad Set," *San Francisco Chronicle*, June 19, 2012.

76. Danny Hakim, "Unions Bankrolled Analyst Vetting Pension Bill," *New York Times*, May 16, 2008.

77. Danny Hakim, "Pension off by $500 Million, City Finds," *New York Times*, June 3, 2008.

78. Office of the New York State Comptroller, *Comprehensive Annual Financial Reports*, http://www.osc.state.ny.us/pension/cafr.htm.

79. Casey Seiler, "Hevesi Draws One-to-Four Pension Pay-to-Play," *Albany Times Union*, April 15, 2011; Danny Hakim and William K. Rashbaum, "Hevesi Pleads Guilty in Pension Case," *New York Times*, October 7, 2010.

CHAPTER 7

1. Lee E. Ohanian, "America's Public Sector Union Dilemma," *The American*, November 26, 2011.

2. Of course, it may be that in government work, where it is much harder to distinguish oneself and truly excel, adequate workers may suffice.

3. Andrew Ferguson, "The Privileged Public Sector," *Weekly Standard*, September 20, 2010.

4. Quoted in Dennis Cauchon, "Private Wages No Match for Feds'," *USA Today*, March 7, 2011.

5. Jonathan Cohn, "Why Public Employees Are the New Welfare Queens," *New Republic*, August 8, 2010.

6. Numerous states have taken policy actions in this area and many major players have endorsed action. See the recommendations of the Senate Republican Policy Committee and the State Budget Crisis Task Force headed by Richard Ravitch and Paul Volker.

7. All figures come from the Bureau of Labor Statistics, US Census Bureau, and http://www.unionstats.com

8. This may be an underestimate of the percentage of private sector workers offered pension plans, as it could result from people underreporting pension offerings in the Community Population Survey. One group of researchers at the Social Security Administration used tax records to supplement self-reporting and found that 58 percent of private sector workers were offered plans. See Irena Dushi, Howard M. Imas, and Jules Lichtenstien, "Assessment of Retirement Plan Coverage by Firm Size, Using W-2 Tax Records," *Social Security Bulletin* 71, no. 2 (2011).

9. John Donahue, *The Warping of Government Work* (Cambridge, MA: Harvard University Press, 2010). See also Morley Gunderson, "Earnings Differentials between the Public and Private Sectors," *Canadian Journal of Economics* 12, no. 2, (May 1979): 228–42.

10. Keith A. Belman and John S. Heywood, "Public Sector Wage Comparability: The Role of Earnings Dispersion," *Public Finance Review* 32 (2004): 567–87.

11. Jason Richwine and Andrew Biggs, *Are California Public Employees Overpaid?* (Center for Data Analysis Report 11–01, Heritage Foundation, March 17, 2011); Robert Costrell and Michael Podgursky, "Golden Handcuffs," *Education Next* 10, no. 1 (Winter 2010): 60–66; Podgursky and Matthew Springer, "Teacher Compensation Systems in the United States K-12 Public School System," *National Tax Journal* 65, no. 1 (March, 2011): 165–92; Podgursky, *Reforming Educator Compensation* (Report, George W. Bush Institute, no. 1, February 2014); Matthew Chingos and Martin R. West, "Do More Effective Teachers Earn More Outside the Classroom?" *Education Finance and Policy* 7, no. 1 (2012); Chingos and West, "Teacher Effectiveness, Mobility, and Attrition in Florida," in *Performance Incentives: Their Growing Impact on American K-12 Education*, ed. Matthew G. Springer (Washington, D.C.: Brookings Institution Press, 2009), 251–71.

12. Keith A. Bender and John S. Heywood, *Out of Balance: Comparing Public and Private Compensation over 20 Years* (Report for the National Institute

on Retirement Security, April 2010); John Schmidtt, *The Wage Penalty for State and Local Government Employees* (Report for the Center for Economic and Policy Research, May 2010); Sylvia A. Allegretto and Jeffrey H. Keefe, *The Truth about Public Employees in California: They Are Neither Overpaid nor Overcompensated* (Policy Brief, Center on Wage and Employment Dynamics at the University of California, Berkeley, 2010); Jeffrey H. Keefe, *Debunking the Myth of the Overcompensated Public Employee* (Report for the Economic Policy Institute, Briefing Paper #276, September 15, 2010); for other reports on various states by Jeffrey H. Keefe, see http://www.epi.org/people/ jeffrey-h-keefe/.

13. Justin Falk, "Comparing Benefits and Total Compensation in the Federal Government and the Private Sector" (Working Paper 2012–4, Congressional Budget Office, Washington, DC, 2012); Falk, "Comparing Wages in the Federal Government and the Private Sector" (Working Paper 2012–3, Congressional Budget Office, Washington, DC, 2012); Maury Gittelman and Brooks Pierce, "Compensation for State and Local Government Workers," *Journal of Economic Perspectives* 26, no. 1 (2011): 217–42; Jason Richwine and Andrew Biggs, *Are California Public Employee Overpaid?* (Center for Data Analysis Report 11–01, Heritage Foundation, March 17, 2011); Jason Richwine and Andrew Biggs, *Public Sector Compensation: Correcting the Economic Policy Institute, Again* (Backgrounder #2539, Heritage Foundation, March 31, 2011); James Shrek, *Inflated Federal Pay: How Americans Are Overtaxed to Overpay the Civil Service* (Center for Data Analysis Report #10–05, Heritage Foundation, July 7, 2010); and Jason Richwine, *Same Worker, Higher Wage: A Study of Workers Who Switch from Private to Federal Employment* (Center for Data Analysis #11-02, Heritage Foundation, June 15, 2011).

14. All figures are from the Bureau of Labor Statistics, 2008.

15. Jason Richwine and Andrew Biggs, "A National Survey of State Employee Pay," (working paper, American Enterprise Institute, October 2013).

16. This is the crux of the work by Richwine and Biggs, which draws on the finance literature and methods applied to pension financing. The Economic Policy Institute takes another approach that yields different results. However, the Congressional Budget Office has endorsed the "market value" approach used by Richwine and Biggs. See also Don Bellante and James Long, "The Political Economy of the Rent Seeking Society: The Case of Public Employees and Their Unions," *Journal of Labor Research* 1, no. 2 (1981).

17. It should be noted that some economists hold that government pays a higher premium for experience than the private sector.

18. Richwine and Biggs, "A National Survey of State Employee Pay."

19. Sharon P. Smith, "Pay Differentials between Federal Government and Private Sector Workers," *Industrial and Labor Relations Review* 29, no. 2 (1976): 179–97.

20. Government Accounting Office, *Federal Personnel: Federal/Private Pay Comparisons* (Report to Congressional Committees, GAO/OCE-95-1, Washington, DC, December 1994).

21. Brent R. Moulton, "A Reexamination of Federal/Private Wage Differentials in the United States," *Journal of Labor Economics* 8, no. 2 (1990): 270–93. However,

Moulton's results depend on assuming that job tenure contributes to higher pay, rather than higher pay resulting in lower quit rates and longer job tenure. If he did not assume that in his model, he'd find a higher federal premium. No other studies have accepted his approach. Using more sophisticated assumptions, the 2012 Congressional Budget Office report found a similar (2 percent) wage premium. That report, like others, finds that the thing really tipping the scales is the benefits public employees receive.

22. George J. Borjas, "The Wage Structure and Sorting of Workers into the Public Sector," (Working Paper No. 9313, National Bureau of Economic Research, Cambridge, MA, 2002).

23. Lawrence F. Katz and Alan B. Krueger, "Changes in the Structure of Wages in the Public and Private Sectors," in *Research in Labor Economics*, ed. Ronald Ehrenberg (Greenwich, CT: JAI Press, 1991), 131–72.

24. James M. Porterba and Kim S. Ruben, "The Distribution of Public Sector Wage Premia: New Evidence Using Quantile Regression Methods" (Working Paper No. 4734, National Bureau of Economic Research, Cambridge, 1994).

25. William J. Moore and Robert J. Newman, "Government Wage Differentials in a Municipal Labor Market: The Case of Houston Metropolitan Transit Workers," *Industrial and Labor Relations Review* 45, no. 1 (1991): 145–53.

26. Jason Richwine and Andrew Biggs, "A National Survey of State Employee Pay" (working paper, American Enterprise Institute, October 2013).

27. William Even and David Macpherson, *Methodology for Estimating Compensation Differentials for State and Local versus Private Sector Workers* (MacIver Institute, November 2012).

28. Andrew G. Biggs, "Lining Up for Government Jobs," post in *The Enterprise Blog* (http://blog.american.com), American Enterprise Institute, February 28, 2011.

29. Steven Venti, "Wages in the Federal and the Private Sectors," in *Public Sector Payrolls*, ed. David A. Wise (Cambridge, MA: National Bureau of Economic Research, 1987); Alan B. Krueger, "Are Public Sector Workers Paid More Than Their Alternative Wage? Evidence from Longitudinal Data and Job Queues," in *When Public Sector Workers Unionize*, ed. Richard B. Freeman and Casey Ichniowski (Chicago: University of Chicago Press, 1988).

30. Alan B. Krueger, "The Determinants of Queues for Federal Jobs," *Industrial and Labor Relations Review* 41, no. 4 (July 1988): 567–81.

31. Center for Retirement Research at Boston College, *Comparing Wealth in Retirement: State-Local versus Private Sector Workers* (Issue Brief SLP-21, Chestnut Hill, MA, 2011). See also E. J. McMahon, *Optimal Option: SUNY's Personal Retirement Plan as a Model for Pension Reform* (Special Report, SR 11-12, Empire Center for New York State Policy, February 2012); Ron Lieber, "Battle Looms over Huge Costs of Public Pensions," *New York Times*, August 6, 2010; E. J. McMahon, "Gold-Plated Pensions," *New York Post*, October 8, 2008.

32. "Pension Calculator," Empire Center of New York Policy, http://www.empire-center.org/pensioncalculator/.

33. Other calculations suggest that a private sector worker would need even greater savings to equal the benefits of a defined benefit plan.

34. "Personal Savings Rate," Economic Research, Federal Reserve Bank of St. Louis, updated June 26, 2014, http://research.stlouisfed.org/fred2/series/PSAVERT/

35. Andrew G. Biggs, "Do Public Employees Actually Have More Job Security?" post in *The Enterprise Blog,*, American Enterprise Institute, September 22, 2011, http://blog.american.com; Biggs, "The Value of Public Sector Job Security," post in *The Enterprise Blog*, American Enterprise Institute, July 28, 2011, http://blog.american.com.

36. Steven G. Allen, "Unions and Job Security," in *When Public Sector Workers Unionize*, ed. Richard B. Freeman and Casey Ichniowski (Chicago: University of Chicago Press, 1988), 294.

37. Joshua McGee and Marcus A. Winters, *Better Pay, Fairer Pensions: Reforming Teacher Compensation* (Civic Report No. 79, Manhattan Institute for Policy Research, September 2013).

38. Michael L. Marlow and William Orzechowski, "Public Sector Unions and Public Spending," *Public Choice* 89 (1996): 1–16; Sarah Anzia and Terry Moe, "Public Employee Unions and the Costs of Government," *Journal of Politics* (Forthcoming, 2015); Chris Edwards, "Public Sector Unions and the Rising Costs of Employee Compensation," *Cato Journal* 30, no. 1 (Winter 2010); Paul N. Courant, Edward M. Gramlich, and Daniel L. Rubinfeld, "Public Employee Market Power and the Level of Government Spending," *American Economic Review* 69, no. 5 (December 1979).

39. US Bureau of Labor Statistics, Archived News Releases, Union Members Annual (2010), http://www.bls.gov/schedule/archives/all_nr.htm#UNION2.

40. For a summary of the literature, see Richard C. Kearney, *Labor Relations in the Public Sector* (Boca Raton, FL: CRC Press, 2009).

41. Casey Ichniowski, "Economic Effects of the Firefighters' Union," *Industrial and Labor Relations Review* 33 (1980): 29–42; Jeffrey S. Zax, "Wages, Compensation, and Municipal Unions," *Industrial Relations* 27 (1988): 301–17; Orley Ashenfelter, "The Effect of Unionization on Wages in the Public Sector: The Case of Firefighters," *Industrial and Labor Relations Review* 24 (1971): 191–202; Ronald Ehrenberg, "Municipal Government Structure, Unionization, and the Wages of Fire Fighters," *Industrial and Labor Relations Review* 27 (1973): 36–48; Daniel G. Gallagher, "Teacher Bargaining and School District Expenditures," *Industrial Relations* 17 (1978): 216–39; Jeffrey S. Zax and Casey Ichniowski, "The Effects of Public Sector Unionism on Pay, Employment, Department Budgets, and Municipal Expenditures," in *When Public Sector Workers Unionize*, ed. Richard Freeman and Casey Ichniowski (Chicago: University of Chicago Press, 1988); Anzia and Moe, "Public Employee Unions and the Costs of Government"; H. Greg Lewis, "Union/Nonunion Wage Gaps in the Public Sector," *Journal of Labor Economics* 8, no. 1 (January 1990): 260–328.

42. Dale Belman, John S. Heywood, and John Lund, "Public Sector Earnings and the Extent of Unionization," *Industrial and Labor Relations Review* 50, no. 4 (July 1997); David B. Lipsky, "The Effect of Collective Bargaining on Teacher Pay: A Review of the Evidence," *Educational Administration Quarterly* 18, no. 1 (1982): 14–42; Stephen J. Trejo, "Public Sector Unions and Municipal Employment," *Industrial and Labor Relations Review* 45, no. 1 (1991): 166–80.

43. Kevin O'Brien, "Compensation, Employment, and the Political Activity of Public Employees Unions," *Journal of Labor Research* 13 (June 1992): 189–203; Don Bellante and Philip Porter, "Public and Private Employment over the Business Cycle: A Ratchet Theory of Government Growth," *Journal of Labor Research* 14 (Fall 1998): 613–28; Linda N. Edwards and Franklin R. Edwards, "Wellington-Winters Revisited: The Case of Municipal Sanitation Collection," *Industrial and Labor Relations Review*, 35, no. 3 (April 1982): 307–18.

44. Laura Feiveson, "General Revenue Sharing and Public Sector Unions" (working paper, Department of Economics, MIT, November 2011).

45. Richard B. Freeman and Eunice S. Han, "Public Sector Unionism without Collective Bargaining" (working paper, Economics Department, Harvard University, December 2012).

46. Harris L. Zwerling and Terry Thomason, "Collective Bargaining and the Determinants of Teachers' Salaries," *Journal of Labor Research* 16, no. 4 (1995): 467–84.

47. Michael F. Lovenheim, "The Effect of Teachers' Unions on Education Production: Evidence from Union Election Certifications in Three Midwestern States" *Journal of Labor Economics* 27, no. 4 (2009): 525–87; John T. Delaney, "Teachers' Collective Bargaining Outcomes and Tradeoffs," *Journal of Labor Research* 9 (1988): 363–77.

48. Hirschel Kaspar, "The Effects of Collective Bargaining on Public School Teachers Salaries," *Industrial and Labor Relations* 24, no. 1 (1970), 57–71; T. A. Brown, "Have Collective Negotiations Increased Teachers' Salaries?" *Journal of Collective Negotiations* 4, no. 1 (1975): 53–65.

49. John H. Landon and Robert N. Baird, "Monopsony in the Market for Public School Teachers," *American Economic Review* 51, no. 5 (1971): 966–71; Roger W. Schmenner, "The Determination of Municipal Employee Wages," *Review of Economics and Statistics* 55, no. 1 (1973): 83–90.

50. Morris M. Kleiner and Daniel L. Petree, "Unionism and Licensing of Public School Teachers: Impact on Wages and Educational Output," in *When Public Sector Workers Unionize*, ed. Richard B. Freeman and Casey Ichniowski (Chicago: University of Chicago Press, 1988).

51. William Baugh and Joe Stone, "Teachers, Unions, and Wages in the 1970s: Unionism Now Pays," *Industrial and Labor Relations Review* 35, no. 3 (1983): 368–76.

52. It does not, however, connect unions to specific units of government and gauge whether those units' expenditures rise or fall; it only explores whether union membership results in higher wages or compensation in general.

53. Robert G. Gregory and Jeff Borland, "Recent Developments in Public Sector Labor Markets," in *Handbook of Labor Economics*, vol. 3, ed. Orley Ashenfelter and David Card (Elsevier, 1999); David G. Blanchflower and Alex Bryson, "What Effect Do Unions Have on Wages Now and Would Freeman and Medoff Be Surprised?" *Journal of Labor Research* 25 (Summer 2004): 383–414; Bahman Bahriami, John D. Bitzan, and Jay A. Leitch, "Union Worker Wage Effect in the Public Sector," *Journal of Labor Research* 30 (2009): 35–51; John D. Bitzan and Bahman Bahrami, "The Effects of Unions on Wages by Occupation in

the Public Sector," *International Business and Economics Research Journal* 9 (2010): 107–19.

54. Ichniowski, "Economic Effects of the Firefighters' Union"; Ann Bartel and David Lewin, "Wages and Unionism in the Public Sector: The Case of the Police," *Review of Economics and Statistics* 63 (1981): 53–59; William J. Hunter and Carol H. Rankin, "The Composition of Public Sector Compensation: The Effects of Bureaucratic Size," *Journal of Labor Research* 9 (1998): 29–42; Jeffrey S. Zax, "Wages, Compensation, and Municipal Unions."

55. Regarding the political attractiveness of promising future benefits, see D. Roderick Kiewiet, "The Day after Tomorrow: The Politics of Public Employee Retirement Benefits," *California Journal of Politics and Public Policy* 2 (2010): 1–30; Hunter and Rankin, "The Composition of Public Sector Compensation"; Bartel and Lewin, "Wages and Unionism in the Public Sector"; Bellante and Long, "The Political Economy of the Rent Seeking Society"; and Ichniowski, "Economic Effects of the Firefighters' Union."

56. Anzia and Moe, "Public Employee Unions and the Costs of Government."

57. However, it could be that cities that have collective bargaining actually paid higher wages and health benefits before the adoption of collective bargaining and the connections the authors find between collective bargaining and higher compensation is simply an artifact of those prior decisions. Yet, Anzia and Moe take this on by adding new control variables: the cities' per capita payroll and cities' total fire and police employment per capita in 1957 (before the adoption of public sector collective bargaining). The new controls do little to change the overall results.

58. Robert Novy-Marx and Joshua Rauh, "Public Pension Promises: How Big Are They and What are They Worth?" *Journal of Finance* 66, no. 4 (October 2011): 1211–49; Robert Novy-Marx and Joshua Rauh, "Policy Options for State Pension Systems and Their Impact on Plan Liabilities," *Journal of Pension Economics and Finance* 10, no. 2 (April 2011).

59. Walt Bogdanich, "A Disability Epidemic among a Railroad's Retirees," *New York Times*, September 20, 2008.

60. Susan Edelman, "New schools boss to collect double de Blasio's pay," *New York Post*, January 5, 2014.

61. Alison Vekshin, James Nash, and Rodney Yap, "Police Chief's $204,000 Pension Shows How Cities Crashed," *Bloomberg News*, July 31, 2012.

62. Kiewiet, "The Day after Tomorrow."

63. "The Unsteady States of America," *The Economist*, July 27, 2013.

64. Hunter and Rankin, "The Composition of Public Sector Compensation."

65. Alicia H. Munnell, Jean-Pierre Aubry, Josh Hurwitz, and Laura Quinby, *Comparing Compensation: State-Local versus Private Sector Workers* (Center for Retirement Research, no. 20, September 2011); Alicia H. Munnell, *State and Local Pensions: What Now?* (Washington, D.C.: Brookings Institution Press, 2012), 75–100.

66. Robert Novy-Marx and Joshua D. Rauh, "The Liabilities and Risks of State-Sponsored Pension Plans," *Journal of Economic Perspectives* 23, no. 4 (2009): 191–210. These data include 116 major state-sponsored plans and 77

large local plans with assets over $1 billion. As a proxy for union public employee union strength, Anzia and Moe used the percentage of public sector workers belonging to unions according to the Current Population Survey. Because more strongly Democratic states tend to both have strong unions and provide generous pension benefits (think of California and New York), they introduce a control variable. They also control for worker friendliness of the state, the state's cost of living, proportion of the state's workforce in the public sector, and the state's dependence on federal government revenue.

67. Ryan Murphy and Paul Bachman, *The Public Sector 'Union' Effect: Pushing Up Unfunded Pension Liabilities and State Debt* (Beacon Hill Institute Report, May 2013).

68. Dan Morain, "OT Pushes Guards Pay Past $100,000," *Los Angeles Times*, December 23, 2006.

69. Steve Malanga, "The Indebted States of America," *City Journal* 23, no. 3 (Summer 2013).

70. Richard B. Freeman and Eunice S. Han, "The War on Public Sector Collective Bargaining in the U.S.," *Journal of Industrial Relations* 54, no. 3 (Spring 2012).

CHAPTER 8

1. David Crane, "California's $500 Billion Pension Time Bomb," *Los Angeles Times*, April 6, 2010. See also David Crane, "California: A High Revenue, Low Services State," *Bloomberg News*, February 20, 2013.

2. See, for example, Robert Samuelson, "Obama's Failure of Leadership," *Washington Post*, December 31, 2012.

3. Lowell R. Ricketts and Christopher J. Waller, "State and Local Debt: Growing Liabilities Jeopardize Fiscal Health," *The Regional Economist: The Debt Crisis* (St. Louis Federal Reserve, October 2012).

4. Richard Riordan and Tim Rutten, "A Plan to Avert the Pension Crisis," *New York Times*, August 4, 2013.

5. The conception of crowding out used here is distinct from the way the term is used by most economists. In a tradition that goes back to Adam Smith, many economists worry about the growth of government insofar as it threatens to displace private business activity—that's what they mean by crowding out. Here, however, crowding out refers to policy items within a government's budget. Specifically, when spending on certain items increases without increasing revenues or debt, other items must be cut or held at current funding levels.

6. James Q. Wilson, *Political Organizations*, rev. ed. (Princeton, NJ: Princeton University Press, 1995).

7. Nicholas Eberstadt, *A Nation of Takers: America's Entitlement Epidemic* (Philadelphia: Templeton Press, 2012).

8. *Fiscal Year 2013: Mid-Session Review, Budget of the U.S. Government* (Office of Management and Budget, July 27, 2012). Operating with slightly different categories and assumptions, the House Republican budget would have similar effects over the next decade, see, *Concurrent Resolution on the Budget—Fiscal Year 2013*,

(Report on the Committee of the Budget, House of Representatives, H. Con. Res. 112, Washington, DC: US Government Printing Office, 2012).

9. Gerald B. Sieb, "Liberals Find Themselves in a Spending Trap," *Wall Street Journal*, March 25, 2013.

10. Eduardo Porter, "Goodbye Government, under Either Fiscal Plan," *New York Times*, December 18, 2012.

11. Congressional Budget Office, *Federal Grants to States and Localities* (March 2013).

12. US Census Bureau, "Census of Governments," (2012), https://www.census.gov/govs/

13. E. J. McMahon, *Iceberg Ahead: The Hidden Costs Retiree Health Benefits in New York* (Special Report SR-12, Empire Center for New York Policy, September 2012); The Widening Gap Update: States are $1.38 Short in Funding Retirement Systems," (Report, Pew Charitable Trusts, June 18, 2012); Rebecca Sielman, "2012 Public Pension Funding Study," Milliman, (October 2012).

14. Robert Novy-Marx and Joshua Rauh, "The Liabilities and Risks of State-Sponsored Pension Plans," *Journal of Economic Perspectives* 23, no. 4 (2009); Robert Novy-Marx and Joshua Rauh, "Public Pension Promises: How Big Are They and What Are They Worth?" *Journal of Finance* 66, no. 4 (July 2011), 1211-49.

15. "After Detroit, Who's Next?" *Wall Street Journal*, July 21, 2013.

16. Monica Davey, "Chicago Sees Pension Crisis Drawing Near," *New York Times*, August 5, 2013.

17. Josh Barro, "Does Obama Know Why the Public Sector Isn't Doing Fine?" *Bloomberg News*, June 11, 2012.

18. Nicole Gelinas, "No Time to Waste," *New York Post*, January 4, 2011,

19. Steve Malanga, "Compensation Monster Devours Cities," *City Journal* 21, no. 3 (Summer 2011).

20. Jeffrey L. Barnett and Phillip M. Vidal, *State and Local Government Finances: Summary 2010* (US Census Bureau, Governments Division Report, September 2012).

21. *Report of the State Budget Crisis Task Force* (State Budget Crisis Task Force, revised July 31, 2012), http://www.statebudgetcrisis.org/wpcms/.

22. *Report of the State Budget Crisis Task Force.*

23. See, for example, E. J. McMahon and Josh Barro, *Blueprint for a Better Budget: A Plan for Action for New York State* (Special Report, SR 1-10, Empire Center for New York Policy, January 4, 2010).

24. Elizabeth McNichol, *Some Basic Facts on State and Local Government Workers* (Report, Center on Budget and Policy Priorities, June 15, 2012).

25. E. J. McMahon and Josh Barro, *New York's Exploding Pension Costs* (Special Report, SR 8-11, Empire Center for Policy, December 2010).

26. Government Accountability Office, *State and Local Government Retiree Benefits; Current Funded Status of Pension and Health Benefits* (GAO-08-223, Washington, DC, 2008); Government Accountability Office, *State and Local Government Retiree Health Benefits: Liabilities Are Largely Unfunded But Some Governments are Taking Action* (GAO-10-61, Washington, DC, 2009); Robert L. Clark and

Melinda Morrill put total liability at $440 billion. See *Health Insurance for Active and Retired State Employees: California, North Carolina and Ohio* (Washington, DC: Center for State and Local Government Excellence, Congressional Budget Office, 2011).

27. The Pew Center on the States found that states' liabilities increased by $22 billion (4 percent) from 2009 to 2010.

28. Jerrell D. Coggburn, *How Local Governments Are Addressing Retiree Health Care Funding* (Washington, DC: Center for State and Local Government Excellence, Congressional Budget Office, 2010).

29. Whether a state is in trouble with its retiree health plan depends on how much of the insurance premium is paid by the state. Some states such as New Jersey, Rhode Island, California, Pennsylvania, and Illinois pay the entire premium. At the other extreme, Idaho, Montana, Wisconsin, and Minnesota don't pay any of it. A majority of states pay anywhere from half to 99 percent of the premium.

30. Josh Barro and Stuart Buck, *Underfunded: Teacher Pension Plans: It's Worse Than You Think* (Civic Report No. 61, Manhattan Institute, April 2010); Kathryn M. Doherty, Sandi Jacobs, and Trisha M. Madden, *No One Benefits: How Teacher Pension Systems Are Failing BOTH Teachers and Taxpayers* (Washington, DC: National Council on Teacher Quality, 2012).

31. Dara Zeehandelaar and Amber M. Winkler, *The Big Squeeze: Retirement Costs and School District Budgets* (Report, Thomas B. Fordham Institute, June 2013).

32. Robert Costrell and Larry Maloney, *The Big Squeeze: Retirement Costs and School District Budgets: Paying the Pension Price in Philadelphia* (Report, Thomas B. Fordham Institute, June 2013).

33. Matt Carroll, "Health Costs Soar, Squeeze Localities: Groups Lobby for Legislation," *Boston Globe*, May 13, 2007.

34. Arturo Perez, "State Budget Update," Presentation, Go. 25084, at the National Conference of State Legislatures, Washington, DC, August, 2012.

35. "How They Failed You," *Chicago Tribune*, January 22, 2012.

36. Richard C. Dreyfuss, *Fixing the Public Sector Pension Problem: The (True) Path to Long-Term Reform* (Civic Report 74, Manhattan Institute for Policy Research, February 2013).

37. Stephanie A. Minor, "Cuomo to Cities: Just Borrow," *New York Times*, February 13, 2013.

38. Kris Maher, Bobby White, and Valerie Bauerlien, "Hard Times Spread for Cities," *Wall Street Journal*, August 10, 2012.

39. "A Widening Gap in Cities: Shortfalls in Funding for Pensions and Retiree Healthcare," (Report, Pew Charitable Trusts, January 16, 2013).

40. Krish Maher, "Pittsburg Challenges UPMC Tax Status," *Wall Street Journal*, March 20, 2013.

41. New York City Comptroller, *Certified Annual Financial Report*, 2012, http://comptroller.nyc.gov/reports/comprehensive-annual-financial-reports/

42. Hunter Walker, "Mayor Bloomberg Launches Coalition to Back Pension with TV Ad Blitz," Politicker.com, March 13, 2012, http://politicker.com/2012/03/mayor-bloomberg-launches-coalition-to-back-pension-reform-with-tv-ad-blitz/.

43. Richard Riordan and Alexander Rubalcava, "Los Angeles on the Brink of Bankruptcy," *Wall Street Journal*, May 5, 2010.

44. Steve Malanga, "Will Los Angeles Join Detroit as a Fiscal Zombie City?" RealClearMarkets.com, http://www.realclearmarkets.com/articles/2013/03/07/will_los_angeles_join_detroit_as_a_fiscal_zombie_city_100184.html.

45. Gretchen Tegeler, "Police and Fire Pensions are Crowding Out Local Budgets," Taxpayers Association of Central Iowa, February 1, 2013. http://taxpayersassociationofcentraliowa.org/police-and-fire-pensions-are-crowding-out-local-budgets-january-31-2013/

46. Stephanie Banchero and Caroline Porter, "Chicago Moves to Close 11% of Elementary Schools in Fall," *Wall Street Journal*, March 22, 2013.

47. *Report to the Mayor's Office on the State of Retiree Healthcare* (Retiree Healthcare Benefits Commission, Office of the Comptroller, Department of Finance of the City of Chicago, January 11, 2013). See also Hal Dardick, "Panel: City Retiree's Health Insurance Too Costly," *Chicago Tribune*, January 14, 2013.

48. Ryan Murphy and Paul Bachman, "The Public Sector "Union" Effect: Pushing Up Unfunded Pension Liabilities and State Debt," Report, Beacon Hill Institute (Boston, MA: May 2013).

49. Jeffery S. Zax, "Employment and Local Public Sector Unions," *Industrial Relations* 28 (Winter 1989): 21–31; Zax and Casey Ichniowski, "The Effects of Public Sector Unionism on Pay, Employment, Department Budgets, and Municipal Expenditures," in *When Public Sector Workers Unionize,* ed. Richard Freeman and Casey Ichniowski (Chicago: University of Chicago Press, 1988); Richard B. Freeman and Ichniowski, "The Effect of Public Sector Labor Laws on Labor Market Institutions and Outcomes," in *When Public Sector Workers Unionize,* ed. Freeman and Valetta (Chicago: University of Chicago Press, 1988); Robert Valetta, "Union Effect on Municipal Employment and Wages: A Longitudinal Approach," *Journal of Labor Economics* 11 (July 1993): 545–74; Stephen J. Trejo, "Public Sector Unions and Municipal Employment," *Industrial and Labor Relations Review* 45, no. 1 (1991): 166–80.

50. Paul Pierson, *Dismantling the Welfare State? Reagan, Thatcher, and the Politics of Retrenchment* (New York: Cambridge University Press, 1994).

51. Eric Patashnik, "Budgeting More, Deciding Less," in *Seeking the Center: Politics and Policymaking at the New Century,* ed. Martin A. Levin, Marc K. Landy, and Martin Shapiro (Washington, DC: Georgetown University Press, 2001).

52. R. Kent Weaver, "The Politics of Blame Avoidance," *Journal of Public Policy* 6, no. 4 (October 1986).

53. Michael McDonald, "Gina Raimondo's Math Convinces Rhode Island of America's Prospects," *Businessweek*, January 18, 2012.

CHAPTER 9

1. Transcript, Albert Shanker on Meet the Press, September 1, 1974, AFT News, AFT Speeches Collection, Walter P. Ruether Library, Wayne State University.

2. Quoted in Michael Rothfield, "A Power Struggle over Prisons," *Los Angeles Times*, September 25, 2007.

3. Philip K. Howard, *The Rule of Nobody: Saving America from Dead Laws and Broken Government* (New York: W. W. Norton & Co., 2014).

4. Andrea Louise Campbell and Michael W. Sances, "State Fiscal Policy during the Great Recession: Budgetary Impacts and Policy Responses," *Annals of the American Academy of Political and Social Science* 650, no. 1 (2013): 252–73.

5. William B. Eggers and Daniel Bylers, "The Real Story of the State and Local Workforce," *Governing*, August 14, 2013.

6. John Donahue, *The Warping of Government Work* (Cambridge, MA: Harvard University Press, 2008), 5.

7. For contrasting perspectives on the benefits of this new economy, see Jagdish Bhagwati, *In Defense of Globalization* (New York: Oxford University Press, 2007); and Joseph E. Stiglitz, *Globalization and Its Discontents* (New York: W. W. Norton & Co., 2003).

8. Joseph A. Schumpter, *Capitalism, Socialism and Democracy,* 3rd ed. (New York: Harper Perennial, 2008), 83–84.

9. Peter H. Schuck, *Why Government Fails So Often* (Princeton, NJ: Princeton University Press, 2014), 198–228.

10. "Steven Eide Interviews former Indianapolis Mayor Steve Goldsmith," June 12, 2013, http://www.publicsectorinc.org/podcasts/061813_goldsmith_eide.php#.Ue_kI4UbFr4.

11. "The Tussle for Talent," *The Economist,* January 6, 2011.

12. Paul C. Light, *The New Public Service* (Washington, DC: Brookings Institution Press, 1999); see also Don Bellante and Albert Link, "Are Public Sector Workers More Risk Averse Than Private Sector Workers?" *Industrial and Labor Relations Review* 34 (April 1981): 408–12; Jessica M. Blank, "An Analysis of Workers' Choice between Employment in the Public and Private Sectors," *Industrial and Labor Relations Review* 38, no. 2 (1985).

13. *Montgomery County Education Association v. Board of Education* (1987), 986.

14. Martin H. Malin, "Public Sector Law Doctrine and Labor-Management Cooperation," in *Going Public: The Role of Labor Management Relations in Delivering Quality Government Services,* ed. Jonathan Brock and David S. Lipsky (Champaign, IL: Industrial Relations Research Association, 2003), 267–94.

15. Howard, *The Rule of Nobody,* 34–43, 74–96.

16. Walt Bogdanich, "A Disability Epidemic among a Railroad's Retirees," *New York Times,* September 20, 2008.

17. "Nassau in a Ditch, Again," *New York Times,* February 1, 2011.

18. Harry P. Hatry, "The Status of Productivity Measurement in the Public Sector," *Public Administration Review* 38, no. 1 (1978): 28–33; John M. Gleason and Darold T. Barnum, "Toward Valid Measures of Public Sector Productivity: Performance Measures in Urban Transit," *Management Science* 28, no. 4 (April 1982): 379–86.

19. See the last 30 years of *Public Productivity and Management Review.*

20. David N. Ammons, "Productivity Barriers in the Public Sector," in *Public Productivity Handbook,* 2nd ed., ed. Mark Holzer and Seok Hwan Lee (New York: Marcel Dekker, 2004).

21. Morely Gunderson, "The Two Faces of Union Power in the Public Sector," *Journal of Labor Research* 26 (2005): 393–412.

22. James Q. Wilson, *Bureaucracy* (New York: Basic Books, 1989), 115.

23. The following discussion draws from Wilson, *Bureaucracy*, 315–26. See also, Schuck, *Why Government Fails So Often,* 127–326.

24. Herbert Kaufman, *Red Tape: Its Origins, Uses, and Abuses* (Washington, DC: Brookings Institution Press, 1977).

25. See two early reports by the US Department of Justice on the effects on managerial discretion of prison officer unionization: John M. Wynee Jr., *Prison Employee Unionism: The Impact on Administration and Programs* (Washington, DC: US Department of Justice, January 1978); M. Robert Montilla, *Prison Employee Unionism: Management Guide for Correctional Administrators* (Washington, DC: US Department of Justice, January 1978). For more recent evidence of the erosion of managerial rights in California's prison system, see Corrections Independent Review Panel, *Reforming California's Youth and Adult Correctional System* (Sacramento: Corrections Independent Review Panel, 2004).

26. Dale Belman and Richard Block, "The Impact of Collective Bargaining on Competitiveness and Employment: A Review of the Literature," in *Bargaining for Competitiveness: Law, Research, and Case Studies,* ed. Richard Block, (Kalamazoo, MI: Upjohn Institute for Employment Research, 2003; Toke Aidt and Zafiris Tzannatos, *Unions and Collective Bargaining: Economic Effects in a Global Environment* (World Bank Report 1, 2002). A labor-backed think tank also found that "[a]nalyses of the union effect on firms and the economy have generally found unions to be a positive force, improving the performance of firms and contributing to economic growth." See Lawrence Mishel with Matthew Walters, "How Unions Help All Workers," *Economic Policy Institute* 15 (2003).

27. James A. Schmitz, "What Determines Productivity? Lessons from the Dramatic Recovery of the U.S. and Canadian Iron Ore Industries Following Their Early 1980s Crisis," *Journal of Political Economy* 113, no. 3 (June 2005): 582–625.

28. Barry T. Hirsch, "What Do Unions Do for Economic Performance?" *Journal of Labor Research* 25, no. 3 (2004): 415–55. For a study of public libraries that found that unionization had no effect on productivity, see Ronald G. Ehrenberg, Daniel R. Sherman, and Joshua L. Schwartz, "Unions and Productivity in the Public Sector: A Study of Municipal Libraries," *Industrial and Labor Relations Review* 36, no. 2 (January 1983).

29. Nonetheless, there is reason for skepticism about whether private sector unions really create efficiencies for firms that the firms themselves would not otherwise adopt. Making this case, however, involves a longer discussion of some of the threats to the validity of the studies of private sector unions and productivity than I have time for here.

30. This episode is recounted in Blanche Blank, "Bureaucracy: Power in Details," in *Urban Politics New York Style,* ed. Jewel Bellush and Dick Netzer (Armonk, NY: M. E. Sharpe, 1990), 109.

31. *Agreement between State of California and California Peace Officers Association,* July 1, 1990 through July 2, 2001 at § 12.7.

32. Mark Arax, "Tales of Brutality Behind Bars," *Los Angeles Times,* August 21, 1996; Kim Christensen and Marc Lifsher, "Prison Guards: Licensed to Kill?" *Orange County Register,* October 23, 1994.

33. Kiley Russell, "8 Guards Cleared of Cruelty," *San Diego Union-Tribune,* June 10, 2000.
34. Michael Pearson, "Wins, Losses, and Draws in Chicago School Strike," CCN.com, September 19, 2012, http://www.cnn.com/2012/09/19/us/illinois-chicago-teachers-strike/
35. Letter from Franklin D. Roosevelt to L. C. Stewart, president, National Federation of Federal Employees, August 16, 1937.
36. The essentiality issue is discussed by Leonard D. White, "Strikes in the Public Service," *Public Personnel Review* 10 (January 1949): 3–10.
37. A. H. Raskin, "The Revolt of the Civil Servants," *Saturday Review* 51, December 7, 1968.
38. Peter Donohue, "Some Do's and Don'ts That Continue to Haunt TWU Six Years after Transit Strike," *New York Daily News,* April 23, 2012.
39. The following discussion draws from Joseph McCartin, *Collision Course: Ronald Reagan, the Air Traffic Controllers, and the Strike That Changed America* (New York: Oxford University Press, 2012), 340–2, 350–1, 363.
40. This point was reinforced to me in interviews with nearly a dozen labor lawyers that I interviewed. Both management and labor-side lawyers with years of public sector negotiating experience confirmed it.
41. The following discussion draws on Terry Moe, *Special Interest: Teachers Unions and America's Public Schools* (Washington, DC: Brookings Institution, 2011). See also Frederick M. Hess and Martin R. West, *A Better Bargain: Overhauling Teacher Collective Bargaining for the 21st Century* (Program on Education Policy and Governance, Harvard University, Cambridge, MA, 2009). See also Jal Mehta, *The Allure of Order: High Hopes, Dashed Expectations, and the Troubled Quest to Remake America's Public Schools* (New York: Oxford University Press, 2013).
42. For samples of teachers' contracts in the nation's largest school districts, see the National Council on Teacher Quality, http://www.nctq.org/districtPolicy/contractDatabaseLanding.do. For a journalistic account of these rules effects, see, Steven Brill, *Class Warfare: Inside the Fight to Fix America's Schools* (New York: Simon and Shuster, 2001).
43. Stephen Brill, "The Rubber Room: The Battle over New York's Worst Teachers," *The New Yorker,* August 31, 2009; Seyward Darby, "Schools out Forever," *The New Republic,* May 20, 2009.
44. Moe, *Special Interest,* 174–79.
45. Katherine O. Strunk and Jason A. Grissom, "Do Strong Unions Shape District Policies?" *Educational Evaluation and Policy Analysis* 32, no. 3 (September 2010): 389-406; Terry M. Moe, "Collective Bargaining and the Performance of Public Schools," *American Journal of Political Science* 53, no. 1 (2009): 156–74; Sean Nicholson-Crotty, Jason A. Grissom, and Jill Nicholson-Crotty, "Governance and the Impact of Public Employee Unions on Organizational Performance," *Public Performance and Management Review* 35, no. 3 (March 2012): 422-48.
46. Kate Walsh, *Steps That Congress Can Take to Improve Teacher Quality—Without Overstepping Its Bounds* (Fordham Foundation Report, April 2007); Paul

E. Peterson, *Saving Schools: From Horace Mann to Virtual Learning* (Cambridge, MA: Harvard University Press, 2007), 293–94.

47. Such salary schedules are common in other areas of the public sector labor force.

48. Caroline M. Hoxby and Andrew Leigh, "Pulled Away or Pushed Out? Explaining the Decline of Teacher Aptitude in the United States," *American Economic Review* 94, no. 2 (2004): 236–40.

49. Jay P. Greene, "The Imaginary Teacher Shortage," *Wall Street Journal*, October 8, 2012. See also Greene with Greg Foster and Marcus A. Winters, *Education Myths: What Special Interest Groups Want You to Believe about Our Schools— And Why It Isn't So* (Lanham, MD: Rowman and Littlefield, 2005), 50, 54–57. For how pension and health costs of teachers crowd out other spending priorities, see Dara Zeehandlaar and Amber Winkler, *The Big Squeeze: Retirement Costs and School District Budgets* (Report, Thomas B. Fordham Institute, June 2013).

50. Raegen T. Miller, Richard J. Murnane, and John B. Willett, "Do Teacher Absences Impact Student Achievement? Longitudinal Evidence from One Urban School District," *Educational Evaluation and Policy Analysis* 30, no. 2 (June 2008).

51. Kevin Carey, "An Admirable Move for the Country's Biggest Teachers' Union (Yes, You Read That Correctly)," *New Republic*, July 11, 2011.

52. Similar results occur across the nation. In 2003–04, 99 percent of Los Angeles teachers were rated satisfactory. In Seattle in 2009, only 16 out of 3,300 teachers received unsatisfactory ratings.

53. Al Baker and Marc Santora, "No Deal on Teacher Evaluations; City Risks Losing $450 Million," *New York Times*, January 17, 2013.

54. Lisa Fleisher, "Teacher Evaluation Deal Falls Apart," *Wall Street Journal*, January 17, 2013.

55. "A School Reform Landmark," *Wall Street Journal*, June 10, 2014.

56. "(Government) Workers of the World Unite!" *The Economist*, January 6, 2011.

57. "Protecting Bad Teachers," Teachers Unions Exposed blog, Center for Union Facts, http://teachersunionexposed.com/protecting.php. See also Mehta, *The Allure of Order.*

58. For a contrary perspective, see Nicholson-Crotty, Grissom, and Nicholson-Crotty, "Governance and the Impact of Public Employee Unions on Organizational Performance."

59. Caroline M. Hoxby, "How Teachers' Unions Affect Education Production," *Journal of Quarterly Economics* 111, no. 3 (1996).

60. Moe, "Collective Bargaining and the Performance of the Public Schools."

61. Although far from as methodologically sophisticated and sound as the Hoxby and Moe studies, Randall Eberts's also concludes that union bargaining increases teacher pay, improves their working conditions, and enhances their job security. As a result, unionization raises the cost of public schooling by more than 15 percent. However, he finds that the effect of unions on student performance is more mixed. Students of average ability perform better on standardized tests, but low-achieving and high-achieving students perform worse. Overall, the modest gain in achievement for middling students does not make up for the higher cost to other students scores and the public fisc. See Eberts, "Teachers Unions

and Student Performance: Help or Hindrance?" *Excellence in the Classroom* 17, no. 1 (Spring 2007). See also Randall Eberts and Joe A. Stone, *Unions and Public Schools: The Effect of Collective Bargaining on American Education* (Lexington, MA: Lexington Books, 1984).

62. See data compiled by the National Fire Protection Association. Alex Tabarrok, "Firefighters Don't Fight Fires," Marginal Revolution Blog, July 18, 2012, http://marginalrevolution.com/marginalrevolution/2012/07/firefighters-dont-fight-fires.html; Fred S. McChesney, "Smoke and Errors," Liberty Economics Blog, June 24, 2002, http://www.econlib.org/library/Columns/Mcchesneyfire.html.

63. Hillel Aron, "Mission Creep at the L.A. Fire Department," *LA Weekly,* August 8, 2013.

64. John Donovan, "Fire Department Takes Medical Calls in Stride," ABC Nightline, March 24, 2010, http://abcnews.go.com/Nightline/firefighters-medical-calls-health-costs/story?id=10181852#.UABoKB3ywle.

65. Teri Sforza, "Only 2 Percent of Fire Calls Are for Fires, Grand Jury Finds," *Orange County Register,* June 6, 2012.

66. Cited in Howard, *The Rule of Nobody,* 17.

67. Anthony Cormier and Matthew Doig, "Unfit for Duty: Unions Protect Problem Officers," *Miami Herald-Tribune,* December 6, 2011.

68. David Packman, "The Conflicting Interests of Public Safety and Police Unions," Cato Institute Blog, October 26, 2009, http://www.policemisconduct.net/the-conflicting-interests-of-public-safety-and-police-unions/.

69. Joshua Page, *The Toughest Beat: Politics, Punishment, and the Prison Officers Union in California* (New York: Oxford University Press, 2011). See also Tim Kowal, "The Role of the Prison Guards Union in California's Troubled Prison System," The League of Ordinary Gentleman Blog, http://ordinary-gentlemen.com/timkowal/2011/06/the-role-of-the-prison-guards-union-in-californias-troubled-prison-system/.

70. Page, *Toughest Beat,* 7. See also chapter 6

71. Ann E. Marimow and John Wagner, "13 Corrections Officers Indicted in MD, Accused of Aiding Drug Gang's Scheme," *Washington Post,* April 23, 2013.

72. Erin Julius, "House Passes Corrections Officers' Bill of Rights Unanimously," *The Herald-Mail,* April 13, 2010; Charles Lane, "A Baltimore Jail Scandal Aided by Union Politics," *Washington Post,* May 6, 2013.

73. Cited in Charles Lane, "Baltimore Behind Bars," *City Journal* 24, no. 2 (Spring 2014).

74. Ian Duncan, "Legal Protections for Baltimore Corrections Officers Goes Too Far, FBI Says," *Baltimore Sun,* April 24, 2013. See 2010 Maryland State Code, Title 10, Subtitle 9, http://law.justia.com/codes/maryland/2010/correctional-services/title-10/subtitle-9/.

75. *U.S. v. Tavon White et al.,* U.S. District Court, District of Maryland, Criminal No. ELH-13-0150, filed April 2, 2013.

76. "Retired Corrections Officers: Some Review Protocol Unprecedented," WBAL-TV 11, May 1, 2013, http://www.wbaltv.com/news/maryland/baltimore-city/

retired-corrections-officers-some-review-protocol-unprecedented/-
/10131532/19956446/-/115mlwxz/-/index.html.

77. Lane, "Baltimore Behind Bars," 36.

78. Wilson, *Bureaucracy*, 318.

79. E. S. Savas, *Privatization in the City: Successes, Failures, Lessons* (Washington, DC: CQ Press, 2005); Savas, *Privatizing the Public Sector* (Chatham, NJ: Chatham House Publishers, 1982); John Donahue, *The Privatization Decision: Public Ends, Private Means* (New York: Basic Books, 1989); Donald Kettl, *The Next Government of the United States* (New York: W. W. Norton, 2008).

80. David Osborne and Ted Gaebler, *Reinventing Government: How the Entrepreneurial Spirit Is Transforming the Public Sector* (New York: Plume 1993).

81. John Donahue, "Outsourcing the Wrong Jobs," *New York Times: Room for Debate*, April 4, 2011, http://www.nytimes.com/roomfordebate/2011/04/03/ is-privatization-a-bad-deal-for-cities-and-states/outsourcing-the-wrong-jobs. For a further discussion, see John Donahue and Peter Zeckhauser, *Collaborative Governance: Private Roles for Public Goals in Turbulent Times* (Princeton, NJ: Princeton University Press, 2011).

82. Douglas Belkin, "Chicago Mayor Trashes Politics of Waste Removal," *Wall Street Journal*, October 13, 2011.

83. American Federation of State, County and Municipal Employees, *Passing the Bucks: The Contracting Out of Public Services* (Washington, DC: AFSCME, 1983); Robert W. Sauter, "Union View: Subcontracting the Work of Union Members in the Public Sector," in *Industrial Relations Research Association: Proceedings of the 1988 Spring Meeting* (Madison, WI: Industrial Relations Research Association, 1988), 487–97.

84. Page, *The Toughest Beat*, 138, 143–49, 156–59.

85. Werner Z. Hirsh, "Factors Important in Local Governments' Privatization Decision," *Urban Affairs Quarterly* 31 (November 1995): 226–43.

86. Timothy Chandler and Peter Feuille, "Cities, Unions, and Privatization of Sanitation Services," *Journal of Labor Research* 25, no. 1 (Winter 1994): 53–71.

87. Eric Boehm, "Labor Unions Keep Strong Hold on PA Politics," *Philadelphia Inquirer*, July 11, 2013.

88. Two researchers emphasize the importance of transparency of the public service itself and voter knowledge in the privatization decision. See Werner Z. Hirsch and Evan Osborne, "Privatization of Government Services: Pressure Group Resistance and Service Transparency," *Journal of Labor Research* 21, no. 2 (Spring 2000): 316–26.

89. *Working Together for the Public Service: The Secretary of Labor's Task Force on Excellence in State and Local Government through Labor-Management Cooperation* (US Department of Labor, 1995).

90. Jonathan Rauch, *Demosclerosis: The Silent Killer of American Government* (New York: Times Books, 1994), 146.

91. James Q. Wilson, *Political Organizations*, rev. ed. (Princeton, NJ: Princeton University Press, 1995), 333–34.

CHAPTER 10

1. Bruce E. Kaufman, "The Early Institutionalists on Industrial Democracy and Union Democracy," *Journal of Labor Research* 21, no. 2 (2000): 189–209.

2. Joseph E. Slater, "Public Sector Labor in the Age of Obama," *Indiana Law Journal* 87, no. 1 (2012); Sylvia A. Allegretto, Ken Jacobs, and Laurel Lucia, *The Wrong Target: Public Sector Unions and State Budget Deficits* (Policy Brief, Institute on Labor and Employment, University of California-Berkeley, October 2011); David Lewin, Jeffrey H. Keefe, and Thomas A. Kochan, "The New Great Debate about Unionism and Collective Bargaining in U.S. State and Local Government," *Industrial and Labor Relations Review* 65, no. 4 (October 2012), 749–778.

3. Jake Rosenfeld, *What Unions No Longer Do* (Cambridge, MA: Harvard University Press, 2014), 50.

4. After the passage of the Taylor Law in New York State, there were an average of 20 public sector strikes a year in New York State. See, Terry O'Neil and E.J. McMahon, "Taylor Made: The Costs and Consequences of New York's Public Sector Labor Laws," (Special Report, SR4-07, Empire Center for New York State Policy, October 2007), 10.

5. Daniel DiSalvo, *Are Unions Democratic? Internal Politics of Labor Unions and Their Implications* (Civic Report No. 91, Manhattan Institute for Policy Research, September 2014).

6. See, for example, Steven M. Teles and Timothy S. Prinz, "The Politics of Rights Retraction: Welfare Reform from Entitlement to Block Grant," in *Seeking the Center: Politics and Policymaking at the New Century*, ed. Martin A. Levin, Marc K. Landy, and M. Shapiro (Washington, DC: Georgetown University Press, 2001), 215–38.

7. *Knox v Service Employees International Union Local 100* 567 U.S. (2012); *Harris v. Quinn* 573 U.S. (2014).

8. Supreme Court of the United States, "Oral Argument Transcript: Harris v. Quinn," (Washington, D.C., January 21, 2014), http://www.supremecourt.gov/oral_arguments/argument_transcripts/11-681_8mj8.pdf

9. *Measuring Performance: The State Management Report Card for 2008* (Pew Center on the States, March 3, 2008).

10. "The Unsteady States of America," *The Economist*, July 27, 2013.

11. Take New York State. In the face of a state constitutional requirement that voters approve new debt issues, they've authorized only 5 percent of New York State's $63 billion in outstanding debt—down from 10 percent a decade ago. See Steve Malanga, "The Indebted States of America," *City Journal* 23, no. 3 (Summer 2013), 28.

12. Bill Keller, "Inequality for Dummies," *New York Times*, December 23, 2013.

13. Nelson Lichtenstein, "Can This Election Save the Unions?" *Dissent* (Summer 2012).

14. James Pierson, "Future Tense X: The Fourth Revolution," *The New Criterion* 30 (June 2012).

15. Conn Carroll, "America's Governing Party," *Washington Examiner*, February 2, 2013.

16. "Mayors and Mammon," *The Economist*, July 13, 2013.

17. Gerald Carlino, Satyajit Chatterjee, and Robert Hunt, "Urban Density and the Rate of Invention," Working Paper 06-14, Federal Reserve Bank of Philadelphia, August 2006; Gerald Carlino, Federal Reserve Bank of Philadelphia; Edward Glaeser, *The Triumph of the City* (New York: Penguin, 2011).

18. Lane Kenworthy, *Social Democratic America* (New York: Oxford University Press, 2014).

19. Frank R. Baumgartner and Bryan D. Jones, *Agendas and Instability in American Politics* (Chicago: University of Chicago Press, 1993). On path dependence, see Paul Pierson, *Politics in Time: History, Institutions, and Social Analysis* (Princeton, NJ: Princeton University Press, 2004); Pierson, "Increasing Returns, Path Dependence, and the Study of Politics," *American Political Science Review* 94, no. 2 (2000): 251–67.

20. Cited in Ron Lieber, "Battle Looms over Huge Costs of Public Pensions," *New York Times*, August 6, 2010.

21. For issues related to tensions between public sector collective bargaining and the First Amendment, see, *Knox v. Service Employees International Union, Local 100*, 576 (2012) and *Harris v. Quinn* 573 (2014).

22. The Public Employees Fair Employment Act, N.Y. Civil Service Law §§ 200–2014, Section § 209-a.

23. E. J. McMahon and Terry O'Neil, *Triborough Trouble* (Report, Empire Center for New York Policy, January 11, 2012).

24. Bruce Katz and Jennifer Bradley, *The Metropolitan Revolution: How Cities and Metros Are Fixing Our Broken Politics and Fragile Economy* (Washington, DC: Brookings Institution Press, 2013).

25. *The Financial State of the States* (Report, Institute for Truth in Accounting, 2011).

26. E. J. McMahon, *Optimal Option: SUNY's Personal Retirement Plan as a Model for Pension Reform* (Special Report, SR 11-12, Empire Center for New York State Policy, February 2012).

27. Alexis de Tocqueville, *Democracy in America*, trans. Harvey Mansfield and Delba Winthrop (Chicago: University of Chicago Press, 2008).

28. James W. Ceaser, "Obama, Romney, and Inequality," Advancing a Free Society, Hoover Institution Blog, May 14, 2012, http://www.advancingafreesociety.org/exclusive/topics/freedom/obama-romney-and-equality/

29. Quoted in Steve Benen, "The Underlying Social Compact," *Washington Monthly*, September 21, 2011.

30. "The Time-Bomb at the Heart of Europe," *The Economist*, November 17, 2012; Jérôme Fourquet, "Les Françias et l'impôt. De la resignation à l'exaspération?" *Commentaire* 143, no. 36 (Autome 2013). In 2010, only 7.8 percent of French workers belonged to unions, according to the Organization for Economic Cooperation and Development,, a majority of them in the government sector. See, "Trade Union Density," Stat Extracts, OECD, http://stats.oecd.org/Index.aspx?DataSetCode=UN_DEN

31. Mancur Olson, *The Rise and Decline of Nations: Economic Growth, Stagflation, and Social Rigidities* (New Haven, CT: Yale University Press, 1984).
32. For another example, see New York City in the 1970s. E.J. McMahon and Fred Siegel, "Gotham's Fiscal Crisis: Lessons Unlearned," *The Public Interest* No. 158 (Winter 2005).
33. Alexis de Tocqueville, *Democracy in America*, trans. and ed. Harvey C. Mansfield and Delba Winthrop (Chicago: University of Chicago Press, 2000), 663.

INDEX

Nagler, Jonathan, 32
Nassau County (New York
   State), 188–189
National Association for the
   Advancement of Colored
   People (NAACP), 8, 107,
   118, 129, 233n29
National Association of
   Realtors, 58, 73–74, 77–78
National Association of School
   Boards, 50
National Education
   Association (NEA)
   agency fees and, 72
   annual income of, 72
   campaign contributions
      from, 58, 68, 70, 73–74,
      77–78, 123
   collective bargaining and, 50
   Department of Education's
      establishment and, 123
   lack of scholarly research
      on, 15
   lobbying and, 116
   local affiliates of, 65, 81
   membership numbers in,
      39, 207
   presidential and
      Congressional elections of
      1976 and, 123
   presidential election of 1980
      and, 124
   urban strongholds of, 47
National Labor Relations Act
   (Wagner Act, 1935)
   collective bargaining and,
      43, 48
   public sector employees
      and, 50
   Taft-Hartley Act's amend-
      ments to, 65
National Labor Relations Board
   v. General Motors, 240n8,
   246n19
National Labor Table, 70
National Rifle Association
   (NRA), 21, 59, 78
Nebraska, 65, 226
Nelson, Gaylord, 49–52
Nevada, 52
New Deal, 164, 218–219
New Hampshire, 46, 52
New Jersey
   building trades unions in, 34
   Communication Workers of

America in, 57, 59
   debt financing in, 180
   direct democracy ballot ini-
      tiatives in, 95
   election of 2010 and, 6
   election of 2013 in, 34
   health care benefits for pub-
      lic sector employees in,
      171, 178
New Jersey Education
   Association (NJEA) and,
   59, 124, 178
   pensions for public sector
      employees in, 36, 157
   public sector employees in,
      34, 36, 42, 57, 59, 124, 157,
      171, 178
   public sector unionization
      rate in, 42
   teachers and teachers' unions
      in, 34, 59, 124, 171, 178
   unfunded pension liability
      in, 167, 170
New Mexico, 42
Newport Beach (California),
   2–3
New York City
   American Federation
      of State, County, and
      Municipal Employees
      (AFSCME) in, 26, 120,
      131, 136
   City Council elections
      (2013) in, 34
   firefighters in, 31, 166, 175
   "Little Wagner Act" (1958)
      and, 48–49
   mayoral election of 2013 in,
      79–80, 87, 130
   Parks Department employ-
      ees in, 193
   party machine era in, 45
   pensions for public sector
      employees in, 31, 136–
      137, 162, 166, 168, 175
   police officers in, 31, 166,
      175
   public sector employees
      and unions in, 24–26, 34,
      48–50, 73, 79, 87, 119–
      120, 130–131, 136–137,
      155, 166, 168, 175, 193,
      195, 201, 224
   sanitation workers in, 37,
      168, 175

Service Employees
   International Union
   (SEIU) in, 79
   Tammany Hall and, 48
   teachers in, 201
   transit strike (1966) in, 52
   transit strike (2005) in, 195
New York State
   annual lobbying expendi-
      tures in, 114
   charter school cap in, 121–
      122, 255n26
   corrections officers in, 128
   county police officers in, 150
   Democratic Party hegemony
      in, 219
   direct democracy ballot ini-
      tiatives in, 95
   disciplinary hearing rights
      in, 46
   education policy in, 121–122
   gubernatorial election of
      2002 in, 132
   gubernatorial election of
      2010 and, 6, 133
   health care sector in,
      130–132
   juvenile correctional facili-
      ties in, 204
   Long Island Railroad
      employees in, 155, 188
   Medicaid and Medicare
      funding in, 130–133
   pensions for public sector
      employees in, 9, 46, 136–
      137, 148, 157, 178
   public sector debt in, 33–34
   public sector employees and
      unions in, 9, 34, 46, 50,
      57–58, 130–133, 136–137,
      142, 148, 150, 157, 178,
      188–189, 201, 219, 224
   public sector unionization
      rate in, 42, 50
   Service Employees
      International Union and,
      130–133
   tax policy and, 7–8
   Taylor Law in, 50, 52–53,
      224
   teachers and teachers unions
      in, 46, 57–58, 73, 79–80,
      119, 201
   tenure rights for public sec-
      tor employees in, 46